LEGAL FOUNDATIONS
of
COMPULSORY SCHOOL ATTENDANCE

Kennikat Press

National University Publications

Multi-disciplinary Studies in the Law

General Editor

Rudolph J. Gerber
Arizona State University

LEGAL FOUNDATIONS
of
COMPULSORY SCHOOL ATTENDANCE

LAWRENCE KOTIN & WILLIAM F. AIKMAN

National University Publications
KENNIKAT PRESS // 1980
Port Washington, N. Y. // London

This work was developed under a grant from the National Institute of Education, Department of Health, Education, and Welfare. However, the content does not necessarily reflect the position or policy of that Agency, and no official endorsement of these materials should be inferred.

Manufactured in the United States of America.

Published by
Kennikat Press Corp.
Port Washington, N.Y. 11050

Library of Congress Cataloging in Publication Data

Kotin, Lawrence, 1940-
    Legal foundations of compulsory school attendance.

    (National university publications: Multidisciplinary studies in the law)
    Bibliography: p.
    Includes index.
    1. Educational law and legislation--United States--States. 2. Education, Compulsory--United States--States. 3. Children--Employment--United States--States. I. Aikman, William F., 1945-   joint author. II. Title.
KF4150.Z95K67 344'.73'079 79-884
ISBN 0-8046-9233-5

TABLE OF CONTENTS

PREFACE

This is a report prepared pursuant to a grant from the National Institute of Education (Grant No. NEG - 00 - 3 - 016) to the Massachusetts Center for Public Interest Law, Inc. The Center is a non-profit, tax-exempt corporation founded to assist federal, state and local agencies, non-profit organizations and other groups operating in the public interest by performing research and analysis, providing advice and representation, conducting training programs and drafting legislation, regulations and other technical legal documents. The work of the Center has been concentrated in the areas of law and education, law and the handicapped person and law and the implementation of public policy.

The principal investigators for this report were William F. Aikman, Esq. and Lawrence Kotin, Esq. The Center would like to express its appreciation to all of the individuals who directly and indirectly contributed to the content of the final report. In particular, special appreciation is expressed to the following individuals who assisted with some of the research: Geraldine Azzata, Gale Halpern, Kathleen Miller, Steven O'Donnell and Betsy Sharawara. In addition, the Center would like to express its appreciation to the following individuals who were support personnel for the project: Marianne Cardosi, Sylvia deMurias, Deborah Haggett, Chester Selbst and Nancy Wilson.

Finally, appreciation is expressed to Ronald Anson and Robert Lindquist of NIE for their encouragement and support during the course of the project.

L.K. & W.F.A.

1. INTRODUCTION

This report is an examination of the legal structure underlying state compulsory school attendance requirements and the likely legal and policy consequences which might result from repeal or amendment of the statutes which form that structure. Although a significant body of literature has accumulated during the past decade concerning a multitude of issues relating to the manner in which elementary and secondary education is provided in the United States, there has been virtually no attention paid to the significance of compulsory attendance laws in that system. While it is true that some educational reformers have challenged the concept of compulsory attendance, they have frequently used the phrase loosely as being synonymous with public education and have not examined in any detail the structure underlying that concept and the specific implications of altering that structure.

This report undertakes such an examination first by reviewing the historical evolution of compulsory attendance laws and of the related system of laws regulating child labor, then by examining the present statutory and constitutional underpinnings of those systems and, finally, by analyzing the principal legal and policy implications of repealing or substantially modifying compulsory attendance laws.

Compulsory attendance laws are examined historically from their theoretical foundations in the English poor laws of the sixteenth century, through the religion-based statutes of colonial America, which required that children be taught to read, in order to be able to study the Bible. The historical overview also focuses upon the enactment, from the mid-nineteenth and into the early twentieth centuries, of the present-day compulsory attendance laws. Examined in this part are the social, economic and political conditions prevalent during periods of active legislating, the development of the belief that education was necessary to insure the continuation of a democratic form of government, the concern, during periods of increased immigration, that there be a method for insuring a common background and citizenship for a diverse population and the movement to curtail abuses in industries employing children during and after the industrial revolution of the nineteenth century.

Because of the symbiotic relationship between compulsory attendance and child labor laws, an historical review of the development of child labor laws is provided. This review traces the history of child labor legislation from its roots in the British statutes of the sixteenth century, emphasizing the movements in the late eighteenth and nineteenth centuries to prohibit the use of child labor in industry and the parallel between the enactment of child labor laws and compulsory attendance laws. It concludes with a summary of the current status of child labor laws and the recent trends away from some of the early restrictions.

The report then provides a comprehensive and systematic comparative analysis of all of the primary reference sections of the compulsory attendance statutes of each state. This analysis focuses, in detail, upon the specific requirements imposed by those statutes upon parents, children and the state; the varieties of educational programs permitted by those statutes to satisfy such requirements; and the elements of those statutes which serve to prevent, circumscribe or encourage the future development of alternatives to traditionally structured public school programs.

This review of compulsory attendance provisions in state statutes is followed by an extensive analysis of all of the major cases which have interpreted those provisions. This analysis discusses the circumstances in which courts have been willing or unwilling to expand the varieties of programs permitted by the statutes to satisfy the attendance requirement; and the implications of those state court decisions for the development of future alternative educational programs.

In addition to the statutory and case analysis of compulsory attendance provisions, the report provides an analysis of the few analogous provisions contained in state constitutions. Also, reference is made to the few cases construing those provisions.

Following the analysis of state statutes and constitutional provisions and the interpretive state case law defining the basic compulsory attendance requirements, the report catalogues and examines the exemptions from those requirements. This examination is designed to further define the dimensions of the attendance requirement.

Once the basic attendance requirements are defined and analyzed, the report summarizes the system through which the requirements are enforced. This summary, as well as all the other major parts of the report, is supplemented by comprehensive charts contained in the appendices, which describe specific provisions of the statutes of all American jurisdictions.

Because of the importance of child labor laws to the maintenance and enforcement of the compulsory attendance system, the report outlines and compares the basic provisions of the child labor laws of the fifty states, Puerto Rico and the District of Columbia, noting the specific connections between those laws and compulsory attendance requirements. Some of those connections are, for example, the fact that, in a particular jurisdiction, the maximum compulsory school attendance age and the minimum age for permitted full-time employment are often the same; school officials are responsible, frequently, for administering and enforcing the requirements of child labor laws; and the requirements for work during school hours or part-time after school hours include achievement of a minimum educational level (e.g. sixth grade).

The next part of the report is an examination of the relationship between the state systems of compulsory attendance laws and the United States Constitution. In this part, the report focuses upon direct and indirect references to state compulsory attendance laws in decisions of the United States Supreme Court and in decisions of the lower federal courts in areas where the Supreme Court has not rendered a definitive decision. The purpose of this part is to describe and analyze the significance of compulsory attendance laws in various landmark federal court decisions in the area of elementary and secondary education; and to lay the basis for a later discussion of the federal constitutional implications of repeal or amendment of those laws.

The final part of the report analyzes the principal legal

implications of repeal or amendment of compulsory attendance laws
by reviewing the proposals for repeal or amendment made by various
educational theorists, as well as the broader reform context in which
such proposals are made; describing the changes in the legal structure which would be required to effectuate such proposals for repeal or amendment; commenting on the principal new legal issues
which would be raised by repeal or amendment; and summarizing the
significance of compulsory attendance laws in the overall debate
about the quality and viability of elementary and secondary education in the United States.

Each chapter of the report contains within it a detailed
commentary and a variety of specific conclusions about its content.
The following is a summary of some of the principal general conclusions we have reached:

1. While the basic structure of the compulsory attendance
and child labor provisions is similar from state to state, the details of those provisions are substantially different so that na-
tionally, the compulsory attendance and child labor laws present
a dense network of laws which are not easily susceptible to classification.

2. In each state, the age provisions contained in the compulsory attendance and child labor statutes are directly keyed
to each other so that one system acts as an enforcement mechanism
for the other. This reflects the parallel historical development
of the two systems.

3. Repeal or amendment of compulsory attendance laws would require relatively minor state constitutional and statutory changes. Such repeal or amendment, for example, would not require the repeal or amendment of laws relating to the establishment, operation and financing of the public schools.

4. Repeal of compulsory attendance laws would not result in the total elimination of compulsion in the public schools, absent repeal of laws requiring certain courses to be taught, repeal of the rules and regulations governing the daily lives of students and a complete restructuring of the relationship of students to teachers and administrators.

5. Most state statutes compel attendance at either public school or private school but are very ambiguous with respect to allowing attendance at other types of educational programs. In those few states where these statutes have been interpreted by state courts, however, the courts have generally been liberal in interpreting compulsory attendance laws to allow attendance at such other types of educational programs. In general, the compulsory attendance laws, themselves, are not a major obstacle to the development of alternative educational programs.

6. Amendment of compulsory attendance laws could serve to make the system of compelled attendance more flexible than it is currently, by, for example, expanding the learning arrangements which are permitted to satisfy the attendance requirement. Such amendment, however, to be effective in practice as well as in theory, would require major changes in laws and public policy concerning school finance and governance, so that less affluent parents

and children could receive public funds and thereby be able to afford to exercise the choices provided by such amendments.

7. In general, the existence of compulsory attendance laws has not been a major influence in the decisions of the Supreme Court and of the lower federal courts in the area of elementary and secondary education, except in those few areas where the pro- visions of a compulsory attendance law were directly in issue.

8. The Supreme Court has taken a restrictive view of the scope of Constitutionally-mandated exemptions from compulsory atten- dance, by trying to limit those exemptions to claims under the free exercise clause of the first amendment and by interpreting that clause in a very restrictive manner.

9. Repeal or amendment of compulsory attendance laws would result in the raising of new legal issues. For example, repeal would raise the issue of whether the choice of the parent or child is controlling in situations where there is a difference of opinion between the two on whether the child should attend school.

This is a technical report in the area of law and educa- tion, written for an audience of lawyers, educational scholars, policy makers at all levels, educational professionals, parents of school age children and others vitally interested in the system of elementary and secondary education in the United States. Its purpose is twofold. First, it is to provide in a clear and precise manner, a useful presentation of the massive amount of federal and state constitutional, statutory and case law directly relating to compulsory school attendance. Second, its purpose is to analyze

and comment on this body of law in such a manner as to provide the
legal basis for an examination by the diverse constituencies, described above, of the desirability of the requirement of compulsory attendance as it is currently defined in the United States.

2. THE ORIGIN AND DEVELOPMENT OF COMPULSORY EDUCATION IN THE UNITED STATES

I. Introduction

Compulsory education in the United States - which is mandated by an elaborate system of state laws requiring attendance at either public schools or at some other acceptable learning arrangement - has its roots in English legislation of the 16th and 17th centuries. Americans in the colonial and early national periods enlarged upon these laws, adapting them to the peculiar needs of a rapidly-developing nation with a philosophy of equal opportunity and individual achievement. The refinement of these laws into our present universal compulsory free educational system took place in an evolutionary manner - with occasional reverses of direction - over a period of two and a half centuries.

II. The English Foundations

The English "Poor Laws" of 1563 and 1601[1] provided the theoretical base for all educational legislation in colonial America. The earlier of the two, the Statute of Artificers (1563), provided for a nation-wide system of apprenticeship by requiring a seven-year period of compulsory service in husbandry for all persons between the ages of twelve and sixty who were not otherwise employed. The Poor Laws of 1601 provided minimal maintenance for the poor and their children, as well as requiring their training in a trade. Similar apprenticeship provisions were

---

[1] Statute of Artificers, 1563 5 Eliz. I, c. iv.

encompassed in the earliest education laws in each of the colonies.[2] By the end of the 16th century, the English Poor Laws
had clearly established both in legal precedent and in political
discourse a number of major principles which would shape Anglo-
American educational legislation for the next 300 years:

1. Fostering economic independence in the individual and
developing moral character are acceptable bases for wide-ranging
legislation.

2. The state may compel local communities to care for
their poor and unemployed residents by requiring that funds for
education and training be raised by a general tax.

3. The state may control the movements and the terms of
employment of minors and of destitute adults.

4. The state may intervene in family life and remove
children from the custody of parents who are unable to support them.

5. The state is the final arbiter of the type of learning
conveyed to children and the uses to which that learning is put.[3]

Thus the colonists embarked in their new land with a
heritage of compulsory, publicly-enforced training which was
already several generations old.

-----

[2]See, e.g., Laws of the Province of Pennsylvania, 1683, c. CXII,
and other colonial statutes cited _infra_.

[3]A more elaborate treatment of the contribution of the early
colonial legislation in terms of principles for later legislation
can be found in Ensign, Forest C., Compulsory School Attendance
and Child Labor. The Athens Press, Iowa City, Iowa, (1921), p. 16.
(hereinafter Ensign).

III.   Colonial America

   A. Early Educational Legislation

   The first compulsory education law in America was
enacted in 1642 in the Colony of Massachusetts Bay.[4] This statute
required all parents and masters to provide an education both in
a trade and in the elements of reading to all children under
their care. The local selectmen were required, under penalty of
a fine, to determine whether parents and masters were teaching
their children and apprentices some calling or trade and whether
children were being taught to read and to understand "the principles of religion and the capital lawes of this country."[5] If
the selectmen found that parents or masters were not fulfilling
their obligations, the selectmen were required to remove the children from parental custody and place them as apprentices with someone
who would carry out the law.[6] This 1642 Massachusetts compulsory
education statute expanded the principles established in the
English Poor Laws by requiring both vocational _and_ academic training for _all_ classes of children, not merely the destitute. (It
should be noted that the 1642 statute made no provision for schools
or teachers. The parents or masters were the sole agents for the
education of their children.)

   The motives for compelling education in Massachusetts

---

[4]Records of the Governor and Company of Massachusetts Bay in
New England, 1642 (June 14), pp. 6, 7.

[5]_Id._, p. 6.

[6]_Id._, p. 7.

included some purposes which were not prominent parts of the English scheme. Among the reasons were concerns that youth readily accept the developing religious, political and social patterns and become good citizens of the state and of the newly-established church.[7] Knowledge of reading was frequently stated as required in order to be able to understand the principles of religion and of the colonial laws. The primary burden of caring for poor and neglected children had shifted from town governments to the masters to whom the children were apprenticed. Of course, as in England, vocational training was also seen as essential to teach children trades and skills that would prevent the development of a large unskilled pauper class. As we will see in the next chapter, this notion of the moral and economic desirability of working children was to be reversed two centuries later with the onset of child labor laws.

The 1642 Massachusetts Bay act also differed from its English prececessors in that it contained a fairly elaborate system of penalties to ensure compliance. Neglient parents and masters were subject to court proceedings and fines for failure to comply with the statute, as well as to the more severe penalty of having their children taken away from them to be placed as apprentices elsewhere. And the selectmen, themselves, could be fined for neglecting enforcement of the statute. Altogether, at least five different parties were charged with enforcement duties:

---

[7]Edwards, Newton and Herman G. Richey, The School in the American Social Order. Houghton-Mifflin Co., Boston, 1947, p. 54 (hereinafter Edwards and Richey).

parents and masters, selectmen, grand jurors, magistrates, and courts.[8] This multiplication of persons with enforcement duties was both characteristic of the Puritan scheme of government and indicative of the seriousness with which the colony viewed the statute.[9]

In 1648 the Great and General Court of Massachusetts amended the 1642 legislation to clarify its purposes and add specificity to its provisions. The 1648 amendment stated that children should be able to read English "perfectly" in order to arrive at a knowledge of the capital laws and to learn an orthodox catechism sufficiently to answer questions about it.[10] The compulsory training of apprentices was made more specific by requiring boys to be apprenticed until age twenty-one and girls until age eighteen. Most importantly, the amended act permitted payments from the town treasury directly to a master, thereby laying the foundation for the principle of support of schools and teachers through local taxation.[11]

---

[8]Records of the Governor and Company of Massachusetts Bay in New England, 1642 (June 14), pp. 7, 9.

[9]Jernegan, Marcus W., "Compulsory Education in the American Colonies I", The School Review, Vol. 26, No. 10, Dec. 1918, p. 739. (hereinafter Jernegan I).

[10]Book of the General Lawes and Libertyes Concerning the Inhabitants of the Massachusetts, Collected Out of the Records of the General Court for the Several Years Wherein They Were Made and Established. Cambridge, Mass. (1648).

[11]The Charters and General Laws of the Colony and Province of Massachusetts Bay (1814), ch. 88, §1.

The Massachusetts Acts of 1642 and 1648 were the model for all subsequent educational legislation in New England. For the first time in history the state assumed clear responsibility for the education and training of all children. Previously, this role had been filled by parents, the church, or private agencies, if at all. Between 1642 and 1671 the other New England colonies except Rhode Island were brought under the operation of statutes designed to insure that all children acquired the minimum education regarded as essential to citizenship in the Puritan commonwealth.[12]

The most comprehensive colonial statute in educational terms was enacted by the independent New Haven Colony. The emphasis of this law was on "book" education and there was no reference to vocational instruction. Education was posited as essential for moral development, so that children and apprentices would, as the statute said, "be able duly to read the Scriptures, and other good and profitable books in the English tongue", as well as to understand general religious principles.[13]

The New Haven law certainly had the most advanced enforcement system.[14] It provided specifically for determining

---

[12]Public Records of the Colony of Connecticut to 1655 (Trumbull, ed.), p. 520-521; Records of the Colony and Jurisdiction of New Haven, 1953-1665 (1858), pp. 583-584, The Book of the General Laws of the Inhabitants of New Plimouth (1865), ch. V, §1 (p. 13).

[13]Records of the Colony and Jurisdiction of New Haven, 1653 - 1655, (Hartford, 1858), pp. 583-584.

[14]Jernegan I, pp. 747-48.

the negligence of an errant parent or master, through the use of
colonial deputies rather than local town officials as enforcement
agents, and included, for the first time, a money penalty to be
levied directly on the parent or master after the very first
warning. As with other statutes of the period, officially-
ordered apprenticeship to another master was a possible penalty
for continued negligence by a parent or master. It is interesting
to note, however, that the statute failed to provide penalties for
officials who neglected their duties. In 1660 an amendment to
the New Haven law provided the first colonial requirement of
writing skills, a provision that boys should be taught to "write
a ledgible hand, so soone as they are capable of it."[15]

The New Haven laws became void when that colony was
incorporated into Connecticut and became subject to Connecticut
legislation. The Colony of Connecticut had found the 1648 Massachusetts legislation to be well-suited to its needs, and copied it
almost verbatim in its compulsory education code of 1650. The
Connecticut version required "that children and servants be
taught to read English, that they be instructed in the capital
laws, that they be catechized weekly, and that they be brought up
in husbandry or some trade profitable to themselves and to the
commonwealth".[16]

---

[15] Records of the Colony and Jurisdiction of New Haven, 1653-1655,
(Hartford, 1858), pp. 583-84.

[16] Acts and Laws of His Majestie's Colony of Connecticut (1715),
p. 16.

In 1671 the Plymouth Colony enacted a statute[17] which
was an amalgam of both the Massachusetts (1642 and 1648) and New
Haven (1655) statutes. It directed selectmen to be responsible
for its enforcement, and included money penalties for negligent
parents and masters. If the negligence continued six months after
the original fine, the selectmen could take the child and place
it as apprentice with another master. Like the New Haven law,
the Plymouth statute emphasized reading, writing and religious
education more than vocational training.

Most statutes enacted later in the colonial era were
a similar amalgam of provisions from the Massachusetts and New
Haven laws. For instance, the Pennsylvania education law of 1683
ordered all parents and guardians of children to instruct the
children in reading, primarily for religious education, and in
writing, so that they could write by age twelve, and then in some
trade or skills. Enforcement was through local officials ultimately ending with the county courts.[18]

Rhode Island was the one colony which had no compulsory
education law. It did, however, have laws on apprenticeship of
pauper children.[19] It was not compulsory, and no book or religious
education was mentioned. One scholar attributes Rhode Island's lack

---

[17]The Book of General Laws of the Inhabitants of New Plimouth (1685),
ch. V, §1 (p. 13).

[18]Laws of the Province of Pennsylvania, 1683, c. CXII.

[19]The Charter and the Acts and Laws of the Colony of Rhode Island,
Boston, 1719, p. 10.

of any compulsory education statute to the fact that this was the
one colony which was established primarily as a religious haven
for more than one sect. This atypical early separation of church
and state resulted in "a weak central government, lack of unity
of religious belief, and the tendency toward individualism - all
of which hindered the enactment of general laws on compulsory education."[20]

B. Establishment of Public Schools

Soon after compulsory education measures were enacted,
it became obvious that parents and others could not meet the
requirements of such measures, unless schools were available for
the children to attend. Even before there was legislation requiring it, several towns in Massachusetts and the other New England
colonies voluntarily established, managed and supported town
schools. Support was through four means: 1) town land was used
as endowment; 2) land was donated by private individuals; 3) taxes
were levied on property-holders; and 4) tuition was paid by those
who could afford it.[21] Soon after the need for public schools became
clear, Massachusetts enacted, in 1647, the first compulsory school
act, commonly referred to as "The Old Deluder Satan Act". Its
passage was motivated by the fear of Satan who supposedly used
ignorance to keep people from knowledge of the Scriptures thereby

---

[20] Jernegan, Marcus W., "Compulsory Education in the American Colonies II", The School Review, vol. 27, No. 1, Jan. 1919, p. 39
(hereinafter Jernegan II).

[21] Edwards and Richey, p. 61.

damning the race.[22]

The 1647 legislation provided for schools to be set up and teachers appointed to them. Specifically, it required towns composed of fifty or more households to appoint a teacher to give instruction in reading and writing, such teacher to be paid by the parents of the children instructed or by tax funds if the town meeting voted on that method. Towns composed of one hundred or more households were also required to appoint a schoolmaster to give instruction in Latin grammar in order to prepare boys for college.[23] The statute's enforcement mechanism was a system of fines for non-compliance.[24] Thus, schools, rather than parents and masters, became the agency for providing children with the education deemed essential by leaders of the church and common-wealth - education in religious principles to serve the needs of institutionalized religion, literary education to appreciate moral precepts, and cultural education to prepare the individual to accept the social order and the church-state relationship.

The Massachusetts Compulsory School Act of 1647 affirmed the principle that government had the authority to promote education and regulate its manner of acquisition. In combination with the compulsory education acts of 1642 and 1648, the Massachusetts legislation introduced many principles upon

---

[22] Records of the Governor and Company of Massachusetts in New England, (Nov. 11, 1647), p. 203.

[23] Id.

[24] Id.

which the American educational system continues to be based:

    1.   The education of children is essential to the proper functioning of the state.

    2.   The obligation to furnish this education rests primarily upon parents.

    3.   The state has a right to enforce this obligation.

    4.   The state has a right to determine the type and extent of education.

    5.   Localities may raise funds by a general tax to support such education.[25]

Only two of the major elements of modern education laws are lacking in these 17th century formulations: an attendance requirement, and freedom of the child from labor during the school period. Neither of these provisions appears in American legal systems until the 19th century.

    C. The Colonial South

While Massachusetts and other New England colonies were developing comprehensive compulsory education systems, the southern colonies were taking more limited steps to provide education to children. Virginia and later the other southern colonies enacted apprenticeship statutes very similar to the English Poor Laws and applicable only to certain classes of children - orphans, poor children, illegitimate children and "mulattoes born of white mothers"- who would otherwise have been

---

[25] Ensign, p. 23, quoting Martin, Evolution of the Massachusetts Public School System, 1894, p. 13.

neglected.[26] The intention of the Virginia law was to prevent
pauperism, ease the fiscal burden of poor relief, and increase the
industrial efficiency of the colony.[27] The little enforcement of
these laws which was attempted was exercised by parish officials,
and occasionally by county courts if the parish authorities
neglected their duties.[28] The southern assumption seemed to be
that education, other than that required under the poor laws,
was a private matter and that capable parents would voluntarily
provide for their own children. Accordingly, town governments
paid much less attention to educational matters than did those
in New England. There was no legal provision in the southern
colonies for "book" education of apprenticed children until 1705,
nor was there provision for the establishment or operation of
public schools.[29]

D. Declining Interest in Compulsory Education

Beginning in the last quarter of the 17th century,
and lasting until after the Revolution, there was a steady and
significant decline in interest in compulsory education. Legislation requiring compulsory education was substantially modified
and then repealed outright so that by the 18th century there

---

[26]Laws of Virginia, 1642-43, Act 34; and 1646, Act 27.

[27]Edwards and Richey, p. 187.

[28]Butts, R. Freeman and Lawrence A. Cremin, A History of Education in American Culture. Henry Holt & Co., N.Y., 1953, p. 105
(hereinafter, Butts and Cremin).

[29]Id., p. 193.

were no laws which required compulsory education in New England.[30]

Initially, the existing compulsory education laws in
New England were repealed when the Andros regime assumed power
from 1686-1689.[31] With the enactment of one statute in 1687, all
former colonial laws compelling religious and academic education
for children were invalidated.[32] After the individual colonial
governments were re-established in 1689, Massachusetts (by then
joined with Plymouth Colony) and Connecticut each acted to continue, provisionally, their earlier education laws.[33] Thus, the
compulsory statutes were reinstated in these two colonies.
However, subsequent action by the Privy Council in London
invalidated the Massachusetts continuation laws,[34] and throughout the rest of the colonial period Massachusetts had no law requiring compulsory education - whether in religious, academic or trade
education.[35] Connecticut kept its compulsory education law
in effect, and, in 1690 passed a new law which strengthened

---

[30]Marcus W. Jernegan, Laboring and Dependent Classes in Colonial America, 1607-1783. University of Chicago Press, Chicago, 1931, p. 115.

[31]Edwards and Richey, p. 59.

[32]Public Records, Colony of Connecticut, 1678-89, pp. 427-28.

[33]Act of 1691, (Mass.) Acts and Resolves, Vol. 1, pp. 27, 99.

[34]Privy Council Acts of 1695 (August 22) disallowed the Continu- ation Acts of 1691 and 1692.

[35]From time to time between 1695 and the Revolution, Massachusetts did enact limited statutes dealing with the apprenticeship of pauper children.

the method of enforcement.[36] A revision in 1702[37] changed the
law so substantially as to make it possible to substitute religious instruction for academic education. Nevertheless, the
Connecticut law retained symbolic importance because it kept a
strong system of penalties, and because it applied to all
children, not just to paupers.

The compulsory education legislation of the later
colonial period was much more limited in scope than the earlier
statutes. For instance, when New Hampshire enacted compulsory
education legislation in 1766,[38] it required education only for
poor children who were apprenticed, thus reverting back to the
English system and ignoring the American developments of the
preceding century.

Marcus Jernegan[39] focuses on the preamble to the Connecticut education statutes enacted following the Indian Wars
for an explanation of this loss of interest in education. The
Connecticut General Court took notice specifically of the serious
moral and economic dislocation which had followed the Wars of
1675-1676, and of the increasing difficulty of enforcing compulsory attendance laws. In a subsequent work, Jernegan developed
the theory that the movement of the population away from central

[36] Public Records Colony of Connecticut, 1678-89, pp. 251.

[37] Acts and Laws of His Majesty's Colony of Connecticut in New
England, Boston, 1702.

[38] Laws of New Hampshire, Vol. III, Second Session 1766, c. 14.
p. 14.

[39] Jernegan II, pp. 26-27.

towns made the establishment of schools and the enforcement of the laws impractical.[40] The frontier conditions of an infant country required much physical effort for survival and growth and children were an essential part of the labor force. Emphasis was placed on material rather than cultural development. An organized system of compulsory education for all children was incompatible with this frontier life-style.[41]

Edwards and Richey have observed that religion was less dominant in the lives of later generations of New Englanders than in the lives of their forebears. By the end of the 17th century there was wider toleration of various religious sects and a dilution of Puritan strength. The importance of religion diminished considerably, thus depriving education of what had been its strongest raison d'etre - religious learning.[42]

The Indian Wars which pre-occupied New England begin-ing in 1675, caused serious economic damage to the colonial society. The weakening and breakdown of family, government, religion, and morals which accompanied this economic depression presented grave difficulties in the enforcement of legislation such as compulsory education laws.[43]

---

[40]Marcus W. Jernegan, Laboring and Dependent Classes in Colonial America 1607-1783, Chicago, 1931, p. 115.

[41]Jernegan II, pp. 26-27, 42.

[42]Edwards and Richey, pp. 108-109.

[43]Id., pp. 26-27.

IV.   Growth of Education in the United States

The winning of political independence from England gave rise to a general re-evaluation of the structures and patterns of American life. The new democracy challenged the colonial concept of an aristocratic society based on "class and economic distinctions" and "theological absolutism".[44] The growing confidence in individual achievement and free choice in religion supported an increased advocacy of a public education system maintained by the state. The waves of foreign immigrants who arrived in the nineteenth and twentieth centuries needed to be taught the language, integrated into the dominant culture and trained for ever more skilled jobs. Under the long prevalent theory of the school as "melting pot", the necessity of public education was considered increasingly apparent.

A. State Compulsory Attendance Laws

In the early national period, Massachusetts was, again, the leader in introducing educational legislation. In 1789 Massachusetts enacted the first state-wide school law, requiring towns of fifty families to support an "English school" at least six months during the year, towns of one hundred families to operate "English schools" all year long, towns of one hundred fifty families to support a grammar school for six months and a school for the instruction of English for twelve

---

[44]See Butts and Cremin, generally; Edwards and Richey, generally and their references to the principal historians of the period, e.g. Beards, Turner, Jernegan, Parrington.

years.[45] This law also established, for the first time, a school district system, which was necessitated by the settlement of rural areas which were too far from towns to share a central town school.[46]

Probably the most far-reaching piece of post-revolutionary educational legislation was the Massachusetts School Attendance Act of 1852,[47] the first general compulsory attendance statute in America. This statute was the first to compel attendance by requiring persons having any children under their control who were between the ages of eight and fourteen to send such children to school for twelve weeks annually, six weeks of which had to be consecutive. However, the statute lacked any adequate machinery for enforcement and only compelled attendance on a part-time basis. In 1890 Connecticut passed a full-time compulsory attendance law which also provided the means for administration and methods of enforcement.[48] By 1900 over thirty states and the District of Columbia had followed the Massachusetts example and enacted legislation requiring school attendance for a specified period of time each year for all children

---

[45] Acts and Resolves of Massachusetts, 1789, ch. 19.

[46] Id., p. 19.

[47] [Mass.] St. 1852, c. 240, §§1, 2, 4.

[48] Butts and Cremin, pp. 246 ff, trace the support of schools by compulsory taxation - thereby making them free public schools - in several states as follows: Mass., 1827; Conn., 1868; N.Y., 1867; Penn., 1868; N.J., 1871; Ohio, 1853; Wis., 1848; Ind., 1852; Ill., 1855; Iowa, 1858; Mich., 1869. Although Me., N.H., R.I. and several other states still had systems of only partial tax support into the 19th century, the principle of public support was firmly established by the time of the Civil War.

within specified age groups. The southern states were the last
to enact compulsory attendance measures. They did so between 1900
and 1918, although many of these laws were local and optional in
character (that is, they enabled counties, cites, or towns to
elect whether or not to utilize the state legislation).

B. The Public Debate on Universal Free and Compulsory
Education

Important changes in the national climate gave strong
impetus to the spread in America of universal, free[49] and compulsory education. The greatest expansion in public support and
legislation occurred in the post-Civil War era, from about 1865
to the early 20th century. There was a growing public feeling
that education was essential to protect the democratic form of
government and also to enable individuals to enjoy the "fruits
of democracy." Education was seen by humanitarian social reformers as the means not only for providing an intelligent elec-
torate and leadership, but also for preventing crime and poverty
and the elimination of illiteracy.

This period also saw a massive influx of immigrants to
America. The belief that they would change the nature of American
culture if they were not quickly integrated into the society and
the corrolary belief that the quickest means of integration was
through public schools, each gained wide currency. As is well-
known, both popular and professional historians, including such
eminent figures as Henry Steele Commager, traced the development

---

[49]Id., pp. 356-357, 360.

of education for all to this apparent need to integrate foreign
immigrants quickly and to the subsequent "Americanization"
movement of the early 20th century.[50]

The rapid industrialization of the New World required
increasingly more skilled and literate workers, and so contributed to the demand for more extensive education. In an attempt
to improve the conditions of human life, especially for children,
social reformers and humanitarians and, later, labor leaders
demanded raising the school-leaving age and instituting a compulsory school attendance system to replace the traditional
apprenticeship arrangement.

Amid this changing American scene, public debates began
to arise concerning compulsory school attendance laws. There was
bitter opposition to the compulsory nature of the laws. Many
felt that such legislation deprived parents of their inalienable
right to control their children, and was an unconstitutional
infringement upon the individual liberty guaranteed by the Fourteenth Amendment. Opponents also claimed that compulsory education laws were "monarchical" and that already powerful state
governments were arrogating new powers. Claims that the laws
were "un-American" and inimical to the spirit of free democratic
institutions were raised. Supporters countered those arguments
with similar rhetoric such as by the assertion that compulsory educa-

---

[50]Henry Steele Commager, "A Historian Looks at the High School"
in Francis S. Chase and Harold Anderson, The High School in a
New Era, University of Chicago Press, Chicago, 1958, p. 13.

tion is, in its essence, democratic in spirit and purpose, since
it seeks to destroy artificial class distinctions and give every
child an even start in life.[51] In State v. Bailey,[52] a typical
case, the Indiana Supreme Court reasoned that provision of and
control over education is a valid state function because education
is necessary to the welfare of the state. The Court confirmed the
right of the state to compel a child's attendance despite the
ancient common law rights of the parent, on the theory that those
rights do not include the right to deprive a child of the advantages of education.

Concurrently with this debate, another controversy
centered around the universal and public nature of the schools.
Concern was raised that mixing all classes together in public
schools would turn them into breeding grounds of crime and
"pauperism." Those without children or with children in private
schools objected that their taxes were being used to pay for a
system they could not use.[53] Proponents of religious schools,
particularly Roman Catholics, argued that education should occur
in a religious setting and not necessarily in a non-sectarian
public school.[54]

---

[51]See DeYoung, Chris A., Introduction to American Public Education.
McGraw-Hill Book Co., Inc., N.Y., 1950, p. 166; Deffenbaugh, W.S.,
Compulsory Attendance Laws in the U.S. U.S. Bureau of Education,
Bulletin, 1914, No. 2, p. 10; and Johnson, James A. et al., Intro-
duction to the Foundations of American Education. Allyn & Bacon,
Inc., Boston, 1969, p. 122.

[52]61 N.E. 730, 157 Ind. 329 (1901).

[53]Butts and Cremin, p. 362.

[54]Id., p. 363.

Nevertheless, the logical result of efforts to maintain a homogeneous culture were compulsory attendance laws which required attendance at <u>public</u> schools. But in 1925 in the case of <u>Pierce v. The Society of Sisters</u>,[55] the Supreme Court confirmed the right of individuals to establish and maintain both private non-sectarian and private religious schools, and the right of parents to send their children to such schools. The Court held that the right of the state to require attendance at a school did not include the right to preclude attendance at non-public schools.

V. <u>Modern Development of Statutory Features</u>

1. <u>Generally</u>

The compulsory attendance statutes initially contained generally worded and largely ineffective provisions, but specifications were gradually added to clarify the requirements and to provide for adequate machinery to make them enforceable. The early laws included extremely general provisions regarding exemptions, which made it difficult for officials to determine who should and should not be in school. Penalties for violations and the means to enforce them, if included at all, were inadequate. Despite vigorous advocacy by educators and other interest groups, there was a widespread popular resistance to compulsory education, particularly at a time when parents depended on their children's income for economic survival. Measures added to the laws steadily lengthened the required attendance period to include eight to ten

---

[55]268 U.S. 510 (1925). See chapter 11 , <u>infra</u> for a more detailed discussion of <u>Pierce</u>.

months of full-day schooling; age limits were extended in most jurisdictions to compel chilaren between the ages of six and eighteen to attend school.

The current compulsory education system is based on a complex array of statutes only some of which relate directly to attendance or education. Among the matters which must be covered by statute for a fully functioning system are: 1) compulsory age span; 2) permissive admission age; 3) minimum required school term; 4) minimum attendance required; 5) exemptions from attendance; 6) provisions for children with special needs; 7) appointment and duties of attendance officers; 8) identification of truants; 9) adjudication procedures; 10) penalties; 11) age for work permits; 12) minimal education requirements for permits; 13) continuation or part-time attendance; and 14) school census procedures.[56]

Another important change reflected in current compulsory education legislation is in its spirit. Early statutes were written with the stern religious ideas of Puritan ethics in mind, or for the "benefit" of the poor and their phrasing clearly evidences those purposes. Current laws reflect more secular interests such as securing the physical health and social well-being of children; they focus on the children's needs to acquire the fundamentals of literacy and of some industrial skill.

---

[56]For a similar breakdown of the component parts of the current compulsory system, see Fuller, Edgar and Jim B. Pearson, eds., Education in the States: Nationwide Development Since 1900. National Education Association of the U.S., Washington, D.C., 1969, p. 30.

2. Maintenance of a Public School System

Significant progress in the implementation of compulsory education laws was achieved through the refining and addition of specific means for enforcement and penalties. The Massachusetts Act of 1642 had provided for a fine of five pounds sterling as a penalty for communities failing to support their schools in accordance with the requirements of the act.[57] This measure survives in modern statutes in the form of authority for state departments of education to withhold a portion of state funds from communities recalcitrant in complying with state education regulations. After the discovery in a 1919 survey of widespread illiteracy among the drafted army of World War I, strong public feeling developed concerning the necessity to enforce compulsory education laws.[58] During the 1920's, state governments began, for the first time, to set up effective enforcement divisions which required local officials to monitor compliance with the compulsory school laws.[59]

Newer legislative features which helped to ease the problem of enforcement included the introduction of the school census, the appointment of properly qualified attendance

---

[57]Records of the Governor and Company of Massachusetts Bay in New England, 1642 (June 14), pp. 6, 7.

[58]Willis Rudy, Schools in an Age of Mass Culture (Prentice Hall Inc., Englewood Cliffs, N.J., 1965), p. 145.

[59] Id., p. 145.

officers at state and local levels, child labor laws, especially
the requirement of employment certificates, the enumeration of
penalties and means for imposing them, and the detailed specification of exemptions.[60]

3. The School Census

With acceptance of the idea that it was desirable
to educate all the citizenry, many states established funds to
be distributed to schools for aiding them in providing educational opportunities. As states made more of a financial commitment to education, it became more important to determine on what
basis funds should be distributed and how and when school facilities should be constructed. The school census was developed
as a method of making these determinations based upon local
population size. In the early years, there was no need for a
formal census, because school districts were sufficiently
small that there was little doubt about the number of children.
But as populations and the availability of state monies grew,
an accurate census became imperative.

A census of school-age children was also essential to the enforcement of compulsory school attendance laws.
The census provided an official record against which to check
enrollments and discover which children were not in school.
Later, many states expanded the census to include a report on all

---

[60] Such legislative measures first began to appear toward the
close of the 19th century and their growth continued through
the New Deal.

physically and mentally handicapped persons under a specified age, in order to discover the need for, and to provide, special educational programs and institutions.

The school census began in 1870 as a local instrument, imposed by the state but with little state guidance. Without such direction, results were often unsatisfactory for local use and unreliable for state-wide use.[61] But as states began to take a larger and more direct role in educational planning, guidelines were eventually developed for a reasonably accurate and uniform census instrument to be used state-wide in each jurisdiction.

4. Summary

In the post-Civil War period, there was a general expansion of elementary education and of compulsory attendance laws. Most of the American public recognized the importance of universal education and the common school ideal as necessary tools to bring literacy to the people, to minimize social cleavage and equalize opportunity for all, to induct an increasingly heterogeneous and growing immigrant population into American society, to prevent crime, to provide industry with skilled workers and, generally, to contribute to the welfare of the country.[62]

---

[61]Proffitt, Maris M. and David Segel, "School Census, Compulsory Education, Child Labor: State Laws and Regulations", U.S. Office of Education, Bulletin 1945, No. 9, Government Printing Office, Washington, D.C., p. 20.

[62]Butts and Cremin, p. 360.

Of course, these ideals were never fully realized. Children from racial minorities were never included in this "universal" public education system. Prior to the Civil War, several southern states had laws prohibiting outright the education of Negroes.[63] In the north, separate schools were established for Negroes and many states prohibited integrated schools. "Separate but equal" school systems were constitutional for several centuries. And for hundreds of thousands of children of all racial and ethnic backgrounds who were handicapped or had some special need, the "universal" system was in a different universe.

From 1954 until very recently, most public debate about compulsory education centered on segregation. In the aftermath of Brown v. Board of Education, a number of southern states repealed their compulsory attendance statutes in order to avoid requiring children to attend racially mixed schools. Within the following decade, every southern state, except Mississippi, re-enacted a compulsory attendance statute, although some of them were weakened by provisions making the statute essentially a mere enabling act which could be utilized or not at local option.[64] Mississippi is now the only American jurisdiction which does not have a compulsory attendance statute.

Within the past several years, compulsory attendance has figured prominently in public debate once again as a

---

[63] See Brickman, William W. and Stanley Lehrer, The Countdown on Segregated Education. Society for the Advancement of Education, N.Y., 1960, p. 27.

[64] Brickman and Lehrer, p. 64.

number of major cities struggle with the implementation of court orders requiring the busing of substantial numbers of school children. The phenomenon of large numbers of children and youth of compulsory school age remaining out of school, usually with parental acquiescence if not outright encouragement, has become rather commonplace.

This phenonmenon has prompted a number of officials to inquire, often for the first time, into the nature of the enforcement mechanisms for compulsory attendance. The mechanisms they discover are often vague, complex or unduly harsh as we describe in the chapter on enforcement and its accompanying Appendix. What these officials do not realize is that for most of this century one of the major and perhaps the principal enforcement mechanisms for compulsory attendance has not been the truancy statutes and other direct enforcement measures, but rather has been the complex network of state and federal child labor laws. Because of the critical role, one might almost say symbiotic relationship of child labor laws to compulsory attendance laws, we turn now to a consideration of the development of child labor legislation in the United States.

3. THE DEVELOPMENT OF
CHILD LABOR LEGISLATION

I.   Introduction

The history of the development of child labor legislation begins with the industrial revolution. Although children worked long before the introduction of water power and the spinning wheel, their labor was confined to domestic industry; they worked either for their parents or for master craftsmen to whom they were apprenticed.

The idea that children should work was never seriously disputed prior to the late 18th century. Even when it was not necessary for children to work to help support the family, prevailing social philosophy in both England and the United States insisted that children must learn to work by working. Child labor was encouraged as a means of dealing with children who would otherwise be idle and potentially troublesome.

The campaign against the use of large numbers of young children in factories and mills began as a result of the widespread and extensive abuses perpetrated in such industries. Early reformers, asserting interest solely in the welfare of children, claimed that factory labor, especially very long hours, dim lighting and the other conditions that characterized factory work at the time, was invariably harmful to the health of young children.

As industrialization progressed, other factors took on increasing importance for the opponents of child labor. The growing belief in the desirability of education demanded that part of childhood, at least for poor children, be devoted to

training and education instead of work in mills and factories.
Adult labor organizations eventually joined the move for restriction of child labor, motivated as much by self interest as by a
desire to see conditions for children improved; children constituted such a large segment of the work force, that limitations
on child labor would necessarily increase work opportunities and
maintain wage levels for adults.

One of the first arguments in the United States for cur-
tailing work hours of children and raising the minimum age for
employment was that education was necessary for the proper functioning of a democracy. By the end of the 19th century, despite
opposition of various descriptions, most of the states had
adopted a program of compulsory schooling, and within the following quarter century most also enacted child labor legislation.
Without any clear plan to do so, each jurisdiction slowly developed a relationship of reciprocal reinforcement between its child
labor regulations and compulsory attendance legislation.

Typical early child labor legislation merely established
minimum age and maximum hours of work for children, and certain
limited health and safety standards for industries which employed
children. Many of these laws also required certificates of
employment to be obtained from local school officials before a
child could be legally hired. But there was an enormous variety
in the provisions of this legislation from state to state and in
the manner in which it was supposed to be implemented. About
one thing there was considerable uniformity, however - the near

total lack of serious enforcement efforts.

Because states were slow to implement effective statutes, and because of the lack of uniformity of such laws in different states, reformers sought federal legislation to control the use of child labor. Two attempts at federal legislation were declared unconstitutional in 1918 and 1922,[1] and it was thought that a constitutional amendment was required. The need for the amendment, first proposed in 1924 but never ratified by a sufficient number of states, was obviated by another Supreme Court decision in 1941,[2] overruling the earlier opinion, and finding in the Commerce Clause the power for Congress to regulate child labor in establishments engaged in production for interstate commerce.

Since the end of World War II, most state statutes have been modified to bring them into closer conformity to federal standards and to broaden their scope to include employment other than in industry (retail stores, garages, restaurants, etc.). Increasing emphasis on the necessity of schooling bringing with it extensions of compulsory attendance statutes have caused a steady increase in the level of detail contained within state child labor regulations.

Most recently, state legislatures and the federal government have begun shifting the emphasis of child labor statutes away

---

[1]Hammer v. Dagenhart, 247 U.S. 251 (1918); Bailey v. Drexel Furniture, 259 U.S. 20 (1922).

[2]U.S. v. Darby Lumber Co., 312 U.S. 100 (1941).

from the rigid protectionism of earlier years to somewhat more flexible standards in order to facilitate employment of youth. Particularly important in this regard have been the easing of night work restrictions and removing burdensome obstacles in the procedures for obtaining employment certificates.

II.   Children at Work in England and the United States - 1750-1900

A.   England - early development

Until the great change in industrial life which began in the 18th century, British labor legislation clearly was not enacted to protect the workers.[3] On the contrary, British statutes sought to compel work, to keep wages down and to regulate movement of workers.[4] The only method of regulating the employment of children was that provided by the rules of the various trades within the apprenticeship system. Almost all trades were under the control of guilds, which were associations of workmen organized to insure monopoly and a uniform standard of work. The apprenticeship system involved enrolling young learners under the supervision of a Master Craftsman for a specified period of time to learn the trade of the Master.

---

[3] Abbott, Grace, The Child and The State; Select Documents, Vol. I, Part II, Apprenticeship and Child Labor Legislation in Great Britain (New York: Greenwood Press 1938) Reprint 1968 (hereinafter Abbott, G.), p. 80.

[4] See, e.g., The Ordinance of Labourers, 1349 Close Roll, 23 Edward III, p. 1; Labour Legislation, The Statute of 12 Richard II 1388. Reprinted in Bland, Brown and Towney, eds. English Economic History: Select Documents (London: G. Bell & Son 1914)pp. 164 and 171.

These apprentices then became members of the guild, and thereby also became "freemen", an inherited status carrying with it industrial, social and political privileges. In 1562, the Statute of Artificers[5] made this system of apprenticeship compulsory (one had to have been apprenticed in order to legally engage in a trade). The system varied in effectiveness since its enforcement was left to the guilds themselves. But the system did provide training and occasionally minimal education and eliminated some of the more severe forms of exploitation of children participating in it. These advantages, however, were limited to children apprenticed under guild supervision; for the masses of children working at unskilled labor, no such protection was offered.[6]

With the development of large mills located substantial distances from populated areas, manufacturers began to import large numbers of pauper children from the cities. These children were "apprenticed" to the mill owners, although this apprenticeship did not have the same meaning it had within the guild system. Since poverty was seen as the result of shiftlessness, it seemed particularly in the public interest to apprentice poor children who were dependent on the limited public relief available. The punishments inflicted on these children to keep them at very tedious work for extremely long hours as well as the living

---

[5] 5 Elizabeth I, c. 4 (1562).

[6] Abbott, G., p. 81.

arrangements and dreadful sanitary conditions have been well-documented and eventually led to major reforms beginning in the early 19th century.

The Apprentices Act of 1802[7] was the first effort to control the evils of apprenticing poor children to cotton-mill owners and is the forerunner of all Anglo-American child labor legislation. This act provided for certain basic health and safety measures, and ordered owners to provide some limited education for the children apprenticed to them.[8] As a result of this statute, manufacturers began to employ free children, as opposed to apprenticed paupers, thereby circumventing the provisions of the Act.[9] The British government eventually responded to this practice with the Cotton Mills and Factories Regulation Act of 1819 extending the provisions of the Act of 1802 to include free as well as apprenticed children.[10]

Efforts to control child labor and to improve conditions for working children moved very slowly and met great resistance, both from mill owners and from politicians. The reasons for this

---

[7] 42 George III, c. 73 (1802), "An Act for the Preservation of the Health and Morals of Apprentices and Others".

[8] The provisions of the statute required separate sleeping quarters for male and female apprentices and ordered factory owners to provide instruction in reading and writing.

[9] Abbott, G., p. 83.

[10] 59 George III, c. 66 (1819), "An Act to Make Further Provisions For The Regulation of Cotton Mills and Factories, and for the Better Preservation of the Health of Young Persons Employed Therein". This statute set the minimum age for employment at nine years, restricted hours of actual work to twelve per day, prohibited night work and required several other health and safety measures to be taken.

were mostly economic - England was developing a prosperous export
trade and the principle of _laissez faire_ was regarded as the
foundation of imperial greatness and wealth. "It was accepted
that the first duty of the government was to foster its manufacturing and any measure for the protection of working children
was submitted to the test of whether or not it would place the
British manufacturers at a disadvantage in world markets."[11]

Opponents of child labor reform had several common
objections to all proposals that would regulate manufacturers.
First, they argued that idleness was the root of all evil in
the working class, and that prohibition of child labor would,
therefore, encourage vice. Secondly, they claimed that regulation of child labor was just the first step in a program of
general government regulation, and industry would be ruined by
government interference. This was presented as especially per-
nicuous since manufacturers also argued that the principal object of the state was the promotion of trade. Fourthly, they
claimed that such legislation struck at the very root of family
life by interfering with natural parental authority. And,
finally, they claimed that the necessity for regulation had not
been demonstrated and that conditions, never so bad as they
were represented, were improving.[12] To be fair it should also
be pointed out, however, that fear of government involvement in the

---

[11] Abbott, G., p. 84.

[12] _Id._

private lives of citizens was also a factor in the move to
resist government regulation of child labor.[13]

But as the movement for general education gained momentum, the drive for recognition of children's needs for protection in the workplace became more successful. The Children
and Young Persons Labour Act of 1833,[14] although limited in
scope, was the first major victory for this movement. This law
established age and hours restrictions for child labor, entirely
excluded children under nine years from employment, set up a
system of national factory inspection, required medical certification of health before a child could be employed, and required
attendance at school for at least two hours per day.

By the mid-19th century the value of the English child
labor legislation as precedent for American legislation had diminished markedly. By that time the countries' differing views on
the desirable extent of education and England's industry-by-industry approach to labor regulations made the English system inapplicable to the American situation.

B. <u>United States</u>

In the American Colonies in the 18th century, child
labor was accepted not only as necessary, but desirable, especially for children of poor families. The Puritan consciousness

---

[13]See Robson, A.H., <u>The Education of Children Engaged in Industry
in England, 1833-1876</u> (London, Regan Paul, Trench, Trubner & Co.
1931).

[14]3 and 4 William IV, c. 103 (1833).

equated idleness with evil, and poverty was thought to be the result of shiftlessness. The only way to avoid both poverty and evil was to insist that everyone work, including children. In the early decades of the Puritan era, if parents did not keep their children employed, the selectmen of the town intervened and put the children to work.[15]

Initially, apprentices were imported from alms houses in England to help work the fields and clear land in the new country.[16] Later, after initial local stability had been achieved, children of the colonists were apprenticed to tradesmen and craftsmen. This apprentice system never developed to the elaborate extent it had in England, but it was used as a method of helping to insure a steady supply of workers with required skills.[17]

With the advent of organized industry, the American apprenticeship system declined. However, as in England, children were employed in large numbers in the mills and factories. Industrialization was seen as having the desirable by-product of providing employment for children who would otherwise be idle.[18]

---

[15] Abbott, Edith, Women in Industry: A Study in American Economic History; Appendix A. Child Labor in America Before 1870 (1910) (hereinafter Abbott, E.), p. 328-9.

[16] Abbott, E., p. 189.

[17] Jennings, W.J., A History of Economic Progress in the United States (N.Y.: Crowell, 1926) p. 14.

[18] Abbott, E., p. 238. See also: Communication to the House of Representatives by Alexander Hamilton, cited in Abbott, G. at 276.

Conditions in the mills and factories in the United States were
as bad as they were in England, and legislation to regulate
child labor was as slow in coming. Massachusetts was the first
state to enact any regulation concerning child labor. In 1842,
a Massachusetts statute[19] set at ten per day the maximum number
of hours that a child under twelve years of age could work. In
the next ten years six states established minimum age and maximum hour requirements for child labor.[20] But these statutes
typically did not require proof of age, nor did they provide any
effective enforcement mechanisms so very young children continued to be employed for long hours and in hazardous occupations.[21]

With the great expansion of industry after the Civil
War and the employment of larger and larger numbers of children

----

[19]Chapter 90, Mass. Acts and Resolves, 1842.

[20]The following states set minimum age requirements:
Penn.:   1848, 12 years for employment in textile mills;
          1849, 13 years in paper mills;
N.J.:   1851, 10 years in manufacturing;
R.I.:   1853, 12 years in manufacturing;
Conn.:   1855, 9 years in manufacturing and mechanical estab-
          lishments and, in 1856, 10 years in these establish-
          ments.
The following states enacted maximum hours legislation:
Mass.:   1842, 10 hours per day for children under 12.
Conn.:   1842, 10 hours per day for children under 14.
N.H.:   1847, 10 hours per day for children under 15.
Me.:   1848, 10 hours per day for children 16.
Penn.:   1849, 10 hours per day for children 13 to 16.
Ohio: 1852, 10 hours per day for children under 14.
R.I.:   1853, 11 hours for children 12 to 15.
These laws were limited to manufacturing or textile mills. (From
Report on Conditions of Woman and Child Wage Earners in the United
States; U.S. Bureau of Labor Statistics, in Abbott, G., p. 260.

[21]Id.

in factories, the demand for enforceable child labor legislation
increased. Trade union organizations began to advocate legislation to regulate child labor. They argued that premature
employment was a health hazard to young children, and occasionally also acknowledged that the effects of competition from
children on the job security and wages of adult workers was
economically harmful.[22] One organization, the Knights of Labor,
was particularly active in advocating child labor laws. The
period during which the Knights enjoyed their greatest influence
corresponds to a period of rapid spread in state child labor legislation.[23] Between 1870 and 1889, much of the early state legislation
was enacted and by 1899 a total of twenty-eight states[24] had some
variety of child labor law. Typically, these statutes were

---

[22]That organized labor sought the prohibition of child labor
because it tended to lower the wages and conditions of adult
workers is asserted by many commentators on the development of
child labor legislation. See, e.g.: Abbott, E., p. 261;
Article of Child Labor, Cyclopedia of Education, Munroe, Paul,
ed. (New York, 1911), p. 607; Carroll, Mollie, R., Labor and
Politics. The Attitude of the AFL Toward Legislation and Politics (Cambridge, Riverside Press 1923, Reprint Arno Press, 1969),
pp. 81-83; Fuller, Raymond G., Child Labor and the Constitution;
Otey, Elizabeth, "The Beginnings of Child Labor Legislation in
Certain States" (Report on Conditions of Women and Child Wage
Earners in the United States), U.S. Dept. of Labor, Vols. I-VI
(19 vols., Washington, D.C., Government Printing Office, 1910-
1913).

[23]Johnson, Elizabeth Sands, "Child Labor Legislation", in
Commons, et al., History of Labor in the United States (4 Vols.
N.Y. MacMillan, Co. 1935) III, (hereinafter Johnson, E.S.), p.
404.

[24]Calif., Colo., Conn., Ill., Ind., La., Me., Md., Mass., Mich.,
Minn., Mo., Neb., N.H., N.J., N.Y., N.D., Ohio, Okla., Penn.,
R.I., S.D., Tenn., Vt., Va., Wash., W.Va., Wis. See Ogburn, W.F.,
The Progress and Uniformity of Child Labor Legislation, Columbia
Univ. Studies 1912, Vol. 48, pt. 2, Table 12, p. 71.

limited to children employed in manufacturing; set a minimum age for employment of twelve years;[25] fixed maximum hours at ten per day; contained some sketchy requirements as to school attendance and literacy; and accepted the affidavit of the parent as proof that the child had reached the legal minimum age for employment.[26]

One additional and continuing argument for the curtailment of child labor was the necessity of education. Therefore, advocates of child labor regulations became very interested in compulsory school attendance laws, since child labor legislation could be said to have in common with compulsory attendance legislation the aim of insuring a minimal education for all children. Moreover, compulsory school attendance was seen as a potentially very effective instrument for the enforcement of child labor laws. Certainly if statutory provisions existed for compulsory full-time education up to the age limit at which a child could be admitted to work, not only would children receive an education but their competitive effect on adult labor would be substantially delayed.

As early as 1836, Massachusetts required children under age fifteen to attend school for three months out of the year as a

---

[25]Only nine states had a higher minimum age of fourteen years. These states were Colo., Conn., Ill., Ind., Mass., Minn., Mo., N.Y., Wis. Johnson, E.S., p. 405.

[26] Id.

condition of lawful employment.[27] By 1895, twenty-eight states[28]
and the District of Columbia had enacted compulsory education laws,
but provisions for enforcement were poor, and the length of time
of attendance was usually brief (generally three months). Requirements of attendance for the full length of time school was
in session did not occur until the beginning of the next century.

By the end of the 19th century, the most progressive
states had enacted legislation to prevent exploitation of children by industry,[29] had set a maximum number of hours for children
to work,[30] had raised the minimum age of employment to fourteen,[31]
had established a system of factory inspection to enforce age
and hour laws, and had geared their compulsory school attendance
statutes and child labor laws to reinforce each other.[32] But in
the majority of states, especially in the South, the movement
for effective child labor legislation had barely begun. However, the

---

[27] Chapter 245, Mass. Acts and Resolves, 1836.

[28] Calif., Colo., Conn., Idaho, Ill., Kan., Me., Mass., Mich.,
Minn., Mont., Neb., Nev., N.H., N.J., N.M., N.Y., N.D., Ohio,
Ore., Penn., R.I., S.D., Utah, Vt., Wash., Wis., Wyo. U.S.
Commissioner of Education, Annual Report, 1895-96 cited in Johnson,
E.S., p. 411.

[29] See, for example, N.Y. Statutes 1876, Ch. 122, "An Act to Prevent and Punish Wrongs to Children" which prohibited apprenticing
of children for labor dangerous to their life or health,

[30] See note 24, supra.

[31] See note 25, supra.

[32] For example, N.Y. and Mass. amended their compulsory attendance
statutes to make attendance mandatory up to the age of fourteen
years, which was the minimum legal employment age established by
their child labor statutes.

stage was rapidly being set: "During this period, the social
conceptions that would make significant legislative advance-
ments possible in the future were beginning to work their way
into popular attitudes. Child labor, once viewed as a benefi-
cial social institution, was slowly . . . taking on the stigma
of an unrighteous and harmful consequence of industrial capital-
ism, destructive to child and community."[33]

III.   The American Child Labor Movement

    A.   State Development

        The organized American child labor movement of the
20th century began in the South, where there was no pre-existing
child labor legislation and where the cotton textile industry
was undergoing wildly rapid expansion.[34] By 1900, Southern
textile mills employed over 25,000 children, many of them as
young as eight years and almost all of them illiterate.[35] Publication of these facts aroused much public concern and in 1901
child labor regulation bills were introduced in all four of the
South's leading textile states, North and South Carolina, Georgia and Alabama. The bills were strongly supported by state

---

[33]Wood, Stephen B., Constitutional Politics in the Progressive
Era (Chicago; University of Chicago Press, 1968), (hereinafter
Wood, S.B.), p. 6.

[34]See Wood, S.B., p. 7; Johnson, E.S., p. 405.

[35]Otey, Elizabeth L., "Beginnings of Child Labor Legislation in
Certain States" (Report on Conditions of Women and Child Wage
Earners in the United States), U.S. Dept. of Labor, Vol. I (19
Vols. Washington, D.C., Government Printing Office, 1910-1913),
(hereinafter Otey, E.L.), p. 90.

federations of labor, of course not only because of the evils of
exploitation of children, but also because organized labor
wanted the jobs held by children for the adult workers who be-
longed to their organizations.[36] The legislation was actively
supported also by local reform groups including the newly-formed
Alabama Child Labor Committee, headed by Rev. Edgar Gardner
Murphy, which was the first of many "child labor committees" to
be founded in the United States.[37]

However, resistance to early legislative efforts was
strong in the South. The development of industry was seen as
the way in which the region could restore its ruined economy.
Consequently, new factories took on extraordinary importance and
public opinion vigorously opposed efforts to regulate them.[38]
Traditional southern reluctance to tolerate examination of its
institutions was exploited by textile and commercial interests
and the populace in general remained extremely suspicious of
governmental intervention.

In the North, attempts were being made to raise the
standards for employment of children and to make previously-
enacted child labor laws enforceable. In 1902, the New York
Child Labor Committee was formed; with its main purpose being
to insure enactment of legislation with effective enforcement

---

[36]See note 22, supra.

[37]Wood, S.B., p. 9.

[38]Id., p.4.

mechanisms. In Illinois, the Industrial Committee of the State Federation of Women's Clubs and the Cook County Child Saving League performed similar roles.[39]

In 1904, leaders of the state and local child labor organizations met to consider a national organization to advance the child labor movement. The Rev. Murphy was a leading force in the formation of the nation-wide organization, which was established in April, 1904. The National Child Labor Committee's program called for an investigation to determine the facts concerning child labor, for publication of their findings and for general publicity on the issue to arouse public concern. Its main efforts attempted to bar children below the age of fourteen from employment in industry and commerce and to ensure that children between ages fourteen and sixteen would be protected against excessive hours and night work.[40] During the next half-dozen years (1904-1910) the National Committee and the twenty-five state and local committees worked assiduously toward these goals.

The effects of the work of the Committee can be seen in the volume of child labor legislation enacted by the states during the first ten years of the Committee's existence. Between 1904 and 1909, forty-three states enacted significant child labor legislation, either by new statute or by comprehensive amendments to previous enactments. In less than a twelve-month period in

---

[39]Johnson, E.S., p. 407.

[40]"Objectives of the Committee", National Child Labor Committee leaflet (New York 1904), quoted in Wood, S.B., p. 12.

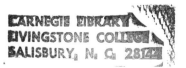

1910, legislative action in thirty states improved child labor legislation.[41] Further legislation in 1912-1914 brought improved protection and enhanced educational opportunities to child workers in every state.[42]

Opponents of state child labor legislation attacked its constitutionality but the statutes were always upheld as a legitimate exercise of the state's police power.[43] In 1913, the first of these cases[44] reached the Supreme Court, which held that there was no doubt about the power of a state to prohibit children from working in hazardous occupations.

Although the pre-1900 child labor statutes had contained elements of the basic principles found in such legislation currently, (i.e., regulation of working age, hours, health and safety standards and education), they had not been elaborated into the specific standards and prescribed methods of administration required to translate principle into actuality. During the

---

[41] "Seventh Annual Report", N.C.L.C., September 1911 in Child Labor Bulletin (Nov. 1911), p. 187, quoted by Wood, S.B., p. 21.

[42] "Child Labor", 3 American Labor Legislation Review, 364, 1913; 5 ALLR 694, 1915.

[43] State courts in virtually every jurisdiction dealt with the question of the constitutionality of state child labor legislation. All found such statutes to be a valid exercise of the police power. See for example, City of N.Y. v. Chelsea Jute Mills, 88 NYS 1085 (1904); State v. Shorey, 48 Ore. 396 (1906); Starnes v. Albion Manufacturing Co., 147 N.C. 566 (1908); Ex parte Spencer, 86 P. 896 (California 1907); Queen v. Coal Co., 95 Tenn. 464 (1908); Gill v. Boston Store of Chicago, 337 Ill. 70 (1929).

[44] Sturges Manufacturing Co. v. Beauchamp, 231 U.S. 320 (1913).

first two decades of the 20th century, most states began to
develop much more specific and precise requirements. The primary
categories of these requirements were:

1. Minimum age for employment was set at fourteen
years in all states, with a requirement in many that the child's
age be documented by more than a mere affidavit of the parent.[45]

2. Maximum hours of eight per day and forty per
week were established in twenty states[46] by 1919 and thirty-
seven states[47] prohibited night work for children, at least in
manufacturing.

3. Progress was made toward extending the scope of
child labor laws to include more than factory employment.[48]
Most states, however, retained exemptions for agriculture and
domestic employment.[49]

4. Certification of sound physical health was made
a condition of employment in most states by 1929.[50]

----

[45]Johnson, E.S., p. 414.

[46]Ariz., Ark., Calif., Colo., D.C., Ill., Iowa, Ky., Md., Mass.,
Minn., Mo., Neb., Nev., N.J., N.Y., N.D., Ohio, Okla., Wis.
U.S. Children's Bureau, Publication No. 10, cited in Johnson, E.S., at
421.

[47]All states except Me., Md., Mont., Nev., N.M., S.D., Tex.,
Utah, Wash. W.Va., Wyo. See Id., at 422.

[48]Other types of employment that statutes were enacted to cover
included employment in offices, laundries, restaurants, hotels,
theatres, retail stores, garages, messenger services and street
trades.

[49]"Child Labor Legislation", The Book of the States, 1945-46
(Chicago: Council of State Government 1946) p. 380.

[50]Johnson, E.S., pp. 426-7.

5. Prohibitions on child labor in certain jobs
defined as hazardous began to be more specific. Prior to 1900,
what prohibitions there were were stated only in general terms
relating to health dangers, but after 1900 states began to
enumerate specific jobs from which children were prohibited.[51]

6. Education requirements, usually in the form of
completion of a certain school grade, took the place of the more
general provision that children be able to read and write.[52]

7. Employment certificates along with compulsory
attendance statutes provided the most effective means of enforcing child labor legislation.[53] The certificate required proof
of age, physical fitness and completion of educational require-

---

[51]In 1903 Illinois became the first state to enact a statute list-
ing which occupations, machines and processes were considered too
dangerous for children. (Ill. Acts of 1903, p. 187). In 1909
Pennsylvania enacted a statute with two lists, one for occupations considered hazardous to children under sixteen, another for
occupations that no minor under age eighteen could engage in. (Pa.
Act of 1909, c. 182). In 1910 Mass. authorized the State Board
of Health to determine whether any occupations were particularly
hazardous and thus should be prohibited to minors under age
eighteen. (C. 404, Mass. Acts and Resolves, 1910). These three
features became the standard type of regulation in the area.

[52]Mass. was the first state to establish as a definite educational
standard the ability to read and write ("legibly") simple sentences
in English. C. 284 Mass. Acts and Resolves, 1906. Such ability
was construed as the required proficiency for entrance into
second grade. By 1915 completion of sixth grade was required in
most states with such standards.

[53]By 1929, compulsory school attendance for the full time that
school was in session was required in all but eight states; and
attendance at continuation school for children who had obtained
employment certificates began to be required. Johnson, E.S.,
p. 412. See also: Ensign, Forest Chester, Compulsory School Attendance and Child Labor (Iowa City: Athens Press 1921), (hereinafter Ensign, F.C.), p. 238.

ments. By 1929, forty-five states[54] had employment certificate requirements.

8. Employment in so-called "street trades" (newspaper, delivery, peddling, shoeshining) began to be subject to regulation between 1911-1915, although not to the same extent as other occupations. By 1915, twenty-two states had statutory provisions limiting child employment in street trades.[55]

By 1914, exclusion of children under age fourteen from employment had been largely achieved in most states, but progress toward other goals espoused by the National Child Labor Committee during the preceding decade - limitation of hours to eight per day, exclusion from night work for children aged fourteen and fifteen and provisions for adequate inspection and enforcement, although significant, was less marked.[56]

Despite the legislative success of the child labor movement, the 1910 census revealed that the percentage of children employed in 1910 was about the same as it had been in 1900, and the number of children employed in agriculture had actually increased.[57] Although the worst physical abuses were mostly

---

[54]All states except Idaho, Miss., Tex. and Wyo. Child Labor Facts and Figures, U.S. Children Bureau Publication No. 197, 1930, p. 69.

[55]Ala., Ariz., Calif., Colo., Del. D.C., Fla., Iowa, Ky., Md., Mass., Mo., N.H., N.J., N.Y., Penn., R.I., Utah, Wis., Child Labor Legislation, U.S. Children's Bureau Publication No. 10 (1915).

[56]Wood, S.B., p. 24.

[57]Child Labor; Facts and Figures, U.S. Children's Bureau (1933), pp. 70-71.

gone, exploitation of children was still a major problem. One child in every six between the ages of ten and fifteen was gainfully employed.[58]

States were reluctant to enact further legislative reforms, partly out of fear that disparity from state to state in provisions for inspection and enforcement would lead to economic disparity. The economic and competitive advantages often enjoyed by states without protective legislation tended to retard reform efforts in almost all states where manufacturing was of any importance.[59]

These factors led reformers to the conclusion that federal legislation was the only effective mechanism for insuring uniform standards for child labor across the country. In addition, the changing political atmosphere encouraged the view that national legislation would be efficacious for fulfilling reform programs. The equalitarian tendencies of progressivism had produced an interest in the rights of children. Sensing this change, the National Child Labor Committee initiated in 1913 a campaign to establish uniform child labor standards by federal legislation.

---

[58] Id.

[59] Fuller, Raymond G., "Child Labor", Encyclopedia of the Social Sciences, Vol. III, p. 419, Erwin R.A. Seligman and Alvin Johnson, eds. (15 vols. New York, Macmillan Co., 1937).

B. Federal Child Labor Legislation

1. 1914-1938

Whether the federal government should act to regulate child labor was a question that had been considered for some
time by proponents of child labor regulation. A national child
labor law had been part of the program advocated by the Knights
of Labor in the 1880's. In 1906, the first proposal for federal
legislation[60] was submitted to Congress, but failed to gain significant public support, or even the active support of the
National Child Labor Committee.[61] By 1914, however, the National
Committee, discouraged by slow improvement in state legislation
and lack of uniformity in standards between states, was ready
to support federal legislation. In that year, the Palmer-Owen
Bill[62] was filed in the House of Representatives. Its chief
provision read:

> "That it shall be unlawful for any
> producer, manufacturer, or dealer to ship
> or deliver for shipment in interstate com-
> merce the products of any mine or quarry

---

[60]The Beveridge Bill, introduced by Senator Albert Beveridge
in 1907 (Congressional Record, 59th Congress 2nd Session, S.
6562) proposed that the Commerce Clause be used to bar from
interstate shipment the products of manufacturing establishments
that employed child laborers.

[61]The organizing principles of the NCLC encompassed only state
legislative action, not federal; the founders believed that the
conditions of industry varied so greatly and decisively from
state to state, that federal legislation would be "inadequate if
not unfortunate". Murphy, Edgar G., Problems of the Present
South (N.Y., Macmillan Co., 1904), p. 129.)

[62]Palmer-Owen Federal Child Labor Bill, 63rd Congress, 2nd
Session, H.R. 12292 (February 1914).

which have been produced in whole or in
part by the labor of children under the
age of 16 years, or the products of any
mill, cannery, factory or manufacturing
establishment which have been produced
in whole or in part, by the labor of
children under the age of fourteen
years, or by the labor of children between the age of fourteen and sixteen
years who work more than eight hours in
any one day or more than six days in
any week, or after the hour of seven
o'clock post meridian or before the hour
of seven o'clock ante meridian."[63]

The bill imposed penalties for violation - a fine
up to $1,000, or imprisonment up to one year, or both. The 1914
session ended, however, before the Senate could vote on the
legislation. The bill was re-introduced in 1916 as the Keating-
Owen Bill.[64]

Opposition to the bill during both Congressional
sessions came mainly from Southern cotton mill owners. They
attacked the bill on two grounds: first, that it was unnecessary
because industrial conditions in the South were satisfactory,
and impolitic because it was certain to prove injurious to
textile mills, their workers and the southern community; and
second, that it was unconstitutional because it exceeded congressional authority and invaded the exclusive jurisdiction of
the states. The Commerce Clause, they argued, did not extend
congressional authority to the conditions of production - but

---

[63] Id.

[64] Keating-Owen Federal Child Labor Bill, 64th Congress, 1st
Session, S.1083 (December 1915) and H.R. 8234 (January 1916).

only to the actual flow of articles in interstate commerce.[65]

Despite the opposition, the bill passed both Houses by a substantial majority[66] and was signed into law[67] in September 1916. Three days before the act was scheduled to become operative, a Federal District Court Judge in North Carolina enjoined its operation in that state.[68] Despite widespread hope and belief that the Supreme Court would uphold the law, it was declared unconstitutional in June 1918 in a five-to-four decision in the case of Hammer v. Dagenhart.[69] The court found that the statute was not a regulation of commerce but a prohibition of it. Justice Day, writing for the majority, held that the Act was repugnant to the Constitution in a twofold sense. "It not only transcends the authority delegated to Congress over commerce, but also exerts a power as to a purely local matter to which the federal authority does not extend."[70]

The following year, Congress enacted another child labor bill, this one based on the federal taxing power.[71]

---

[65] Wood, S.B., p. 48.

[66] The House voted 337 to 46 in favor of the Bill. Congressional Record, 64th Cong. 1st Sess. Vol. 53, part 2, p. 2035 (1916). The Senate approved it by vote of 52 to 12. Cong. Record, 64th Cong. 1st Sess., Vol. 53, part 12, p. 12313.

[67] 39 Stat. L. 675 (1916).

[68] Hammer v. Dagenhart, Unreported, (W.D.N.C. 1917).

[69] 247 U.S. 251 (1918).

[70] Id. at 276.

[71] The Federal Child Labor Tax Bill, 40 Stat. L. 1657 (1919).

This statute, part of the Revenue Act of 1918, levied a tax of 10% on the annual net profits of industries which employed children in violation of the age and hours standards of the bill. This statute came before the Supreme Court in the case of <u>Bailey v. Drexel Furniture Co.</u>, in 1922.[72] The Court concluded that the Act was not a taxing statute at all, but was a police regulation, and since it covered a matter not within federal jurisdiction must necessarily be unconstitutional.

Although the longest either law was in effect was three years,[73] the period during which they were in operation was sufficient to demonstrate their usefulness in eliminating employment of children from industries producing for interstate commerce.[74]

After the Child Labor Tax Law had been declared unconstitutional, the only remaining avenue thought to be available for federal regulation of child labor was a constitutional amendment to allow Congress to legislate in this area. The increase in child labor after the two federal statutes were declared unconstitutional and the increase in hours worked

---

[72] 259 U.S. 20 (1922).

[73] The Child Labor Tax Bill, enforced by the Child Labor Tax Division of the Department of Internal Revenue, operated from April 1919 until May 1922.

[74] Replies to a questionnaire sent out by the National Industrial Conference Board, Inc. indicated that a large majority of state officials found that federal laws helped materially in enforcement of their state laws. National Industrial Conf. Brd. Inc. <u>The Employment of Young Persons in the U.S.</u>, (New York 1925) pp. 70-71.

by children gave evidence that there was still a need for legislation.[75] The proposed child labor amendment read as follows:

> Section 1. The Congress shall have the
> power to limit, regulate, and prohibit the
> labor of persons under 18 years of age.
> Section 2. The power of the several States
> is unimpaired by this article, except that the
> operation of State laws shall be suspended to
> the extent necessary to give effect to legis-
> lation enacted by the Congress.[76]

The National Child Labor Committee, American
Federation of Labor, American Federation of Teachers, Democratic and Republican National Committees, National Education
Association, and many other organizations urged favorable
action by Congress.[77] After some objections concerning the
language of the amendment, the above form was adopted by the
necessary two-thirds vote in both Senate and House and was
submitted to the states for ratification.[78]

The ensuing struggle over ratification was
intense and often bitter. The same organizations that supported
the two federal statutes launched a campaign for ratification
of the amendment by the states. Opposition to the amendment
came largely from manufacturers' associations, farmers and

---

[75]Johnson, E.S., p. 443.

[76]House Joint Resolution 184, 68 Cong. 1st Session, 1924,
Congressional Record, Vol. 65, Part 7, p. 7176.

[77]Abbott, G., p. 466.

[78]Congressional Record, 68th Congress, 1st Session, 1924, Vol.
65, pp. 10122, 10142.

southern textile interests.[79] These groups launched intense propaganda campaigns. They claimed that the amendment was a communist-inspired move to take control of children away from their parents and give it to the federal government. One leaflet, published by the "Citizens' Committee to Protect Our Homes and Children"[80] cited the following arguments in opposition to the amendment:

> If this amendment is ratified it will give to Congress, 500 miles away, the power --
> 1. To take away the sovereign rights of the states and destroy local self-government which is the strength of our democracy.
> 2. To take away from you the control of the education of your children and give it to a political bureau in Washington.
> 3. To dictate when and how your children shall be allowed to work.
> 4. To subject your children and your home to the inspection of a federal agent.
> Wise Child Labor Laws are necessary but the proposed amendment gives the power to Congress to take away the rights of parents and to bring about the nationalization of their children . . .
> The passage of this amendment would be a calamity to the Nation. Don't be deceived. If you love your children . . . put a cross (x) opposite No on REFERENDUM 7."[81]

Massachusetts was regarded as a key state by both sides and a vigorous campaign was waged there. In November 1924, by a referendum vote of 3-1, the amendment was defeated.

---

[79] Johnson, E.S., p. 446.

[80] This group, very active in Massachusetts, is thought to have been an instrument of the Associated Industries of Massachusetts, Id.

[81] Leaflet, Citizen's Committee to Protect Our Homes and Children, 1925, quoted in Johnson, E.S., p. 447.

By 1925, only four states[82] had ratified and
twelve[83] had rejected the amendment, and by 1931, only six
had ratified. Between 1930 and 1932, when unemployment spread
rapidly, large numbers of employed children were discharged,
but in 1932, there was a counter-move to capitalize on the
cheap labor of children and employ them for much less than
employers felt they could offer their parents.[84] With the
combination of this development and the coming to power of
the New Deal Administration, sixteen more states ratified the
amendment. The revival of interest in turn caused renewed
efforts by the opposition and 1934 saw no state ratifications.
By 1938, only twenty-eight states had ratified the amendment,
still eight states short of the requisite number.[85]

The chief reasons for failure of states to
ratify were: 1) criticism of the language - it was thought to
be too broad a grant of power to Congress. Congress would have,
in effect, exclusive control over activities of persons under age
eighteen; 2) fear that ratification would effect a general
weakening of states' rights and a further centralization of
power in the federal government; and 3) belief that there was

---

[82]Ark., Ariz., Calif., Wis.

[83]Conn., Del., Ga., Kan., Mass., N.C., S.C., S.D., Tenn.,
Tex., Utah, Vt.

[84]Abbott, G., p. 467-8.

[85]Child Labor Legislation - Its Past, Present and Future,
7 Fordham L. Rev. 217, 1938.

no necessity for a constitutional amendment - that recent
Supreme Court decisions and severe criticism of Hammer v.
Dagenhart would enable enactment of legislation similar to that
declared unconstitutional in 1918 to survive a new Supreme
Court test, thus making amendment to the Constitution unnecessary.[86]
This last opinion proved to be accurate.

2. 1938 - Present

In 1938 Congress enacted the Fair Labor Standards
Act[87] which prohibited, among other things, "shipment or delivery for shipment in commerce of any goods produced in an estab-
blishment in the U.S. in or about which thirty days prior to the
removal of such goods therefrom, oppressive child labor has been
employed."[88] "Oppressive child labor" was defined as employment
of any child under sixteen in any establishment engaged in production of goods for commerce."[89] In 1941, the constitutionality
of this Act was challenged and upheld by the Supreme Court in
U.S. v. Darby Lumber Co.[90] Hammer v. Dagenhart,[91] several times
distinguished or ignored since it was handed down, was specifically overruled in U.S. v. Darby. Justice Stone, speaking for

---

[86] Id.

[87] 29 U.S.C. §201, et.seq.

[88] 29 U.S.C. §212.

[89] 29 U.S.C. §203.

[90] 312 U.S. 100, 61 S.Ct. 451 (1941).

[91] 247 U.S. 251 (1918).

the Court, stated "The conclusion is inescapable that <u>Hammer v.</u>
<u>Dagenhart</u> was a departure from the principles which have pre-
vailed in the interpretation of the commerce clause both before
and since that decision and that such vitality as a precedent
as it then had has long since been exhausted. It should be and
now is overruled."[92]

       The Act set an eight-hours per day - forty hours
per week maximum that children could work and established sixteen as the minimum age of employment in the industries covered.[93]
It also provided that the Children's Bureau (later amended to
the Department of Labor, Children's Employment Division) investigate and make inspections with respect to the employment of
minors and bring actions to enjoin unlawful practices and to
enforce child labor provisions.[94]

       The great majority of child laborers, those em-
ployed in commercial agriculture, intrastate industries, street
trades, mercantile establishments and many others were not
reached by this statute.[95] It has been estimated that of
850,000 children gainfully employed in 1938 no more than 50,000

[92]312 U.S. 100 at 116-117.

[93]29 U.S.C. §203(1).

[94]<u>Id.</u>, §212.

[95]Trattner, W.T., <u>Crusade for the Children: A History of the</u>
<u>National Child Labor Committee and Child Labor Reform in</u>
<u>America</u> (Chicago, Quadrangle Book, 1970), p. 207.

were covered by the Fair Labor Standards Act.[96]

Since 1938, the Act has been amended several times,[97] each amendment extending the provisions of the Act to include more types of employment and reducing the number of exemptions. The number of hazardous occupations in which child labor is prohibited outright has also been steadily increased.[98]

B. Developments in State Legislation Since 1930

Since the development of minimum standards for child labor laws in the first decade of the 20th century, most modifications of state child labor statutes have been geared to changing requirements concerning minimum ages, maximum hours, night work, need for employment certification, etc.[99] Gradually, state standards have come closer to the standards set by the federal Fair Labor Standards Act. Provisions of state statutes have established sixteen as the minimum legal age for children to be employed, have further extended listings of hazardous occupations and have made more specific provision for obtaining employment certificates.

---

[96]Bremner, Robert H., Children and Youth in America: A Documentary History (4 Vol., Cambridge, 1970), Vol. II, pp. 299-303.

[97]See 29 U.S.C. §§212, 213 and accompanying notes.

[98]"Child Labor Legislation", Book of the States, 1970-71 (Chicago Council of State Government 1971), pp. 500-501.

[99]Book of the States, Vols. 1945-1973 inclusive; "Child Labor Legislation".

C. Recent Trends - State and Federal Legislation

More recently, state statutes have been amended to ease impediments to youth employment without substantially impairing fundamental standards. This has been accomplished by modifying night work restrictions and by reducing the minimum legal age for employment in certain limited instances.[100] Programs enabling minors to obtain job training while attending school also illustrate the shift from rigid protectionism to more flexible standards. Youth Corps and work study programs for high school students are examples of this trend. In addition, amendments to regulations under the Fair Labor Standards Act permit employment of younger children (aged fourteen and fifteen) outside of school hours in certain occupations in retail, food service and gasoline service establishments.[101]

One area of employment, agriculture, has been and continues to be under-regulated, by both state and federal statutes.[102] The Fair Labor Standards Act originally exempted

---

[100] Several states have modified their statutes by easing restrictions on employment of minors engaged in vocational training programs; lowering the age for general employment outside of school hours, relaxing night work prohibitions during vacation periods and on nights preceding non-school days; and eliminating the need for employment certificates for after-school work.

At the same time, states with a fourteen years minimum age for employment have increased it to sixteen and most states have recently added to their lists of hazardous occupations from which children are excluded. Book of the States, 1970-71, pp. 500-501, 1972-73, pp. 502-503.

[101] Id.

[102] Child Labor Laws, U.S. Department of Labor, Wage and Labor Standards Administration, Bulletin No. 312 (Washington, D.C., Government Printing Office 1967), p. 23.

children employed in agriculture if they were not legally required to be in school.[103] In 1949, it was amended to prohibit such employment "during school hours".[104] This provision still allows extensive employment of children, especially migrant children, in agriculture. Very few agricultural states have child labor or compulsory attendance statues adequate to deal with the problem of migrant agricultural labor. Migrants are often not considered residents of the states they travel through and in states where the compulsory attendance statutes apply only to residents, migrant children do not fall within the scope of such statutes.[105] Without child labor legislation establishing a minimum age for agricultural employment, there is no protection for these children at all. Only sixteen states[106] provide a minimum employment age for agricultural labor outside of school hours, and many allow exemption from compulsory attendance for children so employed.[107]

---

[103] 29 U.S.C. §213(c) (1938).

[104] 29 U.S.C. §213 (c) (as amended 1949).

[105] Child Labor Laws, U.S. Dept. of Labor, Bulletin No. 312, p. 24.

[106] Alas., Calif., Colo., Conn., D.C., Ha., Ill., Ind., Iowa, Mo., N.J., N.Y., P.R., Tex., Utah, Wis., Ibid.

[107] U.S. Dept. of Labor Bulletin No. 312.

4. COMPULSORY ATTENDANCE: THE STATUTORY NETWORK

I.   Introduction

The purpose of the next two chapters is to describe in detail, analyze and compare the primary reference sections[1] of the compulsory attendance statutes of every state. An enormous amount of statutory material is involved and in order to present it in both a comprehensive and comprehensible manner, we have reduced it to comparative chart form. The chart, which appears as Appendix A, should be consulted by any reader who wishes to know the provisions of any particular jurisdiction with regard to any matter discussed generally in the text.

The first of the next two chapters will present a detailed comparative and interpretive analysis of the states' compulsory attendance primary reference sections in a manner which will provide a national overview of the answers given by various jurisdictions to the following questions:

1. Exactly what do the compulsory attendance statutes legally require of parents, children and the state.

2. What are the permissible varieties of programs through which these requirements may be fulfilled?

---

[1] By "primary reference section" we mean those portions of a jurisdiction's statutes on compulsory attendance which set forth the basic obligations of the parent, child and state with regard to participating in (usually "attending") some educational program and the alternative manners in which the obligation can be discharged. There are in most jurisdictions many other statutes which also establish rights, obligations and exceptions with regard to the compulsion of education but these are principally dealt with elsewhere in this volume. See, e.g., the chapters on truancy, exemptions and child labor, infra.

3. What elements of the present compulsory attendance statutes may be used to prevent, circumscribe or encourage the future development of alternatives to public school programs as they have traditionally been structured.

The second of the next two chapters presents an extensive analysis of all the major cases which have interpreted the compulsory attendance statutes. This analysis seeks to provide answers to the following questions:

1. Under what circumstances have the courts been willing to expand the varieties of programs which will satisfy the basic obligations contained in the attendance statutes?

2. Under what circumstances have the courts refused to effect any expansion of the programs which are permissible under the statute?

3. What are the general implications of this body of case law for the development of future alternative education programs?

An analysis of the precise wording of the primary reference sections of the compulsory attendance statutes[2] of all states[3] is basic to any determination of the underlying goals of education laws in this country and of the officially-sanctioned

_____

[2] In order to conserve space and to avoid overburdening this chapter with the clutter of hundreds of statutory citations, we have provided the citations for all the primary reference sections of the statutes of all jurisdictions in the chart in Appendix A and have omitted them from the text and notes here, except in the few instances where a particular statute is actually quoted.

[3] For purposes of this chapter, the term "states" refers to the fifty states and the District of Columbia and Puerto Rico.

means for achieving these goals. On the basis of this analysis,
it is then possible to determine the extent to which the present
statutory scheme permits the development of alternatives to the
present educational structures and, conversely, the extent to
which our laws must be changed if our educational practices are
to change.

In common usage, it has become customary to employ the
terms "compulsory attendance" and "compulsory education" interchangeably. This practice does not reflect the reality of the
law. The term "compulsory education" rarely appears in the education laws of the states. It is merely "attendance" - at some
facility or program which purports to be educational - which
is generally required, and not "education". Every state except
Mississippi has statutory provisions on compulsory attendance,
but only a dozen of them[4] ever use the term "compulsory _education_"
and of those, only one, California, really uses it in a way that
appears to require something called "education" to occur after
the more easily compelled process called "attendance" has occurred.

The general nature of the "compulsory attendance" statutes
can be derived from a review of the primary reference sections
which constitute the focal points of the whole complex legal scheme.[5]

---

[4]Alas., Ark., Calif., Ind., Iowa, Me., Mich., Neb., N.J., N.Y., Ohio.

[5]In addition to the statutes which are analyzed in this chapter,
and the case law which is analyzed in the next, this legal scheme
includes administrative regulations promulgated by the state
departments of education and, occasionally, county and local
bodies. These regulations merely implement the statutes as construed by the cases and are not within the scope of this study.
It should be pointed out, however, that they do sometimes contain
matter of critical importance to those who are interested in the
establishment of "alternative" forms of education.

In general, they establish the obligation of parents to send children within certain ages to public schools or to alternative programs for specified time periods, except when certain stated conditions justifying non-attendance exist.[6] They also permit, but do not compel, the attendance of children who are within certain age ranges which are below or above the range for compulsory attendance.[7] To insure the attendance of children who are within the compulsory age range, other sections of the statutes create administrative enforcement systems, often staffed by "attendance officers", and impose penalties on non-complying children and/or their parents.

Initially, it should be noted that neither stated legislative purposes nor case law interpretations of the compulsory attendance statutes provide much framework for this analysis. There is a dearth of both. The compulsory attendance statutes of only two states, Alabama and Indiana, contain any legislative intent provisions. And the number of judicial interpretations of compulsory attendance statutes which have included any determination of the state's precise purposes in enacting the statute

---

[6] As stated in the text, this analysis is generally confined to the primary reference provisions. The principal exception to this is when reference is made in a completely separate exemption section to a permissible alternative through which the requirement noted in the primary reference provisions may be accomplished. This occurs in twenty-four states: Alas., Ariz., Calif., Colo., Del., Ha., Ill., Ky., Me., Mass., Mich., Mont., Nev., N.M., N.D., Ohio, Ore., R.I., S.C., S.D., Tex., Utah, Vt., W.Va.

[7] Statutes of every state except Indiana and Rhode Island contain such permissive attendance provisions.

have also been quite limited.[8] To the extent that there have
been judicial endeavors in this direction, they have been very
superficial and have, not surprisingly, rather easily concluded
that the purpose of the statute was to assure that children be
educated without worrying themselves over difficulties such as
the fact that merely compelling attendance doesn't ensure that
"education" will take place.[9] On the other hand, a few courts
have interpreted compulsory attendance statutes somewhat more
literally.[10] Thus the task of answering the questions: What is
actually required by the compulsory attendance statutes? From whom?
and In what manner? can be met only by a close textual analysis
of the statutory provisions themselves.

II.   The Attendance Requirements

The basic requirement found in the primary reference provisions is that the child attend public school or some permissible
alternative facility or program. This requirement can be broken
down into a division between those states which merely require
attendance at public school or an alternative, without specifying
more, and those which go on to characterize, albeit minimally,

---

[8]See, e.g., Morton v. Board of Education of City of Chicago, 69
Ill. App. 2d 38, 216 N.E. 2d 305 (1966); Commonwealth v. Roberts,
149 Mass. 372, 34 N.E. 402 (1893); State v. Massa, 95 N.J. Super.
382, 231 A. 2d 252 (1967); State v. Hershburger, 103 Ohio App.
188, 144 N.E. 2d 693 (1955).

[9]See, e.g., State v. Williams, 56 S.D. 370, 228 N.W. 270 (1929)
and People v. Turner, 277 App. Div. 317, 319, 98 N.Y.S. 2d 886
(1950).

[10]See, e.g., Palmer v. Dist. Trustees of District No. 21, 289 S.W.
2d 344, 349 (Tex. Ct. App. 1956) and Commonwealth v. Kallock, 84
Pitts 167, 27 D § C 81 (1936).

what should transpire in the facility or program attended. This
latter group is composed of that minority of states which specifically indicate that "instruction" or "education" is required.

Not surprisingly, attendance of a school-age child in
some permissible program, as defined by statute, is required by
every state except Mississippi. More surprisingly, however, is
the fact that nothing other than attendance is required in the
majority of states. Only twenty-two states' statutes contain a
requirement that instruction or education be provided children
"upon such attendance". The usual presumption is that the legislatures assumed that there could be no doubt that their intention in
enacting such statutes was to require "education", whatever they
might have thought that term to comprise. On the other hand, most
of the statutes do not, on their face, supply much basis to refute
the claims of the public schools more severe critics that schools exist merely as convenient warehouses where, at best, a certain degree
of socialization is effected.

Of the twenty-two states which require something more than
mere attendance, two-thirds[11] require "instruction" to be given
and one-third[12] require "education" to take place. Although the
distinction between the requirements of instruction versus education has been of negligible effect to date, we note it because
of the possibility that the difference between the two terms may

---

[11]Conn., D.C., Idaho, Ind., Iowa, Me., Mass., Mo., Mont., Nev.,
N.J., N.Y., P.R., W.Va.

[12]Alas., Calif., Colo., Fla., Ind., Okla., Vt.

be of some use to those who are seeking to establish the
acceptibility of certain alternatives to the present systems.

In the fourteen states where there is a requirement of
instruction, this requirement is generally extended to any program the child attends.[13] However, there are another fifteen
states which, although they do not require "instruction" to
take place in public schools, they do require it as a prerequisite to approving home-study or other alternatives to public
school attendance.[14] Curiously, two states, Maryland and Virginia, require the child to attend school or to receive instruction.

In a majority of those fourteen states explicitly requiring instruction in the public schools, the attendance requirement
is stressed and the necessity of instruction is merely noted sub-
sequently, and indirectly. For example, in a number of statutes
this occurs through reference to attendance in a program providing
"instruction equivalent" to that given in public schools as an
acceptable alternative to attendance in public school.[15] Three

---

[13]But note that West Virginia specifies instruction in other than
public school and instruction in the home or other approved place
as exemptions from compulsory public school attendance although
no reference is made to instruction in the public school. Likewise, Nevada refers to equivalent instruction of the kind and
amount approved by the state board of education, although there
is no mention of a requirement that the public schools give "instruction".

[14]Typically these statutes require instruction by a person "teach-
ing courses usually taught in the public schools". See statutes of
Ala., Ariz., Calif., Colo., Del., Ha., Md., N.M., Ohio, Ore.,
Penn., R.I., S.D., Utah, Wis.

[15]Ind., Iowa, Me., Mo., N.J. Massachusetts notes that a child not
attending school may be "otherwise instructed", while Nevada and
West Virginia, as indicated in note 13, stress attendance in public
school while emphasizing instruction in programs other than public
school.

states[16] seem to accord the requirements of attendance and instruction equal emphasis, although in two of them the necessity of instruction is noted first. Only three states[17] appear to emphasize instruction as opposed to mere attendance as the primary requirement of their statutes.

Seven states[18] have a specific statutory requirement of "education" for each child. In addition to Indiana which has specifically stated that education of the child is the primary goal under the compulsory attendance statute,[19] only California uses the term "compulsory education" in the body of its attendance provision: "Every person between the ages of 6 and 16 years not exempted under the provisions of this chapter is subject to compulsory full-time education."[20] Only two states, Alaska and Colorado, specifically require an "academic education" to be provided. Interestingly, in Florida education and instruction evidently have been merged since its statute provides that education must be part of the "school-approved instructional program".

---

[16] Mont. (instruction and enrollment in public school), N.Y. ("attendance upon full-time instruction"), P.R.

[17] Conn., D.C., Idaho.

[18] Alas., Calif., Colo., Fla., Ind., Okla., Vt.

[19] The primary reference section refers to "A child for whom education is compulsory under this section" Ind. Code §20-8.1-3-17 (1971).

[20] Cal. Educ. Code §12101 (1969).

III.   Specific Responsibilities and Rights

    A.   The Children

       The compulsory attendance statutes of all states, ex-
cept South Carolina, indicate generally that a child of compulsory school age (most commonly, ages seven to sixteen) who is
not within any stated exception must attend public school for
the "entire time that school is in session" or at least "during
each school term". Only thirteen states specify that the attendance must be regular,[21] continuous,[22] consecutive,[23] or for every
day that the schools are open.[24] Another five states require
attendance during the specific hours that the public school is
in session.[25]

       Twenty states specifically place the burden of atten-
dance on the child.[26] In fifteen of these states,[27] the child
shares this responsibility with his parent or whomever is in

----

[21]Ariz., Conn., Fla., Md., Mich., N.J., S.C., Utah, Wis.

[22]Kan., Mich.

[23]Mich.

[24]Neb., Vt.

[25]Conn., La., N.J., P.R., Vir.

[26]Ala., Alas., Calif., Colo., Fla., Ga., Ha., Ind., Me., Md., Mass.,
Minn., N.H., N.M., N.Y., Okla., Ore., Penn., R.I., Tex.

[27]The five exceptions are Colo., Minn., N.H., N.Y., Tex., each of
which merely state that the "child is required to attend". All but
two (Ga., Okla.) of the fifteen states first place the responsibility on the child and then on the parent. Note also that some
courts have ruled that marriage, or other acts emancipating a
minor from parental control, exempts a pupil from the compulsory
attendance laws on the theory that under the statute the parents
are only responsible for assuring attendance of children (cont'd.)

loco parentis. Almost all states have truancy provisions[28]
and many of these provisions permit children to be institutionalized for truancy. In addition, several states have statutes
which authorize suspension or expulsion for truancy and most
of those which do not, have the same remedy available by virtue
of regulation.[29] Thus, whether or not the primary reference
section of the compulsory attendance statute places the responsibility for attendance on the child, a child can be made to
bear the burden of non-attendance.[30]

Despite the language of the limited number of court decisions defining the object of the compulsory attendance
statutes,[31] no compulsory attendance law refers to the "right"

---

[27] (cont'd) under their control and emancipation removes children
from parental control. See State v. Priest, 210 La. 389, 27 So.
2d 173 (1946).

[28] Only Alas., Ha., Mass., N.C., P.R. and Wash. have no such provision. See, Children Out of School in America, Children's Defense
Fund of the Washington Research Project, Inc., Appendix J, pp. 226-
228 (October, 1974). It should be noted that the first three of the
six states listed above are among those few states whose statutes
specifically place the burden on the child to attend, although they
contain no penalty for failing to attend.

[29] See, Children's Defense Fund, supra, note 28, Appendix V. pp.
350-356.

[30] See State v. Jackson, 71 N.H. 552, 53 A. 1021 (1902).

[31] For example, People v. Turner, 227 App. Div. 317, 98 N.Y.S. 2d
886, 888 (1950):
> The object of the compulsory education law is to see
> that children are not left in ignorance, that from
> some source they will receive instruction that will
> fit them for their place in society.

Through the compulsory attendance laws the state assures children
of "adequate preparation for the independent and intelligent exercise of their privileges and obligations as citizens in a free
democracy." Commonwealth ex rel Bey, 166 Pa. Super. Ct. 136,
140, 70 A.2d 693.

of children to attend school, or to be instructed or educated.[32]

It is interesting to note in this connection that the statutes

of only two states[33] refer to the child as a "person". (Normally,

under our constitutional scheme of government, only persons have

rights.) Of course, claims have been made that if a child is

required to attend school then he or she must have a concomitant

right to be enrolled; however, these claims have usually involved

various constitutional assertions[34] and there is no case where

such a claim has been upheld solely on state statutory grounds.

As has been well-documented elsewhere,[35] if a child fails

to abide by the rules and regulations of the school, suspension

and/or expulsion is specifically authorized by statute, regulation

---

[32]The only compulsory attendance statute which specifies any
right of the child is the statute of Alabama: "Each child,
through his parents, legal custodian, or guardian, shall have
the right to choose whether or not he shall attend a school provided for members of his own race." Tit. 52, §297 (1956, 2nd Ex.
Sess., p. 446, §3, appvd., April 14, 1956).

[33]Calif., N.M.

[34]See, e.g., Mills v. Board of Education of District of Columbia,
348 F. Supp. 866 (D.D.C. 1972). And see discussion, Chapter 11,
infra.

[35]See, Children Out of School in America, supra, note 28. And
in this connection note Betts v. Board of Education of City of
Chicago, 466 F. 2d 629, 635 (7th Cir. 1972): "The compulsory
attendance statutes are directed to parents or guardians and do
not purport to guarantee students impunity from their schools
regardless of the misconduct they engage in." 466 F.2d at 635.

or local policy in all but a half-dozen states. The compulsory attendance statutes of only fifteen states list suspension and expulsion as reasons for exemption from the attendance requirement; presumably, however, a suspended or expelled student cannot be proceeded against in the other states for violation of the attendance duty although that Orwellian possibility is not inconceivable.

Probably the principal group of children still not specifically included within the operation of the nation's compulsory attendance statutes are the children of migrant workers. Only three states specifically provide that a migrant child or a child whose residence is seasonal is subject to the compulsory attendance laws.[36] However, contrary to the assumption of many, nothing in the compulsory attendance laws of the remaining states indicates that a migrant child would be denied access to the public school system in the district in which he or she resides merely because that residence is temporary. Moreover, such a denial would raise a state constitutional issue in those sixteen states with constitutional enabling statutes providing that any state-provided educational system must be open to "all children".

May a child of his or her own accord and without parental consent choose to attend a private school or participate in some other program which is a statutorily-acceptable alternative

_____

[36]See Pa. Stat. tit. 24 §§13-1326, 1327 (1970); Ky. Rev. Stat. Ann. §159.010 (1971), and Ohio Rev. Code Ann. §3321.02 (1972).

to public school attendance?[37]   No compulsory attendance statute

refers to any such right of the child to so choose.[38]   On the

other hand, no compulsory attendance law specifies that atten-

dance at a private school or other program in lieu of public

school attendance must be with the consent of the parent or

person in loco parentis.   The manner in which a child may be

excused from public school attendance may have bearing on this

question.   Only a small minority of jurisdictions provide that a

child may be excused from attendance only upon the application

of the parent or person in loco parentis.   In those jurisdic-

tions, clearly the child could not implement his or her own

choice; in the other jurisdictions it appears to be an open

question.

    B.   The Parents

       Whatever the precise nature of the common law respon-

sibility of parents to educate their children,[39] there is no

statutory responsibility to educate their children created by the

---

[37]This dicussion does not consider the legal ramifications of
such a choice and a refusal to attend a public school by a child
residing in a state with so-called "stubborn child" statutes and
whose parents object to his or her choice of school or program
and want the child to attend public school.

[38]With the possible exception of Arizona, where a parent or
other person having custody of a child may be excused from his
or her obligation to send the child to public school if "the
child has presented reasons for non-attendance which are satisfactory to a board consisting of the president of the local board
of trustees, the teacher of the child and the probation officer
of the superior court of the county". Ariz. Rev. Stat. Ann.
§15 - 321(5) (1972).

[39]The parents' duty to educate their children up to their (i.e.,
the parents') "station-in-life" is often said to be part of the
common law duty of "parental support" owed by all parents to
their unemancipated children.

compulsory attendance laws. The most that seems to be required
of parents under these statutes is that they be the force that
sets the wheel in motion - the usual statutory language is that
they have the obligation "to cause the child to attend school" or
to "cause the child to be otherwise instructed".

Every state directly or implicitly requires the
parent[40] having control of a child who is not within any exception to send or cause such child to attend school or some prescribed alternative. Just exactly what is meant by the qualification "having control" of a child, which appears in many
statutes, remains unexplicated in every jurisdiction.[41] The vast
majority of states explicitly require the parent to cause the
child to attend school. Those states which do not use the
explicit language achieve the same effect by imposing criminal
penalties (usually misdemeanor level fines and/or imprisonment)
on the parent whose child does not attend.[42] However, jurisdictions which have considered the question have usually concluded
that parents do not have to literally "insure" attendance of
their children at school.[43] If a parent is not a party to his
or her child's violation of the compulsory attendance statutes,

---

[40]Throughout this discussion all references to parent shall include
parent, guardian or other person in loco parentis.

[41]But for some possible insight into the meaning of this term,
see State v. Priest, supra, note 27.

[42]Only Kansas does not impose such penalties and it does not
require parents to "require" their children to attend school.

[43]See, e.g., Comm. v. Mosteller, 34 D & C 2d [Pa.] 711 (1965).

some state statutes excuse the parent from responsibility for the child's non-attendance, even though the statutes provide that it is unlawful for a parent to "fail, neglect or refuse" to send the child to school.[44]

Only Michigan describes in its compulsory attendance statutes "how" the parent shall send the child to the public schools: "equipped with the proper textbooks necessary to pursue his school work."[45] The obligation of paying for textbooks or other fees may be imposed on the parent. While a majority of states have provisions requiring free textbooks for children in grades one through twelve, some states[46] have no such provisions, others[47] require free textbooks only through eighth grade, a few[48] condition the availability of textbooks on the extent of state appropriations, some[49] merely _permit_ the free distribution of textbooks and several states[50] either require or permit free textbooks only for indigents. In the majority of instances

------

[44]See, e.g., Ind. Code §§20-8.1-3-33,34(1973).

[45]However, in Bond v. Public Schools of Ann Arbor School Dist., 178 N.W. 2d 484, 383 Mich. 693 (1970), the court held that since books are an essential part of a system of free public elementary and secondary schools, the school cannot charge for them. But see Hamer v. Bd. of Ed., 47 Ill.2d 480, 265 N.E. 2d 616 (1970.) (Phrase "free school" does not mean free textbooks.)

[46]Alas., Colo., Ha., Utah.

[47]Ariz., Calif., Ore.

[48]Ala., Ky., N.C.

[49]Ill., Ind., Iowa, Kan., Mich., N.D., W.Va.

[50]Ark., Kan., Ky., Va., Wis.

where judicial challenges have been brought against public school
textbook fees, the fees have been held invalid.[51]

Although many states refer to the parents' duty to
arrange for instruction of a child who does not attend public
school, only Connecticut establishes the affirmative duty of the
parent to instruct personally if no other alternative is elected.[52]
The Connecticut provision also illustrates nicely the connection
between child labor regulation and compulsory attendance which
was discussed earlier in this volume: "All parents and those
having the care of children shall bring them up in some lawful
and honest employment and instruct them or cause them to be
instructed"[53] in specified subjects.

Perhaps because the existence of compulsory attendance
statutes is predicated upon the _public_ interest in the education
of children, the concept of parental "rights" concerning the education of their children, which is often referred to in case law,
is absent in the statutes. The parental right doctrine has been a
major underpinning of the jurisprudence of the United States
Supreme Court in this area. In the leading case of _Pierce v._
Society of Sisters[54] the court said: "The child is not the mere
creature of the state; those who nurture him and direct his

---

[51]See cases collected in Annotation, _Validity of Public School_
Fees, 41 ALR 3rd 753.

[52]An example of a more typical provision is Idaho's: "Unless the
child is otherwise comparably instructed . . . the parent or
guardian shall cause the child to attend school", Idaho code
§33-202 (1963).

[53]Conn. Gen. Stat. Ann. § 10-184 (1959).

[54]268 U.S. 510 (1925). See discussion in Chapter 11, _infra_.

destiny have the right, coupled with the high duty, to recognize
and prepare him for additional obligations." The combined effect
of _Pierce_ and _Meyer v. Nebraska_,[55] the other early leading case in
this area, is that the state cannot unreasonably interfere with
efforts of parents to direct the education and upbringing of their
children. Even though this doctrine is not very evident on the
face of these statutes, many state courts have included it in them
by interpretation.[56]

In an indirect way, the parents' right to exercise some
discretion in the matter of education of their children appears
in the attendance statutes, since in most cases it is the parent
who must make the decision as to whether the child will attend
public school or participate in one of the other permitted alternatives. However, even this right of the parent to choose is
circumscribed by the concurrent obligation to submit to state
regulations concerning whichever educational alternative is
chosen.

C. The State

The authority of the state to require some sort of
educational experience for children has never been seriously

---

[55] 262 U.S. 390, (1923). See discussion in chapter 11, _infra_.

[56] See, e.g., _State v. O'Neil_, 187 Ind. 84, 118 N.E. 529 (1918)
("Statutes such as the compulsory attendance statutes do not
invade the right of the parent to govern and control his own
children and they are to be given a reasonable interpretation
to the end that the best interests of the child and the state
alike may be served."); _In re Skipworth_, 180 N.Y.S. 2d 852, 873
(1958) ("These parents have the constitutionally guaranteed right
to elect no education for their children rather than to subject
them to discriminatorily inferior education").

doubted. Even the plaintiffs in the Pierce case didn't question
that proposition; as the Supreme Court observed, "no question is
raised as to the [power of the state] to require that all
children of proper age attend some school."[57] (emphasis added.)
Numerous lower courts have echoed this view by holding that compulsory attendance statutes are clearly within the police power
of the state and are not in violation of any constitutional
prohibition.[58]

The compulsory attendance statutes reflect separate
state constitutional[59] or statutory[60] obligations to establish
school systems. But, despite occasional statutory[61] or case
law[62] pronouncements regarding the purpose of these systems,

---

[57]Pierce v. Society of Sisters, 268 U.S. at 534.

[58]See, e.g., Marsh v. Earle, 24 F.Supp. 385 (D.C. Penn. 1938), and
State v. Hoyt, 84 N.H. 38, 146 A. 170 (1929).

[59]Forty-three states are required by their constitutional provisions to provide some kind of educational system.

[60]The Massachusetts statute is typical of those where the state
requires individual localities to fulfill this mandate:

> Every town shall maintain, for at least the number of
> days required by the local board of education in each
> school year unless specifically exempted as to any one
> year by said board, a sufficient number of schools for
> the instruction of all children who may legally attend
> a public school therein. Mass. Gen. Laws. c. 71, §1.(1974).

[61]For example, the Secretary of Education of Puerto Rico is
"directed to establish and maintain a system of free public
schools in Puerto Rico for the purpose of providing a liberal education to the children of school age." P.R. Laws Ann. Tit. 3,
§141 (1965).

[62]In Re Shinn, 195 Cal. App. 2d 683, 686, 6 Cal. Rpts. 165
(1963) ("A primary purpose of the educational system is to train
school children in good citizenship, patriotism and loyalty to
the state and nation as a means of protecting the public welfare."); Comm. v. Kallock, 84 Pitts 167, 67 D§C 81 (1963) (cont'd)

few state compulsory attendance statutes actually require
the state to fulfill the educational needs of children. All
that is required by most statutes is that there be facilities
for them to attend. On the other hand, more recent court decisions have concluded that certain responsibilities of the state
must logically follow from the compulsory nature of the attendance
statutes:

> [We] need not belabor the fact that requiring
> parents to see that their children attend school
> under pain of criminal penalties presupposes
> that an educational opportunity will be made
> available to the children.[63]

Nevertheless, even this view of the state's responsibility has not yet been extended to the point where the state
would be seen as under an obligation to insure that every child
who wishes to attend school may do so. A notable illustration
of this is provided by the "exception" to the requirement of
attendance which is "given" (i.e. forced on) those children who
live such a distance from the nearest school that the school
transportation system cannot include them.

[62(cont'd)] (The public school system "is designed and intended not
only to furnish equal opportunity to obtain an education by all
children but also to compel all parents to take advantage of that
opportunity, to the end that through education a more enlightened
citizenry may result." State v. Counart, 69 Wash., 361, 124 P.
910 (1912) ("[T]he purpose and end of both public and private
schools must be the same - the education of children of school
age.").

[63] Mills v. Bd. of Educ. of District of Columbia, 348 F. Supp.
866, 874 (D.D.C. 1972). And see Jackson v. Hankinson, 51 N.J.
230, 238 A. 2d 685, 688: "[S]ince the relationship between child
and school authorities is not a voluntary one but is compelled
by law . . . school authorities are obligated to take reasonable
precaution for his safety and well-being.").

IV.   The Permissible Learning Arrangements

In most jurisdictions parents have the option of electing one of three different learning arrangements in order to comply with the compulsory attendance laws: public school, private school and, in a scant majority of states, some non-school learning program. The following analysis of the programs through which the attendance requirements of the compulsory attendance laws may be satisfied excludes three categories of "educational" programs in which attendance may be required by the states under special circumstances: "continuation" or part-time school programs, truancy or "parental school" programs, and special education programs. We exclude these because they are not, in most jurisdictions, an integral part of the general statutory scheme we are examining. Requirements concerning attendance in such programs seldom occur in the primary reference sections of the compulsory attendance laws. But, because of their importance to a substantial number of children, we summarize the statutory situation regarding these children:

1. Special Education Programs. All states have exceptions to their compulsory attendance laws permitting non-attendance in regular school programs for reasons of physical or mental disability. Only thirteen of these states refer to special education programs for children so exempted.[64] Most of these states require attendance of children in such programs

---

[64]D.C., Fla., La., Mass., Mont., N.Y., N.D., Ohio, Ore., P.R., S.C., S.D., Tex.

only under certain circumstances,[65] while only a few seem to
require some special instruction for the child in any situation.[66]
It should be noted, however, that there is a judicial trend establishing the right of handicapped children to an education _in_
public schools based upon the U.S. Constitution and state statutes.[67]

2. Continuation or Part-Time School Programs. A number
of states require attendance at part-time "continuation" schools
for school-age children who have been granted employment permits.
The requirement of part-time continuation school attendance
appears in the primary reference section of the attendance statutes

---

[65]For example, Louisiana (if the state provides programs); Ohio
(unless the child is termed incapable of profiting from further
instruction); Puerto Rico (if an examination shows that the
"minor may benefit from instruction in an ungraded or special
class").

[66]For example, D.C., Ore., and Mass. Note the special language
of several sections of the Massachusetts compulsory attendance
law: A child is excused from school attendance if his or her
"physical or mental condition is such as to render attendance
inexpedient or impracticable, subject to the provisions of section three of Chapter seventy-one B" (emphasis added). Mass.
Gen. Laws c. 76, §1.(1972). Reference to Mass. Gen. Laws c. 71B, §3
indicates that Massachusetts law requires that all children
with special needs be provided with a special education program
to meet those needs. The language of Mass. Gen. Laws c. 76, §2
is unique among the states. This "Duties of Parents" section
provides that

> No physical or mental condition capable of correc-
> tion, or rendering the child a fit subject for
> special instruction at public charge in institu-
> tions other than public day schools, shall avail
> as a defense unless it appears that the defendant
> has employed all reasonable measures for the cor-
> rection of the condition and the suitable instruc-
> tion of the child.

[67]See, _Mills_, _supra_, note 63; _Pennsylvania Assoc. for Retarded
Citizens v. Pennsylvania_, 343 F. Supp. 279 (E.D. Pa., 1972).
And see discussion, chapter 11, _infra_.

in some states,[68] and in others it appears in the "exceptions"
to attendance sections.[69] Curiously, while about half the
states have statutes requiring attendance at such schools, only
fourteen states have enabling statutes authorizing the establishment of the schools.

    3. Truancy or Parental Programs. A few states have
statutes requiring truants, or, in some cases, children who have
been found to be "incorrigible, vicious or immoral"[70] to attend
"truancy or parental school" programs. Unfortunately, these
statutes provide no descriptions of the nature or content of
these schools or programs. This lack of definitional content is
typical of the compulsory attendance statutes, which generally do
not describe the other types of facilities or programs they permit,
as will be seen below.

    A. Public School

    Every state specifies that a "public" school (also
known as "common school") is among the enumerated learning
arrangements through which a child may satisfy the compulsory
attendance requirement.[71] A substantial number of jurisdictions

---

[68]For example, Calif., Wash., N.Y.

[69]For example, Ill., Mo., Ohio, Ore., Utah and Wash.

[70]For example, statutes in Ky., Neb., and Tenn. so provide.

[71]Pennsylvania merely states that the child shall attend a "day
school in which the subjects and activities prescribed by the
standards of the State Board of Education are taught in the
English language." Pa. Stat. tit. 24 §13-1327 (1970). Although
the statute doesn't use the words "public" or "common", it is
obvious from the context that "public" schools are intended.

stress attendance in the public school by referring to the other permitted arrangements as "exceptions" to public school attendance rather than alternatives to it.[72]

The compulsory attendance statutes provide almost no description of these "public schools". In virtually every jurisdiction, the education statutes define "public school" by describing programs,[73] courses,[74] and teacher[75] requirements, or presenting the policies regulating those requirements.[76] The nature of the facility, if there must be one, and the precise meaning of "public" are left unspecified.

Only four states provide any definition of "school" at all for purposes of the compulsory attendance statutes.[77] While three of these jurisdictions merely describe a "school" as a "school" meeting certain requirements,[78] only one actually

---

[72]Alas., Ariz., Calif., Colo., Conn., Del., Ill., Ky., Me., Mich., Mont., Nev., N.D., Ore., R.I., Tex., Vt., W.Va.

[73]E.g., Mass. Gen. Laws, c. 71A, §§1-9

[74]E.g., R.I. Gen. Laws Ann., §§16-22-(1-9) (1963).

[75]E.G., N.D. Cent. Code §15-41-25 (Supp. 1973).

[76]E.g., Wash. Rev. Code §28A.04.120 (1970).

[77]Ala. Code tit. 52 §299 (1927); La. Rev. Stat. §17:236 (1964); Minn. Stat. §120.10(2) (1959); N.C. Gen. Stat. §115-166 (1975).

[78]Ala. (holding a certificate issued by school authorities indicating that the school has certified teachers teaching courses required to be taught in the public schools in the English language and keeping a register of attendance); Minn. (having qualified teachers teaching all the "common branches" in English from textbooks written in English); N.C. (having teachers approved by school officials).

defines the nature of the entity that may be classified as a
school:

> "an institution for the teaching of children,
> consisting of an adequate physical plant,
> whether owned or leased, (certified) instruc-
> tional staff members and (at least fifty)
> students (enrolled as bona fide pupils),

and operating a minimum session of not less than one hundred and
eighty days.[79] Except for Alabama's provisions, all of the above
"definitions" apply to both public and private schools. The
definition of "school" in Louisiana, a jurisdiction which specifies only private school attendance as a permissible alternative to
public school attendance, essentially precludes any future expansion of permissible learning arrangements through interpretation
of the term "private school".

Some jurisdictions do specify the minimum and maximum
enrollments that must be maintained by "graded" and "rural" schools.[80]
To the extent that such statutory requirements are enforced, the
varieties of possible public experimental school programs may be
limited.

A few state attendance provisions refer to regulatory
bodies, primarily local, which may prescribe policies and regulations concerning admission and attendance.[81] Although the primary

---

[79]Louisiana (La. Rev. Stat. §17:236 (1964). Although all states,
except South Carolina, have statutory provisions establishing a
minimum term that a child must attend, only Louisiana requires
that an institution operate a minimum session in order to be
classified as a school.

[80]See, e.g., P.R. Laws Ann., T.18, §80(d) (1961).

[81]The statutes of Ala., Conn., Del., Fla., Ha., Idaho, Iowa,
Mont., Ohio have such references.

reference provisions generally require attendance during the time school is in session, they seldom prescribe the actual length of the school term. (The minimum length of the school term in the vast majority of states is between 170 and 180 days.[82])

One presumes that the term "public school" includes vocational school, but the primary reference sections of only two states' statutes[83] refer to the vocational school component of the public system. In one of those states, the existence of a vocational school within the school district in which the child resides determines the maximum compulsory school age for children residing in that district: if no "vocational, technical and adult education school" exists in the district, the compulsory school age is sixteen years or until high school is completed, otherwise it is eighteen years.[84]

B. Private School

Every state is constitutionally required[85] to permit children to attend private schools in lieu of public school attendance, so long as the private schools meet reasonable state requirements. Consequently, virtually every state's statutes specifically recognize the "private school" as one means of

---

[82]See K. Alexander and K.F. Jordan, Legal Aspects of Educational Choice: Compulsory Attendance and Student Assignment (NOLPE Second Monograph Series on Legal Aspects of School Administration) (No.4 1973).

[83]Wis. and Penn.

[84]Wis. Stat. §40.77(1)(am)(1965), §118.15(1)(b) and (c)(1971).

[85]Pierce v. Society of Sisters, supra, note 57.

acceptable compliance with the compulsory attendance law, and eight jurisdictions[86] appear, on the face of their statutes, to consider it the only acceptable alternative to the public school. In those eighteen jurisdictions[87] which specify "private school" as the only type of school (as opposed to learning arrangements not involving a "school", e.g., home instruction, individual tutors) which may be attended in lieu of public school, the reference is apparently generic and refers to any school which is not public but which complies with applicable regulations. In those twenty jurisdictions whose statutes refer to "parochial"[88] and/or "denominational",[89] "parish",[90] or "other"[91] schools in addition to "private school", the reference to "private school" is apparently meant to refer only to non-religious schools.

In addition, twelve jurisdictions implicitly recognize the private school for purposes of the compulsory attendance requirement by a general reference to "some other school",[92] a

---

[86]Ga., La., Minn., N.H., P.R., Tenn., Tex., Wyo.

[87]Alas., Calif., Ga., Ha., Iowa, La., Me., Minn., Mont. ("private institution"), N.H., N.M., P.R., R.I., S.D., Tenn., Utah, Wis., Wyo.

[88]Ariz., Ark., D.C., Idaho, Ill., Ky., N.D., Tex., Wash.

[89]Ala., Fla., Kan., Mich., Neb., Ore., S.C., Va., W.Va.

[90]Mo.

[91]Okla., W.Va.

[92]Ind., Mass., Nev.

school meeting certain requirements,[93] or a school which is
"independent",[94] "elsewhere",[95] or providing "equivalent education otherwise".[96]

The statutory provisions of sixteen states contain
definitions of the term "private school". Most of these definitions are found in recently enacted amendments regulating
trade and career schools. In twelve of these jurisdictions,[97]
the definition usually refers only to a private school operated
for profit, and generally defines it as any person, firm, part-
nership or corporation doing business by offering instruction to
the public for a fee. All of these twelve jurisdictions exclude
parochial or religiously affiliated schools from their "private
school" definitions. In the remaining four jurisdictions, the
definition of "private school" is simply: any "non-public
school" or any school not funded by public money.

1. The Principal Statutory Requirements

Much of the state control which is exercised over
private schools has its source in regulations rather than in

[93] Conn., N.J., N.C., Ohio

[94] Colo.

[95] Del., Md., N.Y.

[96] Vt.

[97] Ark. Stat. Ann. §80-4301 (1975), Hawaii Rev. Stat. §302-1(2) (1965);
Ind. Code §20-1-19-1 (1971); Kan. Stat. Ann. §72-4919 (1971); Minn.
Stat. §141.01-141.11 (1973); New. Rev. Stat. §394.103(1975); N.C. Gen.
Stat. §115-245 (1961); Ohio Rev. Code Ann. §§3301.07 (1971),3321.01
(1971) and 3321.07 (1967); Okla. Stat. Tit. 70 §3-104 (1972), Tit.
70§21-101 (1971); Ore. Rev. Stat. §§45.010(5) (1973); Pa. Stat. Ann.
Tit. 24§2731 (1951); Wyo. Stat. Ann. §21.1-191 (Supp. 1973).

statutes. To the extent that statutory law puts constraints on
private schools, these constraints tend to fall into four major
categories: requirements regarding some "approval" process, requirements about length of term, requirements concerning curriculum and requirements concerning the teaching staff.

The primary reference sections in nine states'[98]
statutes contain provisions establishing private schools as
acceptable alternative learning arrangements for compulsory
attendance purposes only when the private school is "approved".
The body which grants this approval varies from state to state
and includes school committees,[99] county superintendents of
schools,[100] county boards of education,[101] the state superintendent of education,[102] and the state board of education.[103] A
few statutes which call for approval are unclear about the body
which grants the approval,[104] or merely state that approval shall
be pursuant to regulations established by the state board of education,[105] which presumably, but not necessarily, means the state

---

[98]Ala. (certified), Ky., Mass., N.H., N.D., R.I., S.C., Wash.,
W.Va.

[99]Mass., R.I.

[100]N.D.

[101]W.Va.

[102]Ala.

[103]Ky.

[104]E.g., N.H.

[105]E.g., Wash.

board, itself, grants the approval. Occasionally, approval is by a non-state agency as in South Carolina where the statute permits approval by the South Carolina Independent Schools Association or "some similar organization".

Only four states'[106] statutes specify the minimum requirements that must be met by a private school in order to obtain the requisite approval. All four specify the necessity of a curriculum "equivalent" to that taught in the public schools; one adds that this curriculum must be taught thoroughly and efficiently;[107] two require staffing by certified teachers,[108] and the keeping of a register of attendance.[109] A few statutes contain very vague or even undecipherable provisions such as a requirement that the private school be "regularly organized"[110] or "established".[111]

Obviously, there is a substantial void in the statutory law regarding private schools. There are, however, some requirements which the private school must conform to in order to be an officially acceptable alternative for a compulsory school age child. The most prevalent of these requirements relates to the amount of time a child must spend in the

---

[106]Ala., Mass., N.D., R.I.

[107]R.I.

[108]Ala., N.D.

[109]Ala., R.I.

[110]Ariz.

[111]Utah

school. In a fair number of states[112] this is the only requirement specified in the primary reference sections. Most states[113]
simply apply to the private schools the general time requirement
that governs public schools and specify that the private school
child must be in attendance for the entire time that the public
school is in session.

Requirements regarding curriculum are the next
most prevalent standards found in the primary reference sections,
with about one-half the jurisdictions making reference to the
nature of an acceptable course of study. Thirteen states specifically require that the instruction be "equivalent"[114] or "comparable"[115] to that provided to children in the public school in
the locality where the child resides. Although one often hears
educators and public school critics speak of the "requirement"
that private alternative schools have curriculum "substantially
equivalent" to the public schools, only one jurisdiction, New
York, actually uses that phrase in its statutes.

A few states, such as Nevada,[116] have statutes
which speak of equivalency not only in terms of the kind of instruction being given but also in terms of the "amount", although how

---

[112]Ark., Fla., Ga., Ha., Idaho, Neb., Okla., P.R., S.C., Tenn.,
Va., Wash., W.Va., Wis., Wyo.

[113]All except Alas., Calif., Conn., Del., Ill., Ky., Mass.,
Mich., Mont., Nev., N.J., S.C., Tex., Vt.

[114]Conn., D.C., Ind., Iowa, Me., Mass., N.J., N.Y., Vt.

[115]Alas., Colo., Idaho, Mich.

[116]Nev. Rev. Stat. §392.070 (1956).

this requirement differs from the length of term requirement is unclear. In addition, two states delineate the elements of this equivalency by providing that the instruction be equal or comparable to that given to children of the same age[117] and grade[118] or level of attainment.[119] Massachusetts adds, optimistically, that private school instruction must be "equal in thoroughness and efficiency" to that of the public schools.

In addition, seven jurisdictions[120] provide that private schools must offer instruction in the "same branches of study" which are required to be taught in the public schools. Three of these jurisdictions specifically require that the courses offered be those taught to children of corresponding age[121] and grade[122] in the public school, and one requires that the subjects be taught "in a manner suitable to children of the same ages and stage of advancement".[123]

While refraining from requiring that the same subjects taught in the public schools be offered in the private schools, the remaining states do have curriculum requirements

---

[117]Mich., N.Y.

[118]Mich.

[119]N.Y.

[120]Ala., Calif., Del., Ill., Md., Mich., Ore.

[121]Ill., Md., Mich.

[122]Ill., Mich.

[123]Del.

in the sense that they require a prescribed[124] or "approved"[125]
course to be offered. The compulsory attendance provisions of
six states[126] specifically require the courses in the private
school be taught in English. The only course of study prescribed
for the private schools in Texas is "a study of good citizenship".[127] In addition to "branches of study", Pennsylvania requires private schools to provide "activities" prescribed by
the state Board of Education, but it appears to be alone in this
requirement.

The last major category of requirements with which
private schools must comply involves their teaching staff. The
compulsory attendance provisions of a small number of states
indicate that private schools will be acceptable places of attendance only if their teachers meet certain requirements. Five
states require that teachers be "certified",[128] while one merely
requires that they be qualified.[129] Two other states use the
even less definite term "competent".[130] Another states that

---

[124]Minn., Mont., N.D., Penn., R.I. While some states, for example
Mont. and N.D., refer to other statutory provisions concerning
courses of instruction, the compulsory attendance statute of
Minn. merely requires that the "common branches" be taught, although it does not define that term.

[125]Me. (by commissioner); N.M. (by the state board); N.D. (county
or city superintendent of schools or the state board of education).

[126]Ill., Ind., Minn., Mont., Penn., R.I.

[127]Tex. Educ. Code §21.033(1)(1971).

[128]Ala.,Alas., Iowa, La., N.D.

[129]Ohio

[130]Ariz., Kan.

teacher qualifications must be "essentially equivalent to the minimum standards for public school teachers of the same grades or subjects."[131] While the exact scope of the above terms is not apparent from the compulsory attendance laws, the law of several jurisdictions indicates that whatever the precise meaning of terms such as "capable", these terms do not necessarily imply the necessity of meeting state certification requirements.[132]

A few state compulsory attendance statutes contain other general requirements pertinent to the private school. Although seldom appearing in the primary attendance sections, the requirement that private schools keep registers or records of attendance may appear in other sections of the compulsory attendance statutes.[133] The failure of private schools to keep records of attendance and render attendance reports as are required of public schools¸renders them unacceptable places of attendance for purposes of the compulsory attendance laws in some jurisdictions.[134] Some statutes require that private schools be "open to inspection" by the state attendance officer, local attendance officers or other officials.

---

[131] Minn.

[132] See, e.g., People v. Turner, 121 CA 2d Supp. 861, 263 P. 2d 685 (1953), appeal denied 347 U.S. 972. The California compulsory attendance provisions requiring private tutors to "hold a valid state credential for the grade taught" was not "unreasonable or arbitrary", although teachers in private schools were not required to possess such certificate although they were required to be persons "capable of teaching".

[133] For example, such records are required in Calif. (§12154), D.C. (§31-205), La. (§17:228) and R.I. (§16-19-2).

[134] E.g., Conn., N.C.

2.   Relationship between the Principal Requirements
     and the Establishment of Alternative Learning
     Arrangements

Because no state other than Louisiana defines
the "private school" in terms of a physical facility and a
minimum number of students, the private school option which is
explicitly or implicitly permitted in all compulsory attendance
statutes opens a wide range of possibilities for the extablish-
ment of future alternative learning arrangements. For example,
case law in two states has already interpreted the phrase "private
school" to include home instruction.[135]

Of course, the two primary categories of basic
requirements which might seriously circumscribe or even prevent
the establishment of future innovative alternative learning
arrangements under the "private school" option are those regarding
curriculum, which require "equivalent instruction" or adherence
to a prescribed program of study, and those requiring state certification of the teaching staff.

With regard to the first category, "equivalent
instruction" is, as we have seen, essentially undefined by most
compulsory attendance statutes. But the most likely implication
of the phrase and the one that has been adopted by a number of
regulations which implement these statutes is that it probably

---

[135]People v. Levison, 404 Ill. 574, 90 N.E. 2d 213 (1950);
State v. Peterman, 121 Cal. App. 2d 861, 263 P.2d 685 (1853).
But contra, State v. Garber 197 Kan. 567, 419 P.2d 896 (1966);
State v. Counart, 69 Wash. 361, 124 P. 910 (1912);
Cf. State v. Hoyt, 84 N.H. 38, 146 A. 170 (1929). And, see
discussion, chapter 5, infra.

means, at a minimum, instruction in those subjects offered to children of the same age or grade in the public schools in the locality
where the child resides. If this is all it means, it is probably
a requirement that can be coped with by innovative alternative
learning arrangements seeking legitimacy under the "private
school" rubric. However, if, in addition, it is interpreted to
mean instruction to the same extent and for the same duration
that the subjects are taught in the public school, and instruction
in a "school" environment similar to that of the public school,
it could be a limiting concept so far as the development of
new alternative learning arrangements is concerned. Of course,
very strict adherence to a set of prescribed courses, to the extent and for the duration that similar courses are required to
be taught in the public schools, would be very restricting even
to more conventional private schools and is not often required
of them. It is important to note that very few states specify
both that the courses and the methods of instruction must be
those utilized by the public schools. In general, the most that
is required is that the methods of instruction be approved, not
that they be equivalent.

The difficulties likely to be engendered by the
second category of requirements concerning teacher certification
is obvious. The effectiveness of a contemplated alternative
learning arrangement other than public schools and conventional
private schools may well depend on the use of personnel whose
qualifications do not comply with state certification requirements.

A third and widespread requirement that private
schools be attended for a specified number of days and during
the same basic period the public schools are in session is also
potentially limiting. But the failure of almost every state to
provide a statutory definition of "attendance" for private
school purposes may alleviate this impediment to the establishment of innovative programs. Note that Florida is the only state
with a statutory definition of "regular attendance" in a private
school.[136] Whether the definition of attendance is provided by
statute, as in Florida, or by regulation, as in a number of
states, or by some less formal document, in most instances, the
requirement of presence in a facility (school) is qualified by
a provision which considers engaging in an activity which is
part of the approved curriculum to be compliance with the attendance requirement. This should enable a number of innovative
alternative learning arrangements to avoid violation of the basic
statutory requirements.

On the other hand, it must be remembered that the
policies and regulations established by state and local governing
bodies may circumscribe attendance policies in ways which are
detrimental to the development of future alternative learning
arrangements. Surprisingly, however, of the four states with
primary reference sections which explicitly refer to the establishment of general attendance requirements by regulatory

---

[136]Fla. Stat. §232.02 (1961).

Governmental agencies,[137] only two, Florida and Idaho, indicate
that such policies are to be applied to private schools. Statutory provisions elsewhere in the education codes may establish
limiting policies and requirements concerning attendance in
private schools, but such limitations certainly appear in no
more than a dozen jurisdictions and probably in far fewer than
that.[138] To the extent that these statutes merely require
governmental agencies to promulgate regulations on the attendance issue, any roadblocks to innovation established by such
regulations are probably much easier to overcome than statutory
restrictions.

---

[137]Connecticut, Florida, Idaho, Montana.

[138]In addition to provisions regulating private schools in the
states listed in note 97, statutory provisions affecting
private schools are found outside the compulsory attendance
statutes in fourteen states. However, some of these sections
establishing requirements that must be adhered to by the private
school are extremely limited. For example, South Carolina [S.C.
Code Ann. §21-89 (1962)] requires only that attendance records be
kept and be available to the State Department of Education.
Provisions in Alabama [Ala. Code tit. 52 §547-8 (Cum.Supp. 1973)],
Colorado [Colo. Rev. Stat. Ann. §123-21-14(1964)], Delaware
[Del. Code Ann. tit.14 §4104 (Cum.Supp.1970)], Kentucky [Ky.Rev.Stat.
Ann. §155.080 (1971)], Iowa [Iowa Code §§280.2(1971, 280.10(1970)],
and New York [N.Y. Educ. Code §810 (McKinney Supp. 1975)] generally
provide that private school curricula must be approved by the
State Board of Education, and that attendance and other records
must be kept in the same manner as those in the public school.
Six states establish more extensive statutory requirements: In
California [Cal. Educ. Code §29007.5 (1975)], Maryland [Md. Ann.
Code art. 77 §11-12 (1975)], Maine [Me. Rev. Stat. Ann. tit. 20
§102 (1965)], Nebraska [Neb. Rev. Stat. §§16-19-2 (1970),
16-49-4(8) (1970)], South Dakota [S.D. Code §13-4-1 (1975)], and
Washington [Wash. Rev. Code §28A.02.200 (1970)] private schools
must be accredited and supervised by the State Department of
Education and comply with public school regulations beyond mere
equivalence in curriculum and concerning teacher accreditation,
adequacy of facilities, and compliance with building, health and
sanitary regulations.

Another category of requirements which necessarily will have substantial effect on any program seeking recognition under the private school rubric, is that of the approval processes. For example, in Massachusetts where the approval process is under the jurisdiction of the local school committees, the statute specifies that a school committee may approve a private school only "when satisfied that the instruction in all the studies required by law equals in thoroughness and efficiency and in the progress made therein, that in the public schools in the same town".[139] Although the "studies required by law" are delineated more or less clearly, the provision obviously encourages wholly subjective school committee decisions by use of the terms "thoroughness", "efficiency" and "progress". In jurisdictions with provisions as vague as this, or even more so, of which there are many, the power of the designated approval agency is clearly a major obstacle to the development of alternative learning arrangements even though such arrangements are indisputably permitted under the primary reference sections of the compulsory attendance statutes themselves.

In addition to the difficulties inherent in the approval process itself, further impediments may lie in the appeal process, if any, which is provided for parties aggrieved by a denial of approval. Only Rhode Island's primary reference sections contain provisions regarding approval, but other jurisdictions probably have such provisions either in regulations

---

[139] Mass. Gen. Laws c.76 § 1. (Supp. 1975).

or in their administrative procedure acts since the lack of
an appeal mechanism would be subject to constitutional challenge.
In this connection it is interesting to note that a 1973 amendment
to the North Dakota compulsory attendance laws removed the right
to appeal to the state superintendent of public instruction from
a decision of the county superintendent of schools and made the
county superintendent and the state superintendent co-decision-
makers in the approval process.[140] In removing the initial
approval power from the county superintendent alone, the amendment may have increased the likelihood of flexibility in initial
decision making, but it is unclear to whom, if anyone, an
aggrieved party may now appeal.

Finally, there are occasional references in the
education statutes of some jurisdictions, although only in Massachusetts does the provision actually occur in the compulsory
attendance law itself, regarding the transportation of children
in private schools. These provisions generally permit public
financing for transportation of children to private schools under

---

[140]N.D. Cent. Code §15-34.1-03(1971).

certain prescribed conditions.[141]

The constitutionality of such provisions author-
izing the use of public funds to provide students with transportation to sectarian and other private schools has been upheld in
numerous federal[142] and state[143] decisions, usually on the theory
that the aid(transportation) is being provided to the students
not the private institutions and therefore the public funds
are providing no or only de minimis aid to the private (usually
sectarian) institutions. However, other states have struck

---

[141]See, e.g., Mass. Gen. Laws C.76 §1 (1969): ...In order to
protect children from the hazards of traffic and promote their
safety, cities and towns may appropriate money for conveying
pupils to and from any schools approved under this section.
Pupils, who, in the fulfillment of the compulsory attendance
requirements of this section, attend private schools of elementary
and high school grades so approved shall be entitled to the same
rights and privileges as to transportation to and from school as
are provided by law for pubils of public schools and shall not
be denied such transportation because their attendance is in a
school which is conducted under religious auspices or includes
religious instruction in its curriculum, nor because pupils of
the public schools in a particular city or town are not actually
receiving such transportation.

[142]Board of Education of Central School Dist. No. 1 v. Allen,
392 U.S. 236, 88 S. Ct. 1923 (1968) is typical. In that decision
the Supreme Court stated:

As with public provision of police and fire protection,
sewage facilities, and streets and sidewalks, payment of
bus fares was of some value to the religious school, but
was nevertheless not such support of a religious institution as to be prohibited establishment of religion within
the meaning of the First Amendment. 392 U.S. at 242.

[143]See Rhoades v. School Dist. of Abington Township, 424 Pa. 202,
226 A.2d 53 (1967); Snyder v. Town of Newtown, 147 Conn. 374,
161 A.2d 770 (1961); Bowker v. Baker, 73 Cal. App. 2d 653, 167
P.2d 256 (1946); Adams v. County Com'rs of St. Mary's County,
180 Md. 550, 26 A.2d 377 (1942); Alexander v. Bartlett, 14 Mich.
App. 177, 165 N.W. 2d 445 (1968); Americans United Inc. et. al
v. Independent School Dist. No. 622, 288 Minn. 196, 179 N.W.
2d 146 (1970).

down similar statutes as contrary to the provisions of the state
constitutions.[144] In the most recent of these cases, Epeldi v.
Engelking,[145] the Idaho Supreme Court concluded that the prohibitions in its constitution against public aid to parochial
endeavors were more stringent than those in the federal constitution and precluded even state financing of transportation for
parochial school students.[146] The opinion remains in force,

---

[144]See Epeldi v. Engelking, 94 Idaho 390, 488 P.2d 860, cert.
den. 406 U.S. 957 (1972); Matthews v. Quinton, 362 P. 2d 932
(S.Ct. Alas. 1961); Spears v. Hoda, 51 Hawaii 1, 449 P.2d 130
(1969); Judd v. Board of Education, 278 N.Y. 200, 15 N.E. 2d
576 (1938); Visser v. Nooksack Valley School Dist. No. 506,
33 Wash. 2d 699, 207 P. 2d 198 (1949).

[145]94 Idaho 390, 488 P. 2d 860, cert. den. 406 U.S. 957
(1972).

[146]The Epeldi court considered that, unlike the provisions of
the Federal Constitution, the Idaho constitution contains provisions
specifically focusing on private schools controlled by sectarian
religious authorities and prohibits any appropriation by the
legislature or other governmental entities or payment from any
public fund in "aid of any church" or "to help support or sustain"
any church affiliated school. (Idaho Const. art. 9, §5.) In
striking down the legislation assisting students to attend parochial schools by the provision of free transportation, the court
noted that the legislation also aided those schools by bringing
students to them and was thus prohibited under the provisions
of the Idaho constitution. The court stated:

> [I]t is our conclusion that the framers of our consti-
> tution intended to more positively enunciate the
> separation between church and state than did the framers
> of the United States Constitution. 488 P.2d at 865.

In countering arguments made in State ex rel. Hughes v. Board of
Education, 154 W.Va. 107, 174 S.E. 2d 711 (1970) holding that
denial to parochial school students of the right to ride the
public buses would be in violation of the equal protection
clause of the Fourteenth Amendment to the Constitution of the
United States, the Epeldi Court referred to Idaho's paramount
interest against aiding religious institutions and concluded that

> [A] state has sufficient latitude under the Fourteenth
> and First Amendments to uphold its policy against aid to
> (cont')

certiorari having been denied by the U.S. Supreme Court.[147]
In some states, particularly those which are large and sparsely
populated or with substantial low-income populations, the state's
position on this transportation issue may have important bearing
on the type of alternative learning arrangements which can be
developed.

3. Other Programs

In addition to public and private schools, there are
two other categories of learning arrangements which, under the
terms of the primary reference sections, represent acceptable
alternatives for complying with the compulsory attendance statutes.
The first of these is generally referred to as "private" or
"home" "tutoring" or "instruction"; and the second includes
those vague references to instruction "elsewhere" or "otherwise."
(Solely for reasons of convenience, we will refer to these two
categories as "non-school" alternatives by which we mean they
are not implemented in a physical facility commonly called a
"school".) Even a superficial perusal of the statutes makes clear
that these categories of programs are not held in much favor.
Only a minority of statutes have references to these categories,
and, even when reference is made, it is most often a reference

---

146 (cont'd)   religion although by doing so free exercise of
     religion (attending parochial schools) becomes more
     expensive. 488 P.2d at 867.

[147] 406 U.S. 957 (1972).

to that program as an "exemption" from, rather than an alternative
to, public school attendance. For example, in twelve[148] of the
twenty states[149] whose statutes explicitly refer to non-school
programs as acceptable alternative learning arrangements for
purposes of compliance with attendance statutes, this reference
appears in terms of an exemption. And of the sixteen states whose
statutory language may be interpreted as implying the acceptability
of such programs, nine of them[151] treat them as exceptions not alternatives. In many of these states where "non-school" alternatives
are thus de-emphasized as acceptable learning arrangements, private
schools are accorded similar treatment so that a strong statutory
preference for public school attendance becomes clear.[152] And in
the seven states[153] where private school attendance is listed as
an alternative but "non-school" arrangements appear as an exemption,
again, presumably, a preference is being expressed for learning

---

[148] Alaska, Arizona, California, Colorado, Hawaii, Nevada,
Ohio, Oregon, Rhode Island, South Dakota, Utah, West Virginia.

[149] Alabama, Alaska, Arizona, California, Connecticut, Colorado,
D.C., Florida, Hawaii, Iowa, Missouri, Nevada, Ohio, Oregon,
Pennsylvania, Rhode Island, South Dakota, Utah, Virginia, West
Virginia.

[150] Arizona, Connecticut, Delaware, Idaho, Iowa, Maine, Maryland,
Massachusetts, New Jersey, New Mexico, New York, Oklahoma, South
Carolina, Vermont, West Virginia, Wisconsin.

[151] Arizona, Delaware, Maine, Maryland, Massachusetts, New Mexico,
South Carolina, Vermont, West Virginia.

[152] The states whose statutes reveal this preference are Alaska,
Arizona, California, Delaware, Maine, Maryland, Nevada, Oregon,
Rhode Island, Vermont, West Virginia.

[153] Hawaii, Massachusetts, New Mexico, Ohio, South Carolina,
South Dakota, Utah.

within the framework of some conventional facility.

However, even though a state may so indicate a preference for school attendance over learning through "non-school" programs, if it does permit such programs, its ability to impose this preference on parents, or, conversely, the extent of parents' ability to make a meaningful choice among alternatives, will depend upon the nature and extent of official restrictions applied to such "non-school" programs. Are the restrictions presently applied to "non-school" programs under the compulsory attendance statutes rendering those programs effectively inaccessible? Can the present program requirements be interpreted to permit innovative alternative learning arrangements even beyond those presumptively intended by the statutes? To answer these questions requires a closer look at the nature of these restrictions.

a) Home or Private Instruction or Tutoring

The non-school category composed of arrangements described as "home" or "private" "instruction" or "tutoring" is a _permissive_ category; that is, it authorizes participation in such arrangements in lieu of school attendance for children who _could_, if they wished, attend school. In situations where a child is _unable_ to attend school for some reason,[154] such child may always participate in these non-school alternatives even if such alternatives are not permissible under the primary reference

_____

[154]But in accordance with the national trend toward "mainstreaming" - including disabled children in public school programs - presumably fewer and fewer children will be considered "unable" to attend school.

sections because they would be permissible, as to the disabled child, under some separate "exemptions" section.

The statutes of ten states explicitly permit "home instruction"[155] and those of ten others explicitly permit private instruction or tutoring[156] which presumably includes home instruction. In addition, case law in six more states has interpreted the language of the compulsory attendance statutes to permit home instruction even though it is not specified in the language of the statute. Two states have effected this by interpreting the term "private school"[158] and two others by defining the word "elsewhere."[159] The remaining two have concluded that home instruction is within the meaning of the phrases "other means of instruction"[160] and "instruction in a manner approved by school officials."[161]

---

[155] Arizona, Colorado, Florida, Missouri, Nevada, Ohio, Oregon, Utah, Virginia, West Virginia.

[156] Alabama, Alaska, California, District of Columbia, Hawaii, Iowa, Pennsylvania, Rhode Island, South Dakota. Note that Connecticut refers to such private instruction by specifying that all parents who have the care of children "shall instruct them or cause them to be instructed" in specified subjects (emphasis added). Conn. Gen. Stat. Ann. §10-184(1967).

[157] Ind., Ill., Mass., N.J., N.Y., Okla. And in several jurisdictions there are Attorney General's opinions interpreting the primary reference sections to permit home instruction despite the absence of explicit statutory language so permitting.

[158] People v. Levison, 404 Ill. 574, 90 N.E. 2d 213(1950).; State v. Peterman, 32 Ind. App. 665, 70 N.E. 550 (1904).

[159] State v. Massa, 95 N.J. Super. 382, 231 A. 2d 252 (1967); In re Foster, 69 Misc. 2d 400, 330 N.Y.S. 2d 8 (1972).

[160] Wright v. State, 21 Okla. Crim. 430, 209 P. 179 (1922).

[161] Commonwealth v. Roberts, 159 Mass. 372, 34 N.E. 402 (1893).

As in the case of the private school, a basic and
widespread requirement applied to private instruction[162] concerns the time for which or during which the program must be
attended or the child instructed. At least eleven of the nineteen states whose statutes explicitly permit private instruction
contain this requirement. The majority[163] state it generally
and simply, indicating that the child must attend or be instructed
for the entire time during which the public school in the locality
in which the child resides is in session, or for a period of time
equivalent to that for which the public school is in session.
Three of these states actually specify hours requirements, one
generally, and two, specifically.[164] In a few jurisdictions ,
there is a wide discrepancy between the number of days that
private instruction must be offered and the number of days
public schools must be in session. For instance, in Alabama,

---

[162]Unless explicitly stated otherwise,"private instruction" will
be used throughout the remainder of this section to include home
instruction and tutoring.

[163]District of Columbia, Florida, Missouri, Oregon, Pennsylvania,
South Dakota, Utah, West Virginia.

[164]Note that the Virginia primary attendance section refers to
school attendance and instruction by a tutor at home as alternatives to public school attendance and then specifies that
"such child...shall regularly attend such school during the
period of each year the public schools are in session and for
the same number of days and hours per day as in the public
schools" Va. Code Ann. §§22-275.1(1973) (emphasis added.) Evidently, this transmutes the home or other locale of the private
instruction into a "school" under the Virginia statute.

public schools are required to be in session for 180 days but private instruction need only be given for 140 days. Sometimes the number of days required is the same but the number of hours varies widely. For instance, in California both private instruction and public schools must be operating for 175 days, but private instruction need only be given three hours per day, whereas students in public schools must attend twice that long.

To insure compliance with these restrictions, a number of states require registers or records of attendance to be kept by the private tutor.[165] For example, Alabama requires that "Such tutor shall keep a register of work, showing daily the hours used for instruction and the presence or absence of any child being instructed, and shall make such reports as the state board of education may require."[166] Some states specifically require such registers or records to be kept open for inspection at all times by whichever officials are required to enforce tne compulsory attendance law. One state imposes a penalty on those required to keep such records for failure to do so. In a few states, the parent or other person having control of the child must furnish a "certificate" to the secretary of the school district indicating, among other things, the period of time during which the child has been under private

---

[165] See Ala. Code tit. 52§299 (Cum. Supp. 1973); D.C. Code Ann. §31-205(1973); Fla. Stat. §232.021(1961); R.I. Gen. Laws Ann. §16-19-2(1970); S.D. Code §13-27-3(1975); W.Va. Code Ann. §18-18-1(1975).

[166] Ala. Code Tit. 52 §299 (Cum. Supp. 1973).

instruction and the "details" of such instruction. However,
only one state, Florida, appears to impose any penalty for
parental failure to comply with those record-keeping obligations.

Basic requirements of "approval" of private instruction or of an "established system" of home study appear in the
attendance statutes of only four states.[167] One of these merely
states that this approval must be obtained without specifying
any conditions for approval [168] while two others refer only to
the most cursory and vague standards that must be met: approval
will be given if the instruction is deemed "proper"[169] or "satisfactory"[170] by the appropriate school officials. The remaining
state, Rhode Island, applies to private instruction the same
lengthy requirements which are prerequisite for approval of
private schools including, among other things, the requirement
that specified subjects be taught "thoroughly and efficiently",
in English and substantially to the same extent required in public
school.

---

[167]Colorado, Hawaii, Pennsylvania, Rhode Island.

[168]Colorado (Note: Although Colorado requires such approval for
instruction "under an established system of home study", it
requires no such approval of the alternative mode of instruction
"at home by a teacher certified [pursuant to law.]" Colo. Rev.
Stat. Ann. §123-20-5(j)(1964).

[169]Hawaii.

[170]Pennsylvania.

Seven other states indicate the subjects, usually termed "branches of instruction," required to be taught under the private instruction arrangement. Five of these require that they be the same subjects taught in the public school.[171] The other two states[172] just indicate, generally, that the child is to be instructed in "prescribed" subjects, presumably referring to the provisions in the education laws which prescribe what is to be taught in public schools. Note that two of the above states[173] require that the instruction be given in English, while one, which formerly provided that instruction be given entirely in the English language, now merely requires instruction "given so as to lead to mastery of the English language."[174]

In addition, five states' statutes contain the critical requirement that any private instruction be "equivalent",[175] or "comparable"[176] to that offered in the public schools if it is to be deemed an acceptable arrangement for compliance with the compulsory attendance requirement. What is the nature of this equivalency, and how literally is the word to be taken? No

---

[171] Alabama, Arizona, California, Oregon ("usually taught in public school"), South Dakota.

[172] Ohio, Utah.

[173] Alabama and California.

[174] South Dakota [S.D. Code §13-27-3 (1975) as amended by Stat. 1971 C. 116, §2)].

[175] Connecticut, District of Columbia, Iowa, Nevada.

[176] Alaska.

jurisdiction's statute provides an adequate answer. One state[177] prescribes equivalency "in kind and amount" to that approved by the state board of education. Another state[178] specifies in its primary reference section that the instruction must be comparable to that offered in the public schools in the area. Three of the jurisdictions which demand equivalency[179] do not even provide generalities as vague as those just noted. The state with the most elaborate provision, Missouri, requires that the private instruction "shall, in the judgment of a court of competent jurisdiction, be at least substantially equivalent to the instruction given children of like age in the day schools in the locality in which the child resides".[180] Note that even this provision supplies very little in the way of a usable standard. How could a court ever reach a determination under it when children "of the same age in day schools in the locality" may be engaged in a number of different courses of study and since day schools, according to the primary reference statute, may be "public, private, parochial, or parish"?

---

[177] Nevada (Satisfactory written evidence of this must be presented to the board of trustees in the school district in which the child resides.)

[178] Alaska.

[179] Connecticut, District of Columbia, Iowa.

[180] Mo. Rev. Stat §167.031 (1965).

The most pervasive category of statutory requirements
applied to private instruction concerns the teachers or tutors
who provide the instruction. Fourteen states have some statutory criterion for persons providing private instruction which
must be met if that instruction is to satisfy the compulsory
attendance statute. Five states[181] require that teachers be
"certified", four[182] that they be "qualified", three[183] that
they be "competent", and one[184] merely stipulates that they must
be teaching with the permission of the local school district.
One other, Florida, requires that they be persons meeting "all
requirements prescribed by law and regulations of the state
board for private tutors."[185] It is not apparent from the
statutes whether to be "competent" or "qualified", tutors must
be _certified_ teachers. In those states where private instruction
is permitted as a result of judicial construction of the compulsory attendance statute rather than as a result of explicit provision in the statutes themselves,[186] actual certification is

---

[181]Alabama, Alaska, California, Colorado, Iowa.

[182]Ohio, Pennsylvania, Virginia, West Virginia.

[183]Arizona, Hawaii, South Dakota.

[184]Oregon.

[185]Fla. Stat. §232.02(4)(1973).

[186]See cases cited at notes 158-161, inclusive, _supra_.

never required of tutors (or parents acting as tutors).

Surprisingly, only two states have any provisions regarding examination of children who satisfy the compulsory attendance requirement through private instruction at home or in
some other non-school setting. South Dakota requires that a child
who is privately instructed must take such examination as the
state superintendent may require in order to determine the "competency of such instruction"[187] while Oregon merely requires a
child privately instructed to be examined in the work covered
by the instruction.[188]

b) Miscellaneous Learning Arrangement References

As noted above, sixteen states have general
statutory references to nonspecified programs which may be
characterized as alternative non-school learning arrangements.
Seven of these statutes refer to instruction "elsewhere",[189]
(than in public/private school), three refer to instruction
"otherwise"[190] (than in public/private school), and one[191] to
instruction "in any other manner" (than in public/private school).
Another[192] simply permits "other means of education" as an alternative to schools. The remaining four states have attendance

_____

[187] S.D. Code §13-27-3 (1975).

[188] Ore. Rev. Stat. §339.030 (6) (b) (1973).

[189] Conn., Del., Iowa, Md., N.J., N.Y., Wis.

[190] Idaho, Massachusetts, Vermont

[191] Maine

[192] Oklahoma

statutes referring variously to other "approved" programs,[193]
including those meeting "educational standards of the state department of education"[194] and plans "for pursuing educational
interests that the school is not satisfying."[195] Note that one
of these states[196] specifically permits attendance at a _program_
of instruction offered by a state institution in lieu of attendance at school.

In those three states[197] whose statutes refer to both
private school and home instruction as alternatives to attendance in public school, the terms noted above must refer to
some additional, unspecified learning arrangements other than
public/private school and home instruction. Likewise, nonspecific references in the compulsory attendance statutes of four
states whose statutes have already been interpreted to include
home instruction[198] must be references to the permissibility of

---

[193]Arizona (including "work training, career education, vocational or manual training programs" approved by the state board
of education), New Mexico (by local school committee), South
Carolina ("instruction at a place other than school" approved
by the state board of education), West Virginia (instruction
at home approved by the county board of education).

[194]Arizona

[195]New Mexico (Participation in these programs is only
available to high school students who prove to the satisfaction
of the local board that they have such plans).

[196]New Mexico Stat. Ann. §77-10-2 (Supp. 1975) (It is instructive
to note that N.M. Laws 1972, Ch. 17, §2 amended this section by
substituting "program of instruction" for "school".

[197]Arizona, Connecticut, West Virginia

[198]Massachusetts, New Jersey, New York, Oklahoma

yet another type of learning arrangement. The primary reference sections in three of the states noted in the preceding
paragraph[199] contain no references to private school attendance
as an alternative to attendance in public school, so the non-
specific program references found in these statutes may have
been intended only to mean private school, but they certainly
could be interpreted to apply to additional learning arrangements, including home instruction. The statutes of the remaining five states[200] all explicitly or implicitly refer to "private
school" so that their nonspecific references noted above must
be to non-school alternatives. As such, all of the above terms
could be useful to those who may desire to establish alternative
education programs under the present compulsory attendance
statutes. Again, just how useful such terms will be depends
in part on the nature of the requirements applied to the
alternatives authorized under these rubrics.

Only five of the jurisdictions[201] containing such non-specific

---

[199]Maryland, Delaware, Vermont. Note that although "elsewhere"
is not further defined in the body of the Delaware statute, an
exemption section of the Delaware compulsory attendance law also
containing the reference to "elsewhere" is entitled "Private
school attendance or other educational instruction." (emphasis
added). Del. Code Ann. tit. 14 §2703 (Cum. Supp. 1970).

[200]Idaho, Maine, New Mexico, South Carolina, Wisconsin.

[201]Maine, Maryland, New York, Oklahoma, West Virginia.

learning arrangement references require "attendance" at the permitted arrangement for a specified period of time. In three of these,[202] this period must coincide with the period the schools in the area are in session. Two of the five refer specifically to the "public schools",[203] and one merely to the "schools of the district." In the remaining two states, the time for which the child must attend the non-school instruction must be "equal to the school term of the county"[204] or "for a like period of time."[205] In addition, some states provide that this attendance must be "regular," and one requires that it be "for at least as many hours and within the hours specified" for the public school in the town where the child resides.[206] One other state mandates that private instruction be "during the required period elsewhere," the "required period" apparently being only that approved by the state superintendent.[207] A few states now merely require "regular" private instruction, although their statutes formerly required such instruction to be "during the minimum school time."[208]

---

[202]Maryland, New York, Oklahoma.

[203]Maine and West Virginia.

[204]West Virginia.

[205]Maine.

[206]N.Y. Educ. Code §3210(b)(2) (McKinney Supp. 1975).

[207]Wis. Stat. §40.77(1)(c)(1971).

[208] E.g., Del. Code Ann. tit. 14 §2703 (Cum. Supp. 1970).

In addition to the states generally allowing instruction
in some "approved" program to be substituted for public or
private school, six other states require approval of learning
arrangements which are proposed for acceptability under provisions permitting instruction "elsewhere",[209] "otherwise"[210] or
"in any other manner."[211] In two of these states local officials make the controlling decisions,[212] and in two others they
participate in the decision-making process with state officials,[213]
while in the remaining two states the decision is made by state
officials alone.[214]

The most widespread requirement applied to these various
non-specific learning arrangements concerns instruction standards. Such standards are applied, albeit sparingly, in eleven of
the sixteen states. In general, the situation is quite similar
to that which characterized instruction in private schools vis-a-
vis public school curricula. In six of them "equivalent" or "comparable" instruction is required; in three others the instruction

---

[209]Delaware and Wisconsin.

[210]Idaho, Massachusetts, Vermont.

[211]Maine.

[212]Idaho (board of trustees in the school district where the
child resides) and Massachusetts (superintendent or school committee in district where child resides).

[213]Delaware (the instruction must satisfy the superintendnet of
the school district and an official designated by the state board)
and Maine (equivalent instruction arranged for by school officials
with the approval of the state commissioner).

[214]Vermont (state department of education) and Wisconsin (state
superintendent).

must be "substantially equivalent" and in another two it must
include subjects required to be taught in the public schools.

In all of those states demanding equivalency of instruction,[215] the frame of reference is the instruction given in
public school, with only two states[216] specifying that this
be the public school in the locality where the child resides.
Otherwise, there is very little description, if any, of the
requisite equivalency. One state, Idaho, does provide that the
child shall be "comparably instructed in subjects commonly and
usually taught in the public schools" while another, New Jersey,
requires that the instruction be equivalent to that provided
"for children of similar grades and attainments." The compulsory attendance statutes of three states[217] contain no reference to which administrative body or other authority makes this
determination of equivalency, but the other three do so specify.
In Idaho the determination is made by the board of trustees in
the school district where the child resides, in Maine it is made
by the school committee or the school directors with the approval
of the state commissioner, and in Vermont it is made by the state
department of education.

Two of the states requiring that the instruction be
"substantially equivalent"[218] refer to instruction in the public

---

[215] Connecticut, Idaho, Iowa, Maine, New Jersey, Vermont.

[216] Connecticut and New Jersey.

[217] Connecticut, Iowa, New Jersey

[218] South Carolina and Wisconsin.

or private schools in the locality where the child resides as the measuring rod for this equivalency. Only New York looks solely to the public school in the district where the child resides. Similarly, only New York describes the scope of this equivalency as being in the "amount and quality" of that required in its public schools.

The authority which determines whether the required substantial equivalency exists is generally either the local "school authorities in accordance with regulations of the state education department"[219] or the state board of education,[220] or the state superintendent.[221]

Only two of these states specify the subjects which the private instructor must teach. One, Delaware, indicates that they must be those subjects prescribed for the state elementary schools and the other, Maryland, requires instruction in the subjects usually taught to public school children of the same age.

The attendance statutes of only three states[222] contain qualifying standards that teachers giving private instruction must meet, and these standards consist of single, undefined adjectives such as "certified" (Iowa), "qualified" (West Virginia), or "competent" (New York). Case law in three other states has permitted non-certified persons to instruct children on the basis of judicial construction of such terms as "instruction elsewhere,"[223] instruction

---

[219] E.g. New York.

[220] E.g. South Carolina.

[221] E.g. Wisconsin.

[222] Iowa, New York and West Virginia.

[223] State v. Massa. 95 N.J. Super. 382, 231 A.2d 252 (1967).

"otherwise,"[224] and "other means of education."[225]

Finally, to insure that the above requirements are being met, some jurisdictions require, as they do with regard to private schools, that reports be submitted, and one requires that the child be examined. Some states place this duty to furnish information and records of such instruction directly on the person giving the instruction, while others put this duty on the parent or other person in loco parentis.

Summary

In conclusion, to answer the questions posed at the beginning of this chapter:

1. Are requirements now applied to non-school programs likely to render those programs less accessible than the public or other school programs? There appear to be no really formidable statutory obstacles that must be overcome before innovative alternative learning arrangements are sufficient to achieve compliance with the basic requirements of compulsory attendance statutes. Approval procedures may be time-consuming, and other procedures not contained in the statutes but required by regulation may discourage such innovation, but the statutes themselves do not appear to be a major barrier.

2. Can the present program requirements be interpreted to allow innovative alternative educational programs? This will depend on the nature of the alternative program and the degree of specificity of the particular jurisdiction's requirements. As in the case of private schools, the necessary adherence

---

[224] Commonwealth v. Roberts, 159 Mass. 372, 34 N.E. 402 (1893).

[225] Wright v. State, 21 Okla. Crim. 430, 209 P. 179 (1922).

to a specified (i.e. "equivalent") program, teacher qualifications, and attendance procedures including duration requirements, may all circumscribe, and in some cases prevent, the establishment of innovative alternative learning arrangements. Since the statutes generally shed very little light on the meaning of critically important terms applied to permissible non-school learning arrangements such as "attendance", "instruction", "equivalency", etc., no reliable final conclusion can be reached on this issue on the basis of the statutes alone, and even reference to state administrative regulations and case law does not supply many definitive answers as the next chapter will explain.

But the following conclusions may be drawn from an analysis of the primary reference sections of the state compulsory attendance statutes:

a) Every state except Mississippi directly or implicitly requires the parent or other person in loco parentis as to a compulsory school-age child, not within any exception to the compulsory attendance statutes, to send or cause such child to attend school or some other learning arrangement.

b) Only a minority of states specifically place the burden of attendance on the child directly although by statutory provisions in almost all states the child may be penalized for failure to attend school.

c) No compulsory attendance statute refers to the statutory obligations of the state, once the parent and child have complied with the attendance laws.

d) To comply with the compulsory attendance laws children must participate in one of three basic learning arrangements:

public school; non-public school, including parochial and other private schools; and, in slightly more than half the states, some non-school learning arrangement which may include home instruction or private tutoring.

e) Without exception, the compulsory attendance statutes provide no clear definition of these programs, although the general nature of them may be derived by inference from the minimal requirements applied to them.

Since all states are constitutionally compelled to allow instruction in private schools and the compulsory attendance statutes of at least thirty-two states explicitly, implicitly or by judicial construction allow instruction through non-school learning arrangements, there is ample statutory basis for the establishment of a variety of acceptable alternatives to public school attendance. However, a minimum number of burdensome requirements concerning time of attendance or instruction, program content, teaching staff, and testing as well as program definitions may circumscribe or prevent the establishment of some types of innovative alternative education programs. To what degree these requirements will encourage, circumscribe or prevent the establishment of future alternative learning arrangements will depend on the nature of the alternative arrangement, the inventiveness of its proponents in dealing with bureaucratic systems, and the enforceability of the requirements, which, given their exceptional vagueness, is probably not high.

5. COMPULSORY ATTENDANCE: JUDICIAL INTERPRETATIONS

As indicated in the preceding chapter, state courts have been called upon from time to time, although not nearly so frequently as one might expect, to construe portions of compulsory attendance statutes. In so doing, they have rendered decisions which bear importantly on the nature of the types of learning arrangements which will receive official sanction and, thereby, they have exercised a potentially major influence on the question of future educational innovation. This chapter directs attention to three basic questions concerning this judicial activity: When have the courts been willing to expand the permissible learning arrangements beyond those expressly allowed in the compulsory attendance statutes? Under what circumstances have the courts refused to effect such an expansion and required strict adherence to a conservative reading of the statute? What are the implications of this body of case law for the development of future alternative learning arrangements?

As the previous chapter has detailed, a fair number of state statutes refer to very general kinds of learning arrangements which may be interpreted to permit home instruction or other arrangements quite different from traditional education programs. Case law which either expands or restricts the kinds of arrangements which constitute acceptable compliance with those statutes may also shed light on the meaning to be ascribed

to those similar general standards which are applied to the already existing acceptable learning arrangements. As was described
in the previous chapter, thirty states have statutes containing
such general references, eighteen of them[1] referring only to some
type of private school (variously called "private", "parochial"
or "denominational") and twelve[2] referring to totally non-specified
alternatives such as instruction "elsewhere" or "otherwise". Few
state attendance statutes define program standards in any manner
whatsoever, and, almost without exception, those which do provide
some statutory definition do so very inadequately. Thus, conclusions concerning the nature of alternatives which have been allowed or disallowed by the courts will provide important information concerning possible future development of new alternatives.
With this end in mind, the following analysis will focus particularly on judicial standards concerning instruction, teaching staff,
and educational setting, including the nature and degree of the
orientation of these standards toward the child, the parent[3] and
the state.

This analysis is generally confined to those cases expressly allowing or disallowing participation in various alternative learning arrangements in lieu of public or private school

---

[1] Ark., Ga., Ill., Ind., Kan., Ky., La., Mich., Minn., Neb., N.H., N.C., N.D., P.R., Tenn., Tex., Wash., Wyo.

[2] Conn., Del., Idaho, Iowa, Me., Md., Mass., N.J., N.Y., Okla., Wis., Vt.

[3] The word "parent" as used throughout this chapter refers to any person in loco parentis as to a compulsory school age child.

attendance. It does not include those cases permitting home instruction or other alternatives in isolated situations where requiring attendance at school has been positively determined to be
unreasonable or harmful to the child.[4] Nor does this analysis
include reference to those cases which may, in fact, expand access
to or discourage the utilization of alternative learning arrangements by findings concerning matters unrelated to educational
program standards but which, nevertheless, may be central to the
viability of alternative programs, such as, cases involving
the application of health regulations, zoning ordinances,[5] taxation[6]

---

[4]For example, in In re Richards, 255 App. Div. 922, 7 N.Y.S. 2d
722 (1938), the court held that a mother who taught her eight
year old child at home and was competent to do so could not be
penalized for failing to send the child to school where to do so
would have required the child to walk 1-1/4 miles (to the nearest
bus stop) down an isolated road which was poorly maintained and
without a sidewalk or fence.

[5]See St. John's Roman Catholic Church Corporation v. Town of
Darien, 149 Conn. 712, 184 A.2d 42 (1962).
         (There were reasonable grounds for the separate classi-
fication of private and parochial schools, which were not subject
to the approval of the planning commission or the legislative
body of the municipality, from public schools which were subjected
to building regulations. Therefore, the zoning ordinance requiring
that the applicant for construction of a parochial school obtain
a special permit in order to establish the school in a residential
zone did not deprive the applicant of its property without due
process of law or deny equal protection of the law). See also,
Rose Lee Hardy Home and School Association v. D.C. Board of Zoning
Adjustment, 324 A.2d 791 (D.C.C.A. 1974).

[6]See Verde Valley School v. County of Yovapai, 90 Ariz. 180, 367
P. 2d 223 (1961) ("Rent or valuable consideration" within meaning
of the statute exempting private school property from taxation
except when rent or valuable consideration is received for its
use, referred to income received for nonschool purposes, and did
not embrace substantial tuition charges received by a private
nonprofit educational institution.)

THIS PAGE WAS LEFT INTENTIONALLY BLANK

or transportation[7] provisions, or determinations affecting private
school participation in various state programs.[8]

I.   Expansion of the Permissible Learning Arrangements

The expansion by judicial decision of the permissible
learning arrangements has occurred in two major ways: directly
through interpretation of the terms of compulsory attendance
statutes, themselves, or related provisions of the state education
code; and indirectly by refusal to make findings of noncompliance
with the statutes in situations where the defendant parent or
child is concededly not acting in accordance with any of the
options literally described on the face of the statute. The first of
these categories is, of course, the more significant, but the
second also has impact on the extent of allowable deviation from
conventional educational norms. We will explore judicial expan-
sionist activities, both direct and indirect, by examining the
three principal modes courts have used: expansion by interpretation of the attendance and related statutes, expansion by use of
procedural findings and expansion by limiting state regulation of
private schools.

_____

[7]See Rhoades v. School District of Abington Township, 424 Pa. 202,
225 A. 2d 53 (1967) (transportation of children attending sectarian institution allowed); contra, Epeldi v. Engelking, 94 Idaho
390, 488 P. 2d 860, cert. denied, 406 U.S. 957 (1972), transportation of such pupils disallowed.)

[8]See Special District v. Wheeler, 408 S.W. 2d 60 (S.Ct. Mo. 1966)
(the use of public monies to send speech teachers into the parochial schools to give speech therapy was not a use "for the purpose of maintaining free public schools", within the meaning of
Art. 9, §5 of the state's constitution, and therefore was not
lawful.)

A. Expansion by Interpretation of the Attendance and Other Related Statutes

Most judicial interpretation expanding the learning arrangements permissible under the compulsory attendance statutes has centered on cases involving either home instruction or aspects of the public school system. The former are more numerous, more colorful, more significant in terms of impact for the individual child and parent, and, ultimately, more important in terms of influence on future directions.

1. Home Instruction Cases

For well over three-quarters of a century, state courts have been called upon to determine whether home instruction or similar arrangements are permissible under compulsory attendance statutes which do not expressly permit or prohibit such arrangements. Many of these cases, including the first one which was tried in 1893,[9] turn on construction of terms such as "instruction elsewhere" or "instruction otherwise". The more difficult ones, which appear mostly in this century, involve judicial attempts to extrapolate the legislative intent underlying compulsory attendance statutes which provide merely for attendance at a "private school", without definition, in lieu of attendance at public school. To properly appreciate the development of this case law, it is useful to consider these cases in a chronological perspective.

---

[9] Commonwealth v. Roberts, 159 Mass. 372, 34 N.E. 402 (1893).

The first case to be decided, the Massachusetts case of <u>Commonwealth v. Roberts</u>[10], left a theoretical legacy which has reappeared in numerous subsequent cases interpreting the compulsory attendance laws: "The great object of [the compulsory attendance] provisions of the statutes has been that all children be educated, not that they be educated in any particular way."[11] In interpreting the statutory provision allowing an exemption from school attendance for a child who "has been otherwise instructed for a like period of time in the branches of learning required by law to be taught in the public schools", the Massachusetts court stated:

> [I]f the person having a child under his control, instead of sending him to a public school or to a private day school approved by the school committee, prefers to have him instructed otherwise, it will be incumbent on him to show that the child has been instructed for the specified period in the required branches of learning, unless the child has already acquired them. This permits instruction in those branches in schools or academies situated in the same city or town, or elsewhere, or instruction by a private tutor or governess, or by the parents themselves, provided it is given in good faith and is sufficient in extent.[12]

In enumerating the programs that may constitute being "otherwise instructed", <u>Roberts</u> goes further than many subsequent similar decisions which have limited themselves to

---

[10] 159 Mass. 372, 34 N.E. 402 (1893).

[11] 159 Mass. at 374.

[12] <u>Id.</u>

determinations of whether home instruction is allowed. The
opinion does not delineate the two bases it sets forth for
determining when the terms of the statute have been met: instruction which is given "in good faith" and which is "sufficient in
extent". Note that the Massachusetts compulsory attendance
statute now requires that being "otherwise instructed" must be
approved in advance by the superintendent of schools or the
school committee. The case of Commonwealth v. Renfrew[13] held
that merely providing home instruction in the branches of learning required to be taught in the public day schools without obtaining such prior approval, constituted no defense to prosecution under the compulsory attendance statutes. While Renfrew
apparently accepted the Roberts finding that the statute does
not require education in "any particular way", nevertheless only
education pursuant to a particular system of approval will be
satisfactory.

The next major case in the area built on the
Roberts reasoning, The Indiana Supreme Court, in State v. Peterman,[14] concluded that the purpose of the compulsory attendance
statute in its jurisdiction was "to secure to the child the opportunity to acquire an education, which the welfare of the child
and the best interests of society demand"[15] (emphasis added).

---

[13]332 Mass. 492, 126 N.E. 2d 109(1955).

[14]32 Ind. App. 665, 70 N.E., 550 (1904).

[15]70 N.E. at 552, quoting State v. Bailey, 157 Ind. 329, 61 N.E.
732 (1901).

Although not directly addressed, it is evident from the opinion that the parent has free rein to determine the child's welfare provided this is done consistent with society's interests. As is typical not only of cases in this area but of law, generally, the child's own view isn't considered.

In Peterman, the court found that a parent, in good faith, employed a teacher formerly employed in the public schools to teach his child all the subjects taught in the public schools during regular public school hours. The child attended the teacher's home regularly every school day, and, according to the findings of the court, received instruction equal to that which could have been received at the public schools. The Indiana statute, however, specified only "public, private or parochial" schools as alternative learning arrangements for purposes of complying with the compulsory attendance requirement. Furthermore, it emphasized that "no child in good mental or physical condition shall for any cause, any rule or law to the contrary, be precluded from attending school when such school was in session."[16]

As the court noted, the "whole question" in Peterman was "what is a private school". Whatever the nature of a private school, the jury at the trial level returned a verdict of not guilty. On appeal, the school officials disputed the action of the court in refusing to give the following instruction concerning the definition of "private school":

---

[16]70 N.E. at 550.

> A private school, within the meaning of
> the law under which this prosecution is
> conducted, means a reputable person or
> persons, who possess the necessary quali-
> fications as teacher or teachers, or in
> which such teacher or teachers were pro-
> vided, and who have the proper equipment
> for conducting such a school, and who
> hold themselves out as conducting such
> a school.[17]

To this contention, the court in Peterman replied:

> We think the instruction was properly re-
> fused, because it is radically wrong. A
> school, in the ordinary acceptation of its
> meaning, is a place where instruction is
> imparted to the young. If a parent employs
> and brings into his residence a teacher
> for the purpose of instructing his child
> or children, and such instruction is
> given as the law contemplates, the meaning
> and spirit of the law have been fully com-
> plied with. This would be the school of
> the child or children so educated, and
> would be as much a private school as if
> advertised and conducted as such. We do
> not think that the number of persons,
> whether one or many, make a place where
> instruction is imparted any less or more
> a school.[18]

Thus, the home instruction arrangement in Peterman given by a

capable teacher was a "private school" within the meaning of the

statute, even though the teacher did not "hold herself out" as

keeping a private school, had no regular fixed tuition, nor any

school equipment, and made no arrangements to take other pupils.

The fallacy of the state prosecutor's argument,

according to the court, lay in the assertion that "the law has

to do with the way or place where a child shall be educated".[19]

---

[17] Id. at 551.

[18] Id.

[19] Id. at 552.

The court concluded that the desired end - "to secure to the child the opportunity to acquire an education" - and "not the means or manner of attaining it, was the goal which the lawmakers were attempting to reach":

> The [compulsory attendance] law was made for the parent, who does not educate his child, and not for the parent who employs a teacher and pays him out of his private purse, and so places within the reach of the child the opportunity and means of acquiring an education equal to that obtainable in the public schools of the state.[20]

Twenty years later in the case of Wright v. State,[21] the Oklahoma court interpreted the phrase "other means of education" found in the Oklahoma compulsory attendance statute to permit home instruction in the case of a parent who could show that the child had been taught by competent private instructors, and was proficient in the subjects taught in the public schools to children of similar age. As in Peterman, the decision centered around instructions to the jury profferred by the plaintiff school officials. However, in Wright the instructions were given by the trial court to the jury which convicted the parent of violating the compulsory attendance law. On appeal, the court found that the instructions concerning teacher qualifications, length of sessions, and course of study were erroneous. In reversing the lower court decision, the court stated:

---

[20] Id.

[21] 21 Okla. Crim. 430, 209 P. 179 (1922).

> Under the terms of the statute and under
> the Constitution, a parent may have his
> children instructed by a competent private
> tutor or educated in a sectarian or other
> accredited school, without a strict adher-
> ence to the standard fixed for teachers in
> the public schools of the state. The
> statute makes no provisions fixing the
> qualifications of private teachers, or
> teachers in private schools or academies,
> or to prescribe definite courses of study
> in such cases. Of course, if such schools
> or instruction were manifestly inadequate,
> or such instruction was furnished for the
> sole purpose of evading the proper educa-
> tion of a child, the statute could then be
> properly invoked.[22]

Although the court indicated merely that the

instruction must not be "manifestly inadequate", in concluding

its opinion, it further stated that whether such independent faci-

lities for education are "equivalent to those afforded by the

state, is a question of fact for the jury", and, like the deter-

mination of whether such facilities are supplied in good faith, is

not a question of law for the court.[23] As in its predecessors

Peterman and Roberts, the Wright opinion offered little or no

criteria for the determination of "equivalence" or "good faith".

Again, like its predecessors, Wright is a

decidedly parent-centered case, and contains no discussion of

whether the mode of education was, in fact, in the best interests of

the child involved. In this connection, note teh Court's statement

of the facts in the case and its comments on them:

---

[22]209 P. at 180.

[23]Id. at 180-181.

> The parents were members of the religious
> sect known as Seventh Day Adventists, and
> testified that they were desirous of train-
> ing their children to become missionaries
> and ministers, and claimed that the training
> and moral influences in the public school
> there were not favorable to that end. For
> this and other reasons they decided to give
> this child instruction at home, in lieu
> of a public school training. So long as
> the child's education was not neglected, we
> think these parents, under the Constitu-
> tion and laws of this state, had a right to
> manage and supervise the education of their
> child, if done in a fitting and proficient
> manner. The proof is not at all convincing
> that the education of this child was being
> in any way neglected. It seems to us that
> the state misconstrued the scope and spirit
> of the statute upon which this prosecution
> was based.[24]

Approximately thirty years later, a landmark

decision in Illinois provided the fullest judicial articulation

to date regarding home instruction as compliance with compulsory

attendance laws. In People v. Levison,[25] the Illinois court held

that where a seven year old girl received regular instruction

for five hours a day from her mother who had had two years of

college and some training in pedagogy and educational psychology,

and where the child showed a proficiency comparable to that of

average third grade students, that child was, in effect, attend-

ing a "private school" within the meaning of the Illinois compul-

sory attendance statutes and, therefore, her parents' conviction

for violation of the attendance law was erroneous.

---

[24] Id. at 180.

[25] 404 Ill. 574, 90 N.E. 2d 213 (1950).

In contending that the State had failed to prove that the child was not attending a "private school" within the intention of the legislature, the parents argued that

> . . . a school, in the ordinary meaning of
> the word, is a place where instruction is
> imparted to the young, that a number of
> persons being taught does not determine
> whether the place is a school, and that
> by receiving instruction in her home in
> the manner shown by the evidence, the
> child was attending a private school.[26]

The court adopted this argument and further elaborated the earlier reasoning of Peterman:

> Compulsory education laws are enacted to
> enforce the natural obligation of the par-
> ents to provide an education for their young,
> an obligation which corresponds to the
> parents' right of control over his child.
> Meyer v. Nebraska, 262 U.S. 390, 400, 43
> S.Ct. 625, 67 L.Ed. 1042 (1923). The object is
> that all children shall be educated, not
> that they shall be educated in any particu-
> lar manner or place [citing Roberts] . . .
> We think the term "private school", when
> read in the light of the manifest object
> to be attained, includes the place and
> nature of the instruction given to this
> child. The law is not made to punish
> those who provide their children with
> instruction equal or superior to that ob-
> tainable in the public schools. It is made
> for the parent who fails to properly edu-
> cate his child.[27]

In so finding, the court emphasized that it did not imply that parents may, "under a pretext of instruction by a private tutor or by the parents themselves, evade their responsibilities to

---

[26] 90 N.E. 2d at 215.

[27] Id.

educate their children".[28] The _Levison_ opinion offers very little
guidance regarding the "quality and character" of instruction
required to render home instruction acceptable. Presumably,
however, its statement that parents have no right to deprive
children of "educational advantages at least commensurate with
the standards prescribed for the public schools"[29] establishes
the minimal level of acceptable quality and character.

Since the court found that the evidence
was insufficient to sustain the conviction of the parents, it
refrained from consideration of the contention that the statute was unconstitutional. It is unclear from the opinion
whether the parent's assertion of unconstitutionality was
premised on the fact that the Illinois statute did not expressly
permit home instruction, or on a contention that the statute was
unconstitutional as applied to them because of their religious
convictions.[30]

---

[28] 90 N.E. 2d at 215. The court stated: "Those who prefer this
method as a substitute for attendance at the public school have
the burden of showing that they have in good faith provided an
adequate course of instruction in the prescribed branches if
the evidence fails to show a type of instruction and discipline
having the required quality and character. No parent can be
said to have a right to deprive his child of educational advantages at least commensurate with the standards prescribed for
the public schools, and any failure to provide such relief is a
matter of great concern to the courts." 90 N.E. 2d at 215-216.

[29] 90 N.E. 2d at 216.

[30] The appellants were Seventh Day Adventists and believed "that
the child should not be educated in competition with other children because it produces a pugnacious character, that the necessary atmosphere of faith in the Bible cannot be obtained in the
public school, and that for the first eight or ten years of a
child's life, the field or garden is the best schoolroom, the
mother is the best teacher, and nature the best lesson book".
90 N.E. 2d at 214.

The dissent in _Levison_ predicted serious problems of enforceability of a compulsory attendance statute construed in the fashion of the majority and also worried that permitting such arrangements would cause the public schools to lose
the "power, prestige and jurisdiction which is now theirs".[31]
The majority didn't seem alarmed over these issues and made no
real effort to refute them.

While most commentators would probably agree
with the result in _Levison_, and perhaps with its reasoning as
well, the majority's construction of the statute is unsupported
by the legislative history of the enactment. Illinois' original
compulsory attendance law of 1883[32] did provide that a child
could be instructed at home, but this provision was repealed by
an amendment in 1929[33] which re-wrote the statute incorporating
all the earlier provisions regarding attendance _except_ for the
home instruction provision. Thus, Illinois was probably the
worst possible jurisdiction in which to make the arguments the
Illinois court adopted.[34]

Shortly after the _Levison_ decision, the New
York courts in _People v. Turner_[35] followed an analogous line of

---

[31] 90 N.E. 2d at 216.

[32] Ill. Laws 1909, p.342 §274.

[33] Ill. Laws 1929, p.726 §1.

[34] See, generally, "Private Tutoring, Compulsory Education and the
Illinois Supreme Court", 18 Ill. Chic. L. Rev. 105 (1950).

[35] 98 N.Y.S. 2d 886 (1950).

reasoning to a similar conclusion. In a rather cursory opinion
citing only Wright, Levison and Pierce v. Society of Sisters,[36]
the court reversed a finding of the Children's Court convicting
parents of a violation of the compulsory attendance statutes
for failure to send their compulsory school age children to
school. In lieu of school attendance, the children were being
instructed at home by their mother. The Children's Court had
refused to admit the parents' offer of proof regarding the
character of the instruction and the mother's competency to
instruct on the ground that the question of the equivalency of
the instruction to that given in the public schools was not in
issue since the mother was not officially certified to teach.
The higher court found that this proof should have been accepted
and granted a new trial: "Provided the instruction given is
adequate and the sole purpose of non-attendance at school is
not to evade the statute, instruction given to a child at home
by the parent, who is competent to teach, should satisfy the
requirements of the compulsory education law."[37] The finding
of the court was influenced by the terms of the New York attendance statute allowing a minor to attend "at a public school or
elsewhere" providing that instruction "substantially equivalent"
to that given to children of like age and attainments at the
public school is given by a "competent teacher".[38] The New York

---

[36]268 U.S. 510, (1925).

[37]98 N.Y.S. 2d at 888.

[38]N.Y. Educ. Law §3204(1)&(2)(McKinney 1970).

statute, the court noted, was "obviously broader" than the statute interpreted by <u>Levison</u> to include home instruction.[39] The obviously central issue as to whether, for purposes of the relevant statute, one could be "competent" to teach without being "certified" to teach was simply ignored.

The <u>Turner</u> court did not provide any standard for determination of the nature and sufficiency of instruction which would be required to satisfy the "substantially equivalent" requirement. Several subsequent cases have addressed this issue without any success in resolving it. Typically, a court simply recites the facts concerning the child's home instruction and then announces that they do or do not constitute "substantial equivalence" to what the child would receive in the public schools.[40]

Almost twenty years after the <u>Turner</u> decision, New Jersey became the sixth and most recent jurisdiction to permit home instruction by judicial construction of its compulsory attendance laws. In construing the term "equivalent instruction elsewhere" to require only a showing of <u>academic</u> equivalency, the court in <u>State v. Massa</u>[41] overturned its oft-quoted earlier decisions in <u>Knox v. O'Brien</u>[42] and <u>Stephens v. Bonghart</u>[43] which

---

[39] 98 N.Y.S. 2d at 888.

[40] Cf. <u>Shapiro v. Dorin</u>, 99 N.Y.S. 2d 830 (1950) with <u>In re Foster</u>, 69 Misc. 2d 400, 330 N.Y.S. 2d 8 (1972).

[41] 95 N.J. Super. 382, 231 A. 2d 252 (1967).

[42] 7 N.J. 608, 72 A. 2d 389 (1950).

[43] 15 N.J. Misc. 80, 189 A. 131 (1937).

had established such burdensome standards for equivalency as to
essentially foreclose all access to home instruction as an
acceptable learning arrangement in lieu of school attendance.
The Knox decision contained the clearest statement in any jurisdiction of the view that academic similarity alone could not
establish equivalence: "The entire lack of free association with
other children being denied to [the children in the case] by
design or otherwise, which is afforded them at public school,
leads me to the conclusion that they are not receiving education
equivalent to that provided in the public schools."[44]

   Despite these precedents, in Massa, the state
prosecution had stipulated that a child could lawfully be taught
at home and also that the parents need not be certified teachers
in order to give home instruction. Having so stipulated, the
prosecution then emphasized the criteria for equivalency developed
in the earlier decisions, and contended that the parent's lack of
background for teaching and the lack of social development of
the child who was taught alone rendered the home instruction

---

[44]72 A. 2d at 392. Moreover, the Knox court demanded strict
equivalency of teacher qualifications with those required by the
public school. Although the mother in Knox held two degrees, one
a bachelor's Diploma in Education and had taught school twenty
years earlier, the court noted that her education training only
qualified her to teach in the secondary school grades seven through
twelve, and that she had no certificate qualifying her to teach
in the elementary grades. Noting that during the twenty years
since the mother had taught school great progress had been made
in the development of new teaching techniques and methods, it
found that the qualifications possessed by the parent were "unequal and hence, not equivalent" to those then necessary to teach
the elementary grades of the public schools.

unacceptable. However, in finding for the parent, the court
rejected this argument entirely and repudiated its earlier
decisions stating that the Knox interpretation of the word
"equivalent", to include not only academic equivalency but also
equivalency of social development, "appears untenable in the face
of the language of our own statute and also the decisions of
other jurisdictions".[45]

> Under the Knox rationale, in order for
> children to develop socially it would be
> necessary for them to be educated in a
> group. A group of students being educated
> in the same manner and place would consti-
> tute a de facto school. Our statute pro-
> vides that children may receive an equivalent
> education elsewhere than at school. (empha-
> sis added).[46]

After analysis of the case law in various jurisdictions, the
court concluded that

> to hold that the statute requires equiva-
> lent social contact and development as
> well [as academic equivalence] would
> emasculate this alternative and allow
> only group education, thereby eliminating
> private tutoring or home education. A
> statute is to be interpreted to uphold its
> validity in its entirety if possible . . .
> this is the only reasonable interpretation
> available in this case which would accom-
> plish this end.[47]

Massa is not so much a recognition of an
inherent right of parents to choose a mode of education for their
child, as it is an attempt to adhere to legislative intent and

[45]231 A. 2d at 255.

[46]Id.

[47]231 A. 2d at 257.

established rules of judicial interpretation. Clearly, in the
broadest sense, the difference between <u>Massa</u> and its predecessors is simply that in <u>Massa</u> the court finally decided to pay
more attention to the words in the statute than to explicating
some philosophy of child development. <u>Massa</u> does evidence an
attempt to insure that the child is indeed provided with an
adequate means of education, in the sense of one that is academically equivalent to that provided in the public schools.
However, as is true of all the other cases noted above, the
court makes no attempt to determine that the mode of education
is the one the child would have chosen himself or herself.

2. Public School Cases

In commenting on case law expanding the types
of learning arrangements which may be utilized to comply with
compulsory attendance laws, brief mention should be made of the
few reported cases in several jurisdictions interpreting their
education statutes to permit innovative programs within the public school system. For example, in one of the first in a series
of challenges to non-graded public school systems, the Michigan
court found in <u>Schwan v. Board of Education of Lansing School
District</u>,[48] that a statutory grant of discretionary authority
to the board of education[49] was sufficiently broad to encompass

---

[48]27 Mich. App. 391, 183 N.W. 2d 594 (1970).

[49]Mich. Comp. Laws §340.583 (Stat. Ann. 1968 Rev. §15,3583) provides:
Every board shall establish and carry on such grades,
schools and departments as it shall deem necessary or
desirable for the maintenance and improvement of the
schools; determine the courses of study to be pursued
and cause the pupils attending school in such district
to be taught in such schools or departments as it may
deem expedient.

the establishment and operation of completely nongraded programs in the elementary schools.[50]

In another forerunner case, this one an early challenge to a "dual enrollment" program, an Illinois court in _Morton v. Board of Education of the City of Chicago_[51] held that the state compulsory attendance statute permitted part-time enrollment in a public school and part-time enrollment in a non-public school program under a "dual enrollment" arrangement so long as the student receives a complete education. The dual enrollment program was held consistent with the compulsory attendance provision since

> [a]ny child within the ages of 7 and 16 years is required 'to attend some public school in the district wherein the child resides the entire time it is in session during the regular school term' unless the child falls within one of the four exceptions. In the event that the child does come within one of the exceptions it is not necessary that he 'attend some public school in the district wherein [he] resides the entire time it is in session.' (emphasis added).[52]

---

[50]183 N.W. 2d at 595. This was so even though other provisions of the school code dealing with compulsory education gave the board of education of any school district, except primary districts, specific authority to establish ungraded schools for compulsory school age children who were deemed to be "disorderly juvenile persons." Mich. Comp. Laws §340.745 and 340.746.

[51]69 Ill. App. 2d 38, 216 N.E. 2d 305 (1966).

[52]216 N.E. at 308.

However, a Missouri court reached a contrary
opinion in Special Dist. for Educ. & Training of Handicapped Children
v. Wheeler[53] and interpreted the language of its compulsory
attendance statute requiring that a child "attend regularly some
day school, public, private, parochial or parish" to mean that a
child must attend a single school the entire time the school is
open during the regular school term.[54] The dissent objected
strongly to this, asserting that the word "some" does not always
mean "single" and citing precedent[55] for that proposition. It
is interesting to note that a number of other jurisdictions use
the same language as that contained in the Missouri statute but
none of these other statutes have been subjected to judicial
scrutiny.

B. Expansion By Procedural Findings

In a number of jurisdicitons, individuals seeking
to utilize innovative learning arrangements not expressly permitted in the compulsory attendance statutes have benefitted from
burden of proof findings or from procedural errors by the state
prosecution. For instance, courts have held that, as in the case

---

[53]408 S.W. 2d 6(S. Ct. Mo.1966)

[54]Thus, the court held that where a public school district provided speech therapy for parochial school children in buildings
maintained by the public school district and parochial children
who desired such therapy were released from school for part of
their six hour day, such practice violated the compulsory attendance law requiring each school child to attend school regularly
for six hours in the school day.

[55]Walton v. United States Steel Corp., 362 S.W. 2d 617, 625 (S.
Ct. Mo. 1962): "The term 'some' is uncertain in its specifications.")

of other criminal offenses, where a negative averment is an
essential part of the description of an offense, such averment
must be made, and must be sustained by evidence.[56] Thus, the
court in State v. Pilkinton[57] observed that the statutory duty
with which parents were charged in the Missouri compulsory attendance law was stated in two parallel and co-ordinate clauses,
connected by the simple conjunction "or", in the same sentence:

> That parental duty, as expressed and imposed
> in the alternative, is either (1) to cause
> their children (within the stated age range)
> to attend regularly some day school, not
> less than the entire time the school is in
> session or (2) to provide such children with
> home instruction substantially equivalent
> to that given children of the same age in
> day schools in the same locality; and it is
> clear to us . . . that a violation of that
> duty cannot be described accurately unless
> both statutory alternatives are negatived.[58]

Faced with a similar statute and the similar
failure of the state to allege and prove that children were
neither attending public or private school nor receiving some

---

[56] Sheppard v. State, 306 P.2d 346 (Okla. Crim. 1957), State v.
Pilkinton, 310 S.W. 2d 304 (S. Ct. Mo. 1958), State v. Johnson,
188 N.C. 591, 125 S.E. 183 (1924). On the other hand, the burden
rests upon the defendant with respect to a defense predicated upon
an exemption to the compulsory attendance statute which is not a
part of the statutory definition of the offense but is a proviso
directly segregated and set apart in a numbered subparagraph,
Pilkinton, 310 S.W. 2d at 309. Thus, a complaint charging a violation of the California compulsory attendance law need not negative exceptions stated in separate statutes following that in
which the parental duty is created and defined. See People v.
Turner, 121 Cal. App. 2d Supp. 861, 263 P. 2d 685, 686 (1953),
appeal dismissed 347 U.S. 972 (1954).

[57] 310 S.W. 2d 304 (S.Ct. Mo. 1958).

[58] Id. at 308.

other means of education, the Oklahoma court in <u>Sheppard v.</u>
<u>State</u>[59] held that the state failed to make out a <u>prima facie</u>
case of a violation of the compulsory attendance statute and the
convictions of the parents were reversed.[60]

However, courts in two other jurisdictions have
come to somewhat different conclusions, finding that it is not
always necessary for the prosecution to allege and prove non-
compliance with all the statute's alternatives. In <u>State v.</u>
<u>Vaughn</u>,[61] the court noted that while the primary reference sec-
tion of the New Jersey compulsory attendance statute provided
alternative means[62] for complying with the statute, a subsequent
section[63] provided <u>generally</u> for liability for failure to comply
with the primary reference section. In determining the inter-
play of these two sections, the court placed the <u>initial</u> burden
of proof on the parents, since

> if the burden of proving a violation of either
> of the two alternatives rests upon the State,
> it would be saddled with a fairly impossible

---

[59]306 P. 2d 346 (Okla. Crim. 1957).

[60]See also <u>Commonwealth v. Meeks</u>, 192 Ky. 690, 234 S.W. 292 (1921)
concerning a prosecution under the compulsory attendance statute
in which the indictment was held fatally defective for failure to
negative the statutory exceptions.

[61]44 N.J. 142, 207 A. 2d 537 (1965).

[62]N.J.S.A. 18A; 38-25(1968).

[63]"A parent, guardian or other person having charge and control
of a child between the ages of seven and sixteen years, who shall
fail to comply with any of the provisions of this article relating to his duties shall be deemed to be a disorderly person".. ...
N.J. S.A. 18A; 38-31(1968).

task, for it would be obligated to prove a
negative proposition in circumstances in
which the area of disproof is extremely wide.[64]

However, in accordance with the usual criminal procedural rule

that the _ultimate_ burden always remains with the prosecution, the

Vaughn court held that once the parents do come forward with

evidence, the ultimate burden of persuasion remains with the

state.

The fact that cases involving compulsory attendance

statutes are often tried in juvenile courts where procedural

standards are frequently unclear and even more frequently honored

in the breach, heavily influences these evidentiary matters. For

instance, in _F.&F. v.Duval County_,[65] the court rejected the

parents' position that the lower court erred in holding that the

state had made out a _prima facie_ case establishing that the

children were in need of supervision as persistent truants from

school based on the showing that they had failed to attend the

public school to which they had been assigned. The court stated:

> The strict rules of law relating to the burden
> of proof and admissibility of evidence are
> greatly relaxed in proceedings of this nature
> [under the Juvenile Court Act], and the trial
> is usually conducted in a somewhat informal
> manner.[66]

C. Expansion by Limiting the Regulation of Private
   Schools

The nature, detail and enforceability of state

---

[64] 207 A. 2d at 540.

[65] 273 So. 2d 15 (S. Ct. Mo. 1973).

[66] _Id._ at 17.

regulation of the private school varies considerably from jurisdiction to jurisdiction and depending on the precise configura-
tion of those factors may expand or contract the utilization of
variations which are alternatives for compliance with the compulsory
attendance provision. Ever since <u>Pierce v. Society of Sisters</u>
established in 1925 that the state may promulgate reasonable
regulations concerning private schools so long as it permits
their existence, most state courts have upheld the validity and
reasonableness, under the state's police power, of whatever
regulations were adopted. Those cases which have placed limits
on state regulation of the private schools have generally done
so under circumstances where the regulations were so detailed and
burdensome as to affect the very viability of the organization.
For example, in <u>Farrington v. Tokushige</u>,[67] the Supreme Court
held that the provisions of the Hawaii Foreign Language School
Act were unconstitutional since the numerous provisions of the
statute "give affirmative directions concerning the intimate and
essential details of such schools, entrust their control to public officers, and deny both owners and patrons reasonable choice
and discretion in respect of teachers, curriculum, and textbooks."[68]

Other cases have restricted the regulation of private schools where the regulatory process was left to the unlimi-
ted discretion of administrative personnel. For instance, the
New York Court of Appeals in <u>Packer Collegiate Institute v. Uni-</u>

---

[67]273 U.S. 284 (1927). And see discussion, Chapter 11, <u>infra</u>.
[68]273 U.S. at 298.

versity of State of New York[69] declared unconstitutional a statute

requiring the registration of private nonsectarian schools

where the Commissioner of Education was given the power to grant

or refuse such registration under regulations to be adopted by

him with no statutory guidance of any kind as to standards or,

limitations. The court found that under these circumstances, the

private schools' constitutional right to exist was threatened.

Similarly, in State v. Williams,[70] the Supreme Court of North

Carolina held a statute providing for the regulation of private

business, trade and correspondence schools invalid as an imper-

missible delegation of legislative power where the statute

provided no standards at all for the regulations which were to

implement it.

II. Judicial Refusal to Expand Permissible Learning Arrangements

Very few jurisdictions have given rise to judicial

interpretations of compulsory attendance statutes which so

narrowly construe the statutes, as by holding that "private

school" does not include home instruction, for instance, as to

effect a real restriction on the extent of available learning

arrangements. And in several of those jurisdictions which do

have such decisions, one also finds interesting dicta which may

suggest that a different result would have been reached given a

slightly different fact situation.

The leading case which does make a very restricted

construction of a compulsory attendance statute by giving a

---

[69]298 N.Y. 184, 81 N.E. 2d 80 (1948).

[70]25 N.C. 337, 117 S.E. 2d 444 (1960).

narrow interpretation of the private school alternative, is a
New Hampshire court's decision in State v. Hoyt.[71] In that
case the court found that the fact that a child was instructed
and taught by a private tutor in his own home in the subjects
required to be taught in the public schools to children of the
same age was no defense to a charge of failure to send a child
of school-age to public school or to an approved private school as
required by the New Hampshire compulsory attendance statute.
In upholding the attendance law as constitutional within the
framework of Pierce and against the claim that it offended
against the federal guarantee of liberty found in the Fourteenth
Amendment, the Court relied heavily on the difficulty of
effective supervision of home instruction arrangements:

> In the adjustment of the parent's right to
> choose the manner of his children's education,
> and the impinging right of the state to insist
> that certain education be furnished and super-
> vised, the rule of reasonable conduct upon the
> part of each towards the other is to be applied.
> The state must bear the burden of reasonable
> supervision, and the parent must offer educa-
> tional facilities which do not require unrea-
> sonable supervision.
> If the parent undertakes to make use of
> units of education so small, or facilities of
> such doubtful quality, that supervision thereof
> would impose an unreasonable burden upon the
> state, he offends against the reasonable provi-
> sions for schools which can be supervised with-
> out unreasonable expense. The state may require,
> not only that educational facilities be supplied,
> but also that they be so supplied that the facts
> in relation thereto can be ascertained, and proper
> direction thereof maintained, without unreasonable
> cost to the state. Anything less than this would

---

[71] 84 N.H. 38, 146 A. 170 (1929).

take from the state all efficient authority to
regulate the education of the prospective voting
population.[72]

Thus, while recognizing the rights of parents to
choose the manner in which their children are to be educated, the
Hoyt decision is the most decidedly state-oriented in this whole
area. The court's principal concern appeared to be that "the
state is entitled to establish a system whereby it can be known,
by reasonable means, that the required teaching is being done."[73]
Again, as with all the other cases, the competing interests to
be resolved were seen only as those of the state and the parent;
Hoyt makes no reference to the rights of the child.

The court rather summarily dismissed the defendant
parent's claim that the home tutoring was adequate compliance
with the statute: "The statute makes no such exception to the
duty imposed. The only substitute for the public school is an
approved private school".[74] This literal-mindedness led to the
obvious conclusion:

> If the defendants' allegations that 'said child
> was taught by a private tutor in his own home'
> could be construed to set forth attendance at a
> private school (see State v. Counort, 69 Wash.
> 361, 124 P. 910), there is no allegation that
> the enterprise has been designated as a private
> school 'to be treated as approved within the
> meaning of this title'. Not having been approved
> as required by the statute, it is not 'an approved
> private school.' (emphasis added)[75]

---

[72] 146 A. at 171.

[73] Id. at 172.

[74] Id.

[75] Id.

New Hampshire appears to be the only jurisdiction which has considered it reasonable to omit the home instruction alternative on the grounds of the possibly burdensome expense of state supervision of such programs.

Although <u>Hoyt</u> has been cited[76] for the proposition that home instruction is not within the meaning of "private school", the last sentence of the preceding quotation indicates that even under <u>Hoyt's</u> strictures, private instruction may be approvable if the authority which grants approval to "private schools" could be persuaded. And it is questionable whether the state could deny access to a learning arrangement if, in fact, it could be shown, by "reasonable means" that the required teaching is being done.

In addition to its concern over the administrability of state supervision of home instruction, the <u>Hoyt</u> court also evidenced its preference for group, rather than individual education:

> Education in public schools is considered by man to furnish desirable and even essential training for citizenship, apart from that gained by the study of books. The association with those of all classes of society, at an early age and upon a common level, is not unreasonably urged as a preparation for discharging the duties of a citizen. <u>Fogg v. Board of Education</u>, 76 N.H. 296, 299, 82 A. 173, 175.[77]

Although it was decided over half a century ago, the

---

[76] See Annotation, 14 A.L.R. 2d 1369.

[77] 146 A. at 170-171.

Hoyt reasoning still prevails in New Hampshire. As recently as 1974, the state Supreme Court referred to it with approval in In re Davis,[78] a case involving allegations of child neglect. Citing Hoyt, the Davis court summarily concluded: "It is no answer to a charge brought under [the compulsory attendance law] that equivalent supervised instruction is given by a private tutor."

There are series of cases in two other jurisdictions, Kansas and Washington, which have considered the nature of the private school alternative in compulsory attendance statutes, and have concluded that home instruction and similar arrangements are impermissible.

In the most recent Kansas case, State v. Garber,[79] the defendant father failed, for reasons of religious conviction, to send his fifteen-year-old daughter to any "public, private, denominational or parochial school", as required by Kansas statute. Garber followed earlier decisions in other jurisdictions[80] and concluded that constitutional protection is afforded only to beliefs connected to the act of worship. The court held that, since the compulsory laws did not directly affect the defendant's (Amish) worship, there was no abridgement of religious freedom. This reasoning was expressly rejected by the U.S. Supreme Court in Yoder v.

---

[78] 114 N.H. 242, 318 A.2d 151 (1974).

[79] 197 Kan. 567, 419 P. 2d 896, cert. den. 389 U.S. 51, 88 S. Ct. 236 (1966).

[80] Commonwealth v. Beely, 168 Pa. Super. 462, 79 A. 2d 134 (1951); State v. Hershberger, 102 Ohio App. 188, 144 N.E. 2d 693 (1955).

Wisconsin,[81] so the _Garber_ decision would be overturned were it
rendered today. Nonetheless, it deserves review because of its
approach to the general question of whether home instruction may
be allowed under the private school exception.

The child involved in _Garber_ was both enrolled in a
correspondence course approved by the United States Office of
Education for private home study, and attended a school established by the Amish which was taught by an Amish farmer whose
formal education consisted of eight grades in the public school.
The court found that neither of these programs, "being essentially
home instruction systems," constituted acceptable programs within
the meaning of the statute. "Even if the instruction given through
them could be considered as instruction _equivalent_ to that given
in a public, private, denominational or parochial school", the
court stated, "this would not be [adequate compliance] for the
reason that the legislature has made no provision for such
equivalent instruction as the basis for exemption".[82]

In arriving at its decision, the court relied on its
earlier opinions in _State v. Will_[83] and _State v. Lowry_,[84] neither

[81]406 U.S. 205 (1927). Even prior to _Yoder_, _Garber_ had lost significance for the Amish since an exemption was provided in 1968 by
the Kansas legislature. Kan. Stat. Annot. §72-1111 (Supp. 1968).

[82]419 P. 2d at 900.

[83]99 Kan. 167, 160 P. 1025 (1916).

[84]191 Kan. 701, 383 P. 2d 962 (1963).

of which was on point. Will held that a private school not
meeting the standards of instruction applied to the public
schools could still be a permissible learning arrangement under
the compulsory attendance statutes. Garber cited Will, which
was decided in 1916, for its acknowledgment that the truancy
act prescribing an enforcement procedure for the compulsory
attendance provisions was amended in 1903 by the elimination of
a home study exemption. In citing Lowry, Garber noted: "[Lowry]
applied the reasoning expressed in Will and refused to approve
what amounted to scheduled home instruction as an excuse for
nonattendance in schools . . ."[85]

In attempting to decide whether the defendant parents
were operating a "private school" by instructing their children
at home, Lowry had offered what was, by its own admission, a
"sketchy" definition of private school:

> . . . [W]e are of the opinion that any school in
> order to be classed as a private school must at
> least meet the course of instruction requirements
> of [citing another statute], and the children
> must be taught by a competent instructor in the
> English language for the prescribed time as re-
> quired by [another statute]. It is our further
> opinion that any parent who sends a child to a
> school that does not meet these sketchy require-
> ments is subject to the penalty provisions of the
> truancy act. In the instant case the defendants'
> attempt to operate a private school resulted in
> mere scheduled home instruction . . .[86]

In view of the legislative history of the Kansas provision, especially the amendment deleting home instruction as a

[85] 419 P. 2d at 899-900.

[86] 383 P. 2d at 965.

permissible alternative, clearly the Kansas court would have been better off with a decision premised solely on the development of the statute rather than on its own murky precedents.[87]

In comparison to the Kansas decisions, the Washington decisions provide more interesting reading - and more curious outcomes. The most recent case, and one which is often referred to in a number of other contexts, is State ex rel. Shoreline School District v. Superior Court.[88] Shoreline expresses directly what has been implicit in all the other cases discussed so far: that the interests of the child, as distinct from the freedom ("right") of the parent to "act in the child's interest", and certainly as distinct from any views the child might have himself or herself, need not be considered in applying the compulsory attendance statutes.

In determining that the home instruction provided by the parents was not instruction in a private school, the Supreme

_____

[87]Based on language contained in Lowry, one recent study has indicated that the Lowry court found that certain requirements concerning institutional structure, in addition to the statutory requirements concerning the program of instruction, must be met before a program could come within the definition of "private school". K. Alexander & K.F. Jordan, Legal Aspects of Educational Choice: Compulsory Attendance and Student Assignment (NOLPE Second Monogrpah Series on Legal Aspects of School Administration, No. 4, 1973), p. 27.) It is true that at one point in the decision, the court considered facts and circumstances bearing on the institutional nature of the home instruction program in attempting to determine whether the parents were in fact operating a "private school" for the purposes of the compulsory attendance law. Notwithstanding these earlier statements, however, the concluding paragraph of the Lowry opinion makes it quite clear that the home instruction program could have been acceptable to the Lowry court as a private school had it merely met the minimum requirements regarding courses, instructors and time of instruction.

[88]55 Wash. 2d 177, 346 P. 2d 999 (1959), cert. den. 363 U.S. 814 (1960).

Court of Washington reversed the decision of the juvenile court
which had found that the interests of the child would be best
served by allowing her to remain at home, subject to the continuing supervision of the court. The Supreme Court concluded
that the system of home instruction could not qualify as a private school since the mother, who did all the teaching, did not
have a teaching certificate.

As has been observed by other commentators,[89] one very
surprising but nonetheless clear implication of the Shoreline
decision is the subordination, in effect, of judicial determinations of a child's "best interests" to determinations made by
school superintendents. The history of legislative activity in
Washington on compulsory attendance is, in many ways, illustrative of national trends. In the sixteen years since Shoreline
was decided, the primary reference sections above have been
amended four times. At the time the Shoreline litigation was
commenced, not a word of the statute had been changed in almost
half a century.

In reaching its decision, the Washington court cited
its much earlier and oft-quoted opinion in State v. Counort.[90]
A recent study on compulsory attendance law[91] misreads the Washington decisions, especially State v. Counort, and promotes a

---

[89] See note, "Constitutional Law - Compulsory Attendance Law - Freedom of Religion", 35 Wash. L. Rev. 151 (1960).

[90] 69 Wash. 361, 124 P. 910 (1912).

[91] K. Alexander § K.F. Jordan, Legal Aspects of Educational Choice:
Compulsory Attendance and Student Assignment (NOLPE Second Monograph Series on Legal Aspects of School Administration, No. 4,
1973), pp. 26 and 30.

distorted concept of "private school" for the purposes of the
compulsory attendance laws by citing only this excerpt from the
Counort opinion:

> We do not think that the giving of instruction by
> a parent to a child, conceding the competency of
> the parent to fully instruct the child in all that
> is taught in the public schools, is within the mean-
> ing of the law 'to attend a private school.' Such
> a requirement means more than home instruction;
> It means the same character of school as the public
> school, a regular, organized and existing institu-
> tion, making a business of instructing children of
> school age in the required studies and for the full
> time required by the laws of this state....There may
> be a difference in institution and government, but
> the purpose and end of both public and private
> schools must be the same - the education of children
> of school age. The parent who teaches his children
> at home, whatever be his reason for desiring to do
> so, does not maintain such a school.[92] (emphasis
> added).

Focusing on this alone leads to an inaccurate conclusion. Even
Counort, which the authors quote in part, does not support such
a generalization. The Counort court stated directly:

> Undoubtedly a private school may be maintained in a
> private home in which the children of the instructor
> may be pupils. This provision of the law is not to
> be determined by the place where the school is main-
> tained, nor the individuality or number of the pupils
> who attend it. It is to be determined by the purpose,
> intent and character of the endeavor.[93]

---

[92]Id. at 26.

[93]69 Wash. at 364.

Therefore, clearly Counort does not establish an iron-
clad rule that because of its lack of certain institutional
details home instruction can never come within the definition
of "private school" in Washington. Moreover, Shoreline makes
it clear that home instruction meeting certain statutory requirements applied to the private school will come within the definition of "private school" for purposes of the Washington compulsory
attendance statutes.

The California case of People v. Turner[94] should be
noted at this point because of its strict construction of the
term "private school" to foreclose expansion of the permissible
learning arrangements to allow home instruction by noncertified
teachers in a jurisdiction whose statute allowed home instruction
by certified teachers and attendance at a private school taught
by "capable", although not necessarily certified, teachers.[95]
In holding that the term "private school" connotes institutional
details similar to those provided in the public school, the
court found that parents teaching their children at home and
having no state teaching credentials had violated the compulsory
attendance laws since they came within neither the home instruction
nor private school alternatives. However, since the California
statute specifically allows instruction at home by a private
tutor or other person under certain circumstances in addition to
private school attendance, this definition should not be applied

---

[94]121 Cal. App. 2d Supp. 861, 263 P. 2d 685 (1953).

[95]See In re Shinn, 195 Cal. App. 2d 683, 16 Cal. Rptr. 165 (1961).

to "private school" in those jurisdictions whose statutes only specify private school attendance in lieu of public school.

III. Summary

In summary, then, some courts have refused to construe the term "private school" to include home instruction or similar tutoring arrangements when the home instruction did not meet one or more of the following requirements: 1) the parents, or tutors, did not apply for the "approval" applicable to private schools; 2) the instruction was not given by a certified teacher, or, less often, by one whose competence could be judged other than by evidence of certification; 3) the instruction did not meet statutory curriculum requirements; 4) the instruction was not given for an adequate number of hours or over a term of sufficient duration.

None of these requirements singly nor all of them in combination constitute an insuperable bar to utilizing the "private school" rubric as a vehicle for non-traditional learning arrangements. With the exception of New Hampshire, which does appear to have certain requirements for private schools of an "institutional" nature, the case law of every jurisdiction which has reached negative conclusions on the issue, does, on a close reading, seem amenable to the possibility of having "private school" mean something quite different from the ordinary connotations of that term.

Over a seventy-five year span, courts in a half dozen jurisdictions have expanded the permissible learning arrangements

to include alternatives not expressly contained in the compulsory
attendance statutes by interpreting the words "private school",
and instruction "elsewhere" or "otherwise" to allow home instruction or similar tutoring arrangements. At the heart of all such
decisions is the finding that the object of the compulsory attendance statutes is that all children be educated, not that they be
educated in any particular manner or place, and a recognition of
the right of the parents, acting in good faith, to determine,
within limits, the education of their child.[96]

In essence, the courts are generally satisfied whenever the child has been provided, by a competent teacher, with
an education academically similar to that available in the public
schools so that the child has attained a degree of proficiency in
the subjects taught in the public schools comparable to that attained by a child of the same age or grade in the public schools.
In addition, courts in other jurisdictions have interpreted their
statutes to allow innovative programs within the public school

---

[96]The extent to which the Supreme Court's much-debated opinion in
Wisconsin v. Yoder, 406, U.S. 206, 92 S.Ct. 1526 (1972), expands or restricts parental options within the context of the
obligations imposed by compulsory attendance statutes is considered in a later chapter. It is unclear whether the majority
opinion in Yoder was intended to carve out an exemption to the
requirement of compulsory attendance or whether it, in effect,
found the defendants to be complying with the statute in an
unusual way, not permitted under the Wisconsin statute but required on federal constitutional grounds to be acceptable. At a
minimum, however, it overruled those courts which had disallowed
home instruction in lieu of public school attendance for Amish
children who have completed the eighth grade. See State v.
Garber, 197 Kan. 267, 419 P. 2d 896, cert. den. 389 U.S. 51,
88 S.Ct. 236 (1966); Commonwealth v. Beiler, 168 Pa. Super.
462, 79 A. 2d 134 (1951); Commonwealth v. Smoker, 177 Pa. Super.
435, 110 A. 2d 740 (1955); Meyerkorth v. Nebraska, 173 Neb. 889,
115 N.S. 2d 585 (1962).

system, including dual enrollment and nongraded programs without express statutory authorization for such programs. Finally, courts in several jurisdictions have, in effect, expanded the learning arrangements permissible under their statutes in individual cases by dismissing, on procedural grounds, suits against parents who taught their children at home and by limiting the extent of state regulation of private schools.

6. STATUTORY EXEMPTIONS FROM COMPULSORY ATTENDANCE

Compulsory attendance at public or private school or at some other alternative learning arrangement is required by statute in all of the states except Mississippi. Statutory exemptions from this requirement, however, also exist in every state.[1] The purpose of this chapter is to catalogue and analyze the statutory exemptions. It should be noted that attendance at a private school which has been discussed in previous chapters as an "alternative" to public school attendance is categorized by the statutes of some states as either an "exemption" or an "exception" to their compulsory attendance requirements. Specifically, in thirty-one states[2] reference to non-public school attendance appears in the primary reference section as an "alternative" to public school while in seventeen states[3] the primary statutory reference is to private school attendance as an "exemption" or "exception" from public school attendance. Therefore, it would be technically correct to speak of private school students as "exempt" from compulsory attendance in these seventeen jurisdictions, but that usage would be very confusing since, in fact, the private school students are complying with the attendance

[1]For purposes of this section, the word "state" includes the District of Columbia and Puerto Rico.

[2]Ala., Ark., D.C., Fla., Ga., Ha., Idaho, Ind., Iowa, Kan., La., Mass., Minn., Mo., Neb., N.H., N.J., N.M., N.C., Ohio, Okla., Penn., P.R., S.C., S.D., Tenn., Utah, Va., Wash., Wis., Wyo.

[3]Alas., Ariz., Calif., Colo., Conn., Ill., Ky., Me., Mich., Mont., Nev., N.D., Ore., R.I., Tex., Vt., W.Va.

requirement whereas all the other categories of "exemptions" deal with children who are not in compliance, or at least not in full compliance, with the requirement. Therefore, we will continue to refer to private school attendance as an "alterna-tive".

Some statutes, many commentators and most courts have used the terms "exception" and "exemption" interchangeably. However, the underlying concept is the freeing of the parent and child from the obligations of the attendance requirement, and we believe "exemption" expresses this concept more precisely than "exception" which may carry additional connotations with respect to the state's (school system's) obligations. Hence, we will generally use the term "exemption" unless the context clearly requires use of "exception" for some reason such as reference to a particular statute where the term "exception" is employed.

Statutes specifying exemptions from the attendance require-ment do so on a broad range of grounds, including mental, emo-tional or physical disability, completion of a minimum attendance or educational requirement, employment, suspension or expulsion, distance from the school and lack of transportation, judicial or school administrative decision, temporary absences and certain special circumstances such as children who are incarcerated.

I.   Physical, Mental and Emotional Conditions

Physical and mental or emotional disability is the most common ground for exemption. Every jurisdiction contains some provision, many quite broad and only a few very limited, exempting

children from school attendance or one of its alternatives
for physical, mental or emotional reasons. However, in a few
jurisdictions the future viability of this exemption may be ques-
tioned as a result of recent very broad extensions of the meaning of
the word "education" into areas that might previously have been
considered "therapy" or "training" or some other process other
than education.[4]

In most states, the statutes refer to both the emotional
or mental and physical condition of the child. The statutes of
six states[5] refer only to the child's emotional condition as a
reason for exemption while provisions in two other states[6] refer
only to the "mental condition" of the child.

The physical, mental or emotional condition exemptions in
twenty-nine states[7] refer to vague concepts such as the child's
"inability to profit" from attendance. In the other twenty-two
states the exemption is stated solely in terms of the child's
inability to attend. It is not clear from the statutes in these
twenty-two states whether children are exempted because of
inability to attend related to safety or health reasons, or

---

[4] See Mass. Gen. Laws 71B (1972) and regulations issued
thereunder; Pennsylvania Assoc. for Retarded Citizens v. Pennsylvania, 343 F. Supp. 279 (E.D.Pa. 1972); Mills v. Bd. of
Educ. of District of Columbia, 348 F. Supp. 866 (D.D.C. 1972).

[5] Fla., Idaho, La., Md., Mich., N.M.

[6] Conn. and P.R.

[7] Ala., Ark., Calif., Del., D.C., Fla., Ga., Ind., Kan., La., Md.,
Mich., Minn., Mont., Neb., Nev., N.J., N.M., N.Y., N.C., N.D.,
Ohio, Ore., Penn., Tenn., Tex., Utah, Va., W.Va.

because of a supposed inability to benefit from attendance.

The mental and physical disability provisions in six state statutes[8] refer to the welfare of the other children in the classroom. The language in these provisions is general, using phrases such as "detrimental to other children" or "harmful to others". It is unclear whether the concern is that there may be some detriment to the health and safety of the other children or some detriment to their education.

Thirty-seven states[9] require some documentation of the child's condition before exempting the child from the attendance requirement. The statutes in twenty of these states[10] require the certificate of a county health officer or a physician attesting to the child's inability to attend. Nine[11] of the thirty-seven states provide that the statement of the child's condition must be made by a physician, a psychiatrist or a psychologist.[12]

---

[8]Conn., Md., N.Y., S.D., Tenn., Wyo.

[9]Ala., Alas., Calif., Conn., Del., D.C., Fla., Ha., Idaho, Ill., Ind., Iowa, Kan., Ky., La., Md., Mich., Nev., N.M., N.Y., N.C., N.D., Ohio, Okla., Ore., Penn., P.R., S.C., S.D., Tenn., Tex., Utah, Vt., Va., W.Va., Wis., Wyo.

[10]Ala., Alas., Del., Fla., Ha., Ill., Ind., Kan., Ky., Nev., N.D., Okla., S.D., Tenn., Tex., Utah, Vt., Va., W.Va., Wyo.

[11]Idaho, La., Md., Mich., N.Y., N.C., Penn., S.C., Wis.

[12]Idaho, Md., N.Y., and S.C. accept a statement from either a physician or psychologist. La. and Penn. require a statement from a mental health clinic or from a psychologist or psychiatrist. Wis. will accept the statement of a physician, a psychologist or a Christian Science practitioner. N.C. requires a medical, a social, a psychological and an educational evaluation before the child is exempted from compulsory education. Other jurisdictions may have similar requirements as a result of regulations issued pursuant to special education statutes.

Five[13] of the thirty-seven states require a physical examination
or other tests as proof that a child comes within the exemption.

The statutes in two states[14] provide that the exemption
be based on standards established by the board of education.
In two other states,[15] the statement of the physician is required
only if the school authorities deem it necessary. The provision
in California specifies only "satisfactory evidence of condition".
In all probability, this is the statement of a physician, but
it is not clear from the statute. In Iowa, the parents are required to furnish proof by affidavit of the physical and mental
condition of the child.

The physical or mental condition exemption provisions of
only thirteen states[16] refer to special education programs for
those children exempted. In eight[17] of these states, children
exempted are required, with certain qualifications, to receive
special instruction. In four[18] of the thirteen states, the
child is exempted because of inability to participate in either

---

[13]Conn., D.C., Ohio, P.R. and Va.

[14]N.M. and Ore.

[15]Utah, Wyo.

[16]D.C., Fla., La., Mass., Mont., N.Y., N.D., Ohio, Ore., P.R.,
S.C., S.D., Tex.

[17]D.C., La., Mass., Ohio, Ore., P.R., S.C., S.D.

[18]Fla., Mont., N.D., Tex.

a regular or a special program.

No state specifically mentions blindness or deafness as a reason for exemption from compulsory attendance. Most states, however, have separate provisions in their education codes for blind and deaf children requiring attendance at the state school for the blind, the state school for the deaf, or other similar institutions.

II.   Completion of Minimum Attendance or Education Requirement

Thirty-two states[19] exempt from compulsory attendance those persons who have attained a specified minimum grade or education level. Twenty-two[20] of these states require the completion of high school. Several of the thirty-two states also exempt for education equivalent to that achieved through completion of high school.[21] Florida and California have very recently adopted new laws to permit students subject to the compulsory attendance law to leave school with their parents' permission upon successful completion of an examination demonstrating proficiency in basic skills such as English and mathematics.

---

[19]Ala., Alas., Ariz., Ark., Colo., Ga,, Ha., Iowa., Ky,, Me,, Minn,, Mont., Neb., Nev., N.H., N.M., N.Y., N.D., Ohio, Okla, Ore., Penn., P.R., S.C., S.D., Tenn., Utah, Vt., Wash., W.Va., Wis., Wyo.

[20]Ala., Alas., Colo., Ga., Ha., Ky., Me., Neb., Nev., N.M., N.Y., N.D., Ohio, Okla., Ore., Penn., P.R., S.C., Tenn., Utah, W.Va., Wis. But see note 23.

[21]Hawaii exempts students who have graduated from high school or vocational school. Persons who pass the general educational development test in N.M. are exempted from compulsory attendance. In Ore., persons who demonstrate that they have acquired equivalent knowledge to that taught in grades one through twelve can be exempted. South Carolina requires that the child graduate from high school or receive the equivalent of a high school education from a private school.

In seven[22] of the thirty-two states, completion of the
eighth grade is adequate for exemption.[23] Two[24] of the thirty-
two states require the completion of ten grades of school. The
remaining state, Washington, exempts persons after the completion
of nine grades, but requires part-time school attendance thereafter in certain circumstances.

Exemptions for "legal employment" and "special reasons",
often also require the completion of a certain grade level as
an additional condition which must be met before the exemption
is applicable. The specific education requirements accompanying
these two exemptions are set forth in Appendix

III. Legal Employment, Work Study and Vocational Employment

   A. Legal Employment

   Twenty-seven states[25] exempt from the attendance
requirement children who are lawfully employed. In ten[26] of these
states, however, the exemption is granted only when there is a

---

[22]Ariz., Ark., Iowa, Mont., N.H., S.D., Wyo.

[23]In N.H., the completion of the eighth grade is sufficient only
if there is no high school in the district in which the person lives.

[24]Minn., Vt.

[25]Ala., Ariz., Ark., Calif., Colo., Conn., D.C., Fla., Ha., Ill.,
Iowa, Me., Mass., Mo., Neb., Nev., N.Y., N.D., Ohio, Ore., Penn.,
S.C., Tex., Utah., Vt., Wash., W.Va.

[26]Ark., Ill., Neb., Nev., N.D., S.C., Tex., Utah, Vt., Wash.

need for the child to work for the support of the child's family. In addition to these exemptions found in the compulsory attendance statutes, child labor provisions in a number of jurisdictions provide additional qualifications upon the attendance requirement.[27]

B. Work Study and Vocational Employment

In seven states[28] persons are exempted from compulsory attendance if they engage in some form of work study, vocational training or apprenticeship program.

Requirements for obtaining these exemptions are minimal. For example, only three[29] of the seven states even require the person to be of a certain age and only one[30] requires the attainment of a specified level of schooling. In two, Maine and Texas, approval from school officials and parental consent are necessary for these exemptions to be operable. The Utah provision is an employment and work study hybrid exempting a child from attendance if "proper influences and adequate opportunities for education are provided in connection with the employment of the minor".[31]

---

[27] See Chapters 9 and 10 and Appendix E.

[28] Ariz., Calif., Colo., Me., Nev., Tex., Utah.

[29] In Calif. and Nev. the child must be fourteen while Tex. requires the child to be fifteen.

[30] Nev. requires that the child complete the eighth grade before entering apprenticeship.

[31] Utah Code Ann. §53-24-1(b)(5)(1970).

The exemptions in eight states[32] also provide that
the person excused from compulsory attendance for legal employment
or vocational training must attend school on a part-time basis.
Hour requirements for such attendance are established in six[33]
of the eight states. Two of these states[34] require only four
hours of attendance each week. In Illinois the child must attend
school for a minimum of eight hours per week, while Ohio limits
such attendance to a maximum of eight hours per week. New York
requires twenty hours of attendance per week. Part-time attendance in Utah must amount to 144 hours each year. In addition
to these eight states, some other states have provisions in
their child labor laws establishing part-time schools and/or
requiring part-time attendance.

IV.   Suspension and Expulsion

Statutes in sixteen states[35] specifically exempt children
who have been suspended or expelled from school. For the most
part, these provisions are silent regarding the grounds for
expulsion or suspension, which are commonly specified in the
rules and regulations of local school boards or in state regulations. Those statutes that do specify grounds, however, usually

---

[32]Calif., Ill., Mo., N.Y., Ohio, Ore., Utah, Wash.

[33]Ill., Mo., N.Y., Ohio, Utah, Wash.

[34]Mo., Wash.

[35]Alas., Calif., Colo., Ha., Idaho, Iowa, Md., Mich., Mont.,
N.H., P.R., S.C., Tenn., Utah, W.Va., Wyo.

refer to "persistent misbehavior", "violations of rules and
regulations" or "disruption of the educational process".

An expulsion or suspension exemption allows a state, in
effect, to relieve itself of the duty to provide public education for persons of compulsory attendance age whenever the
behavior of a child makes instruction difficult.[36] In one extraordinary anomaly, the West Virginia statute treats as <u>unlawfully
absent</u> a child suspended for failure to comply with the requirements and regulations of the school board. Some states[37] provide
for the establishment of "truancy schools" or other special
disciplinary schools and some expelled children are required to
attend such institutions rather than being exempted altogether.

In addition to the sixteen states which specifically
refer to expulsion and suspension as a basis for exemption from
compulsory attendance, four other states[38] have exception provisions that may enable school officials to exclude persons from
attendance by administrative rule or regulation. Additional
states may exclude children from compulsory attendance because
of disciplinary problems under other specific exemptions. For
example, provisions that include "mental disability" or an

---

[36]For an extended analysis of use of the suspension power see
Children's Defense Fund of the Washington Research Project, Inc.,
<u>Children Out of School in America</u> chapter 5 (1974).

[37]For example, Ky., Iowa and Neb.

[38]Ga. Code Ann. §32-2106(b)(1969); N.M. Stat. Ann. §77-10-2
(Supp. 1975); Ore. Rev. Stat. §339.030(8)(1971); R.I. Gen Laws
§16-19-1(1970).

"inability to profit or benefit from further school attendance" as reasons for exemption from compulsory school attendance may be construed to apply to disciplinary problems and provide the school officials with the purported authority to discontinue the education of the child who is thus "exempted" from the attendance requirement.

V.   Distance from School or Public Transportation

Fourteen states[39] exempt from compulsory attendance children whose residence is too far from the nearest school or from available public transportation. In some states attendance is required only of those children living within a "reasonable distance"[40] or a "safe and practical distance"[41] from public school. Only Montana's statute specifies that, in the case of this exemption, the child be provided with some education program in lieu of attendance.

Five states exempt children from compulsory attendance if they reside a specified distance[42] from school, if no public transportation is available.

_____

[39]Ala., Alas., Fla., La., Mich., Mont., Nev., Ore., Penn., P.R., Tenn., Utah, Va., W.Va.

[40]E.g., Puerto Rico

[41]E.g., Nev.

[42]Ore. (1-1/2 miles, for children ages seven to ten; 3 miles, for children eleven and over); Penn. (2 miles, age not specified); Ala. and Utah (2-1/2 miles, age not specified); and Mich. (2-1/2 miles, children under nine).

Six states[43] measure the distance from the child's residence in terms of either the distance to school or to the nearest
furnished transportation route. Children in two of these states[44]
are not required to attend school if they live two miles or more
from school or from a school bus route. Thus, if a child lives
three miles from school, but only one mile from a school bus
route, attendance at school would be required. Several states
apply the exemption only to children of specified ages. For
example, Virginia exempts children under age ten who live two
miles from public school or one mile from transportation, and
children aged ten to seventeen who live two-and-a-half miles
from public school and one-and-a-half miles from transportation.
In Louisiana, children living one-and-a-half miles from transportation and two-and-a-half miles from school qualify for an
exemption. Three miles distance from either school or transportation is sufficient to exempt children in Tennessee.

Five states,[45] express the exemption in terms of distance
from any school, rather than from the nearest public school.

VI.   Exemptions for Special Reasons Granted in the Discretion
       of a Court or School Administration

Eighteen states[46] have statutory provisions authorizing

---

[43]Alas., Fla., La., Tenn., Va., W.Va.

[44]Alas. and W.Va.

[45]Alas., La., Tenn., Utah, W.Va.

[46]Alas., Ariz., Fla., Ga., Ha., Iowa, Mont., Nev., N.H., N.M.,
Okla., Ore., P.R., R.I., Vt., Va., Wis., Wyo.

exemptions which are worded generally so that a court or school official can balance all the factors involved and determine, as a matter of discretion, whether the child should be exempt from the law. Unlike the other exemptions discussed above, these exemptions rarely have pre-conditions that must be satisfied before the exemption applies. For example, Puerto Rico exempts children when "the parents or guardians show good and sufficient cause for withdrawal in the judgment of the supervising principal".[47] Several states[48] have more than one of these general discretionary exemption categories.

Only thirteen[49] of the eighteen states provide a basis on which the discretionary determination is to be made, and even those do so only through the use of very vague terms. Typically, the statutes merely require "satisfactory", "sufficient" or "good" reasons before an exemption is given.[50] Similarly, exemptions in four states[51] are to be granted in accordance with the "law and general policies of the board of education". Exemptions can be established in six states[52] merely upon a showing that the child is not "benefitting" from

[47] P.R. Laws Ann. T.18, §80(a)(1961).

[48] N.M., Okla., Ore., Va.

[49] Ariz., Ga., Iowa, Mont., N.H., N.M., Okla., Ore., P.R., R.I., Va., Wis., Wyo.

[50] See statutes of Ariz., Iowa, P.R., Wis.

[51] Ga., R.I., N.M., Ore.

[52] Mont., N.H., N.M., Okla., Va., Wyo.

attendance or that attendance is not "in the best interest" of the child.

In twelve states[53] exemptions can be granted by school administrators, most commonly by the local school board or superintendent. In five states,[54] a judge may exempt persons from compulsory attendance and in two states[55] the determination is made jointly by a judge and a school administrator.

There are only a few states which impose age and minimum education requirements for these exemptions. For example, in Nevada and Oregon a child must have completed the eighth grade and in New Mexico only children under age eight or high school students can be subject to these exemptions.

VII.   Exemptions for Temporary Absences and for Religious Reasons

A.   Temporary Absences

Another conceptual oddity in this area is presented by the statutes in seventeen states[56] which provide an exemption for "temporary absences". In several states,[57] exemptions in this category are referred to as exemptions for "necessary and legal absence". In those states which list the types of absences

---

[53]Alas., Ariz., Ga., N.H., N.M., Ore., P.R., R.I., Vt., Va., Wis., Wyo.

[54]Ha., Iowa, Mont., Nev., Va.,

[55]Fla., Okla.

[56]Alas., Colo., Del., D.C., Ill., La., Me., Md., Mass., Mont., Neb., N.C., Okla., Tenn., Vt., W.Va., Wis.

[57]Del., Me., Md., Mass.

covered,[58] this exemption is granted specifically for illness

or bereavement, and in two states[59] also because of conditions

that affect the welfare and safety of the child, such as hazard-

ous weather conditions.

B. Religious Exemptions

In addition to the alternative to public school

attendance contained in the primary reference sections regarding

full-time attendance at a denominational school, there is a

category of religious exceptions in twelve states[60] which permits

temporary absences for purposes of religious instruction and

services. Only four of these states[61] place an hours limitation

on the amount of time for which the pupil may be excused. For

constitutional reasons, the statutes in several states include

the provision that neither transportation nor facilities for

instruction are to be provided in connection with these religious

exceptions.

The religious provision in Kansas differs from that

found in the other eleven states in that it is closer in nature

to an alternative to than to an exemption from the attendance

requirement. In Kansas, persons who have completed the eighth

---

[58]Alas., Colo., La., Mont., Neb., Vt., W.Va., Wis.

[59]Neb., W.Va.

[60]Ha., Ill., Ind., Iowa, Kan., La., Mass., Mich., Minn., N.M.,
N.Y., W.Va.

[61]Hawaii (4 hours/week), Ind. (2 hours/week), Mich. (2 hours/week),
Minn. (3 hours/week).

grade and whose parents voice objections to public school may
attend a regularly supervised program of instruction provided
by a church and approved by the state board of education.[62]
Although not referring to a "religious" exemption specifically,
Virginia has a similar provision whereby parents who object on
religious grounds to the education at public school may request
the school board to exempt their child.[63]

VIII. Other Exemptions

Only two states, Florida and South Carolina, exempt students
by statute from compulsory attendance because of marriage or preg-
nancy. Among the other infrequent exemptions occurring in a few
jurisdictions are exemptions for gifted students to attend college,
exemptions for legislative pages, exemptions for incarcerated
children and in West Virginia, exemption for children who are
destitute.[64]

---

[62] Kan. Stat. Ann. §62-1111 (1972).

[63] Va. Code Ann. §22-275.4 (1973).

[64] W.Va. Code Ann. §18-8-1 (1970).

7. ENFORCEMENT OF COMPULSORY ATTENDANCE

I.   The Statutes

In addition to the indirect enforcement effect provided
to compulsory attendance laws by the child labor laws, there are
direct enforcement mechanisms for compulsory attendance statutes
which are found in truancy and other juvenile offense provisions.
These enforcement mechanisms may be found in either the primary
reference sections, themselves, or in parts of the education
code or in the juvenile delinquency code.

All of the major provisions of every truancy and related
statute in every jurisdiction with such a statute are set out in
detail in chart form in Appendix D. Readers interested in specific questions concerning particular jurisdictions should consult
the chart. The comments which follow summarize what the chart re-
veals and note the few relevant instances of case law.

In all of the fifty-one jurisdictions which have compulsory attendance laws[1], there are provisions in the education code
for enforcement personnel; most make statutory provision for employment of a truant officer; four jurisdictions[2] delegate responsibility for enforcement to the superintendent of schools or to
another agency with the power to employ truant officers. Generally,
truant officers are authorized to bring a complaint against the
parent for failure to cause the child to attend; in twenty-four

---

[1]Every American jurisdiction, including District of Columbia and
Puerto Rico, except for Mississippi.

[2]Delaware, Hawaii, Idaho, Puerto Rico.

jurisdictions[3] they are empowered to take truant children into custody without a warrant. The parent is given certain due process-type protections in the thirty-four jurisdictions[4] which require notice be sent to the parents warning them to comply with the statute before any complaint can be brought.

Every one of the jurisdictions with a compulsory attendance statute places responsibility on the parent for the child's truancy. Although "failure to cause (a child) to attend" school is always the primary offense, twelve jurisdictions[5] also penalize related offenses, such as "contributing to truancy" or "inducing absence", for which a parent or other adult can be held liable. Forty-nine jurisdictions treat both the basic truancy and any related offenses as criminal, usually at the misdemeanor level, and impose criminal sanctions upon the adult offender[6].

The sanctions imposed upon parents vary widely in their severity: in two jurisdictions[7] the parent can be punished by a

---

[3] Alabama, Arizona, California, Connecticut, Florida, Indiana, Iowa, Maine, Massachusetts, Minnesota, Missouri, Montana, Nebraska, Nevada, New Hampshire, New Jersey, New York, Ohio, Pennsylvania, South Dakota, Vermont, Washington, West Virginia, Wisconsin.

[4] Alabama, Arkansas, Colorado, Delaware, Florida, Georgia, Idaho, Illinois, Indiana, Kentucky, Louisiana, Michigan, Minnesota, Missouri, Montana, Nebraska, Nevada, New Jersey, New Mexico, New York, North Carolina, Ohio, Oklahoma, Oregon, Pennsylvania, South Carolina, South Dakota, Tennessee, Texas, Vermont, Virginia, West Virginia, Wisconsin, Wyoming.

[5] District of Columbia, Idaho, Illinois, Kansas, Louisiana, Maryland, Massachusetts, Minnesota, Nevada, South Dakota, Virginia, West Virginia.

[6] New Hampshire and Colorado are the only jurisdictions which establish civil sanctions for such violations.

[7] Virginia, Kansas.

fine of up to $1,000 and/or a maximum jail sentence of twelve
months, while in one jurisdiction[8] the penalty for a first offense
is merely a "public reprimand". Fourteen jurisdictions[9] allow
for imposition of fines of various amounts for initial and subsequent offenses, but do not provide for incarceration. In all
other jurisdictions a fine and/or a jail sentence may be imposed.

Five jurisdictions[10] impose liability for non-attendance
on the parent alone, and three other jurisdictions[11] provide
for parental liability, only, unless the parent can prove the
child was beyond parental control. In all other jurisdictions,
both parent and child can be charged with the substantive offense
and both can be penalized.

In only twenty-four jurisdictions[12] do the education codes
contain any definition of truancy or a similar offense which results
in sanctions being imposed on the children directly. Eight of
of those jurisdictions[13] actually utilize the term "truancy" and

---

[8] Puerto Rico.

[9] Arkansas, Connecticut, Iowa, Kentucky, Maryland, Massachusetts, New Jersey, North Dakota, Puerto Rico, Rhode Island, Tennessee, Texas, Vermont, Washington.

[10] Hawaii, Oregon, Puerto Rico, Vermont, West Virginia.

[11] Alabama, Indiana, Texas.

[12] Arkansas, California, Colorado, Connecticut, District of Columbia, Idaho, Kansas, Kentucky, Louisiana, Maine, Maryland, Nevada, New Jersey, New York, Oregon, Pennsylvania, Puerto Rico, South Dakota, Tennessee, Utah, Washington, Wisconsin, Wyoming.

[13] California, Connecticut, Iowa, Kansas, Kentucky, Nevada, New Jersey, Wisconsin.

include it as one of the actionable juvenile offenses in the state. In the remaining sixteen jurisdictions[14], terms such as "irregular attendance" or "school delinquent" are utilized. Several jurisdictions have more than one attendance-related offense for children; in these jurisdictions there is a basic truancy offense and a separate offense, usually called "habitual truancy".[15]

Children whose behavior brings them within the purview of enforcement statutes can be divided into two basic categories: those who are labelled "delinquent" and those who are proceeded against under some supposedly less serious category such as children who are "in need of supervision"[16], "wayward"[17], "undisciplined"[18], "unruly"[19], "incorrigible"[20], or "disorderly"[21]. A delinquent child is usually defined as one who has violated any federal, state or local law or regulation[22], or committed any act, which, if committed by an adult would constitute a violation of the law[23]. A

---

[14]Arkansas, Colorado, District of Columbia, Idaho, Louisiana, Maine, New York, Oregon, Pennsylvania, Puerto Rico, South Dakota, Tennessee, Utah, Washington, Wyoming.

[15]See, e.g., statutes in California, Kentucky, Nevada.

[16]Alaska, District of Columbia, Florida, Louisiana, Maryland, Massachusetts, Montana, Nevada, Oklahoma, Pennsylvania, South Dakota, Texas, Vermont, Wisconsin, Wyoming.

[17]Rhode Island.

[18]North Carolina.

[19]Georgia, North Dakota, Ohio.

[20]Arizona and Utah.

[21]Michigan and Tennessee.

[22]See, for example: South Dakota Rev. Stats. § 26-8-7. (1974).

[23]See, for example: Oregon Rev. Stats. § 419. 476 (1975).

"child in need of supervision", (or "wayward", "unruly", etc.,
child) is most often defined as a child who is "habitually diso-
bedient", "ungovernable", "habitually and voluntarily truant from
school or home", or "who conducts herself or himself so as to injure
or endanger her or his morals or health, or those of others"[24].
There is no apparent rationale to explain how a jurisdiction determines whether its truancy offense constitutes delinquency or a
transgression of some lesser order. Thirty states[25] classify the
child as other than delinquent, usually as a "child in need of supervision". Such classifications do not always indicate that the
child will be treated any differently from a "delinquent" child
convicted of violation of some other law[26]. Seventeen jurisdictions[27]
provide that children who violate the compulsory attendance laws may
be placed in "truant" or "parental" schools within the school system.

Only seven states do not provide for institutionalization
of children who violate compulsory attendance laws[28]; fifteen

---

[24]See, for example, New Jersey Rev. Stats. Ch. 2A, §§ 4-45 (1973),
and Arizona Stats. Ch. 2, § 8-201 (1972).

[25]Alaska, District of Columbia, Illinois, Louisiana, Maryland, Mon-
tana, Nebraska, New Jersey, New Mexico, New York, Oklahoma, South
Dakota, Texas, Wisconsin, Wyoming. Other: Arizona, California,
Florida, Idaho, Kentucky, Maine, Michigan, Nevada, North Carolina,
North Dakota, Ohio, Pennsylvania, Rhode Island, Tennessee, Utah.

[26]See, for example, statutes of Idaho, Louisiana, Michigan, Nevada,
Oklahoma, Wyoming.

[27]Alaska, California, Delaware, District of Columbia, Illinois, Iowa,
Kentucky, Michigan, Minnesota, Missouri, Nebraska, New York, Pennsylvania, Tennessee, Texas, Utah, Washington.

[28]Hawaii, Iowa, Ohio, Utah, Vermont, Washington.

states[29] permit institutionalization but specify that truants may not be institutionalized with juveniles convicted of more serious crimes.

II.   The Case Law

Considering the importance of the subject of truancy to the operation of so major an institution as the public schools, there is surprisingly little case law on the subject. Of course, truancy was unknown at common law and is strictly a statutory offense[30], but given the vagueness of the definitions, when there are any, and the age of the statutes, one would expect to find more case law.

Most of the few appellate cases which do exist are appeals by parents of convictions for violation of the compulsory attendance statutes. The prosecution in these cases appears to be premised either on the presumption or on a statutory requirement that a child's absence is the parent's responsibility and the parent must be proceeded against first for the child's non-attendance[31].

In terms of outcomes, these cases generally overturn parental convictions where there was some excuse for the child's absence[32] or where the child was receiving an education outside of public

---

[29]Alaska, California, District of Columbia, Kansas, Massachusetts, Missouri, Montana, Nebraska, New Jersey, New York, North Dakota, Pennsylvania, Texas, Virginia.

[30]See, e.g., Inhabitants of Cushing v. Inhabitants of Friendship, 89 Me. 525, 36 A, 1001 (1897).

[31]See, e.g. Kentucky Stats. § 159. 180 (1971, last amended 1974), Florida Stats. §232. 19 (1973) and In re Alley, 174 Wis. 85, 182 N.W. 360 (1920).

[32]See, e.g. State v, Maguire, 106 Vt. 476, 138 A 741 (1927).

school[33]. Very few jurisdictions appear to have settled the question of whether a child may be considered truant if his or her absence is with full parental knowledge and consent. Often the consideration of this question is tied to a question of liability of school board employees (usually truant officers) for actions taken to force the so-called truant to attend school.[34]

In three appellate cases where the absent children were, themselves, parties, courts have been reluctant to hold that the children were "delinquents" or to impose other sanctions upon the children for their behavior.

In Holmes v. Nestor[35], two children were arrested in their home by a truant officer who was thereafter sued by the parents. The Arizona Supreme Court held that the truant officer was without authority to arrest a child whose parents had expressly instructed her not to go to school. The court concluded that the parents had both the right and the power to temporarily excuse their children from attendance so long as they had good cause for so doing. Moreover, the court indicated[36], that the proper remedy was prosecution of the parent, not arrest of the child.

---

[33]See, e.g., State v. Well, 99 Kan. 167, 170 P. 1025 (1916), Wright v. State, 21 Oklahoma Cr. 430, 209 P. 169 (1922).

[34]Cf. Reynolds v. Board of Education of Union Free School District, 33 App. Div. 88, 53, N.Y. S. 75 (1898) with Delease v. Nolan, 185 App. Div. 82, 172 N.Y.S. 552 (1918)

[35]81 Ariz. 372, 306 P. 2d 290, (1957).

[36]306 P. 2d at 293.

In *In re Alley*[37], a 1920 Wisconsin case, a child who was absent from school on several occasions with his father's consent, was declared an habitual truant and a delinquent and was committed to a reform school. In overturning the conviction, the court stated:

> The statute does not define the words "habitually truant". We think the evidence comes far short in this case of establishing the sort of "habitual truancy" upon which a finding of delinquency may be based. It must be borne in mind that the habitual truancy which amounts to delinquency is a refusal to attend school in defiance of parental authority. It is the intention and purpose of the statute that the child shall not be held a truant except in cases where the parent is unable to compel compliance by his child with the provisions of the compulsory school attendance law. The child . . . in this case, if he can properly be said to be a truant at all, which is very doubtful in view of the fact that his absence was consented to by his father, was certainly far from being habitually truant within the meaning of [the statute].[38]

One year later, however, the Wisconsin Attorney General expressed the opinion that under a different section of the statutes relating to education, a child who refused to attend school could be a truant "without regard to any action or inaction on the part of the parents".[39] That opinion, however, was issued with reference to a seventeen year old girl, whereas the child involved in *In re Alley* was only eight years old.

In *State ex rel. Pulakis v. Superior Court of Washington*,[40] there had been findings by the lower court that a child who was truant was a delinquent, and that her father had failed to provide

---

[37] 174 W. 85, 182 N.W. 360 (1920).

[38] *Id.* at 90.

[39] 10 Opinions of the Attorney General 1069 (Wisconsin 1921).

proper maintenance, education and training for her, and should, therefore, be relieved of custody. In reversing both findings, the Washington Supreme Court stated that although the child had been truant, her half-dozen absences did not constitute "habitual truancy" since that phrase contemplated more serious misbehavior. The Court found that the truancy was never made known to her father, so he could not be found guilty of neglect.

Aside from these few reported appellate cases on truancy it appears that in most states, either by statute or by custom, parents, are generally held responsible and prosecuted for the unexcused absences of their children and must make some showing of lack of ability to compel school attendance before the children, themselves, will be prosecuted.

III.   Summary

In general, the enforcement statutes provide the state with the power to take legal actions, often within the criminal process, against parents and children in situations where the children are not in attendance at some lawful learning arrangement. Either by statutory provision, judicial interpretation, or force of custom, a number of jurisdictions require that action be taken against the parents before any action is instituted against the child. It is quite rare for a truancy-related action to reach the level of a reported appellate case. While there are doubtless many reasons for this, the dearth of cases must be taken, at least, as another indication that the formal, direct enforcement statutes

---

[40] 14 Wash. 2d 507, 128 P. 2d 649 (1942).

are not the principal mechanism for enforcement of the attendance requirement. As we have indicated elsewhere in this study, the statutes are enforced largely through the existence of the child labor laws, which remove the possibility of the principal alternative to school attendance, and through the social value placed on educational achievement.

8. THE STATE CONSTITUTIONS

Throughout the history of the United States, education has been a function of state government. The constitutions of every state contain provisions setting forth the nature of the state's responsibility regarding education.[1] Only nine constitutions,[2] however, contain provisions specifically regarding compulsory attendance. Of these nine, five[3] expressly require the legislature to enact a compulsory attendance statute, or compel attendance directly by their own terms, while four[4] merely enable the legislature to enact a compulsory statute.

The constitutional provisions on compulsory attendance are very simple and straightforward. Typical of the four jurisdictions with permissive provisions is Delaware whose constitution provides:

> (The general assembly) may require by law that every child, not physically or mentally disabled, shall attend the public schools, unless educated by other means.[5]

---

[1] See Appendix F for the texts of all states' constitutional enabling articles concerning education.

[2] The constitutions of Colorado, Delaware, Idaho, Nevada, New Mexico, North Carolina, Oklahoma, Puerto Rico and Virginia.

[3] New Mex. Const. Art. XXI, §4; No. Car. Const. Art. IX, §3; Okla. Const. Art XIII, §4; Puerto R. Const. Art. II, §5; Va. Const. Art. VIII, §3.

[4] Colo. Const. Art. IX, §11; Del. Const. Art X, §1; Idaho Const. Art. IX, §9; Nev. Const. Art. II, §2.

[5] Del. Const. Art. X, §1.

The provision in North Carolina's constitution is typical of those with mandatory provisions:

> The General Assembly shall provide that every child of appropriate age and sufficient mental and physical ability shall attend the public schools, unless educated by other means.[6]

Of these nine jurisdictions with constitutional compulsory attendance provisions, three specify the age range within which the legislature is either required or permitted to compel attendance. In Colorado and Idaho, both "permissive" jurisdictions, the range is between the ages of six and eighteen. In Oklahoma, a "mandatory" jurisdiction, the range is between the ages of eight and sixteen. North Carolina and Virginia limit their requirements to children of "appropriate age" and the other constitutions are silent on this point. Only Colorado specifies one age range during which attendance is compelled (six to eighteen) and another during which it is permitted (six to twenty-one). Puerto Rico, interestingly, provides that education shall be compulsory "to the extent permitted by the facilities of the state"[7] a provision which could be used as justification for limiting the age range of children subject to the basic requirement.

Of the nine jurisdictions with either mandatory or permissive constitutional articles on compulsory attendance, all

---

[6]No. Car. Const. Art. IX, §3.

[7]Puerto Rico Const. Art. II, §5.

but three[8] expressly exempt "exceptional children" from the attendance requirement. In every case, the exemption is phrased in the form of some vague generality such as children who are not "of sufficient mental and physical ability"[9] or children who are "physically or mentally disabled".[10] Oklahoma compels attendance only of children "who are sound in mind and body"[11] while Virginia requires attendance only of "eligible" children, "such eligibility ... to be determined by law..."[12]

The constitutions of three of these nine jurisdictions prescribe the length of time during which the legislature may or shall, whichever is applicable in the particular jurisdiction, compel attendance. Oklahoma provides that the compulsory period be at least three months long,[13] Nevada specifies that it be at least six months long[14] and Colorado provides that it be "for a time equivalent to three years" between the ages of six and eighteen.[15]

---

[8] The only jurisdictions with a compulsory attendance provision which do not exempt exceptional children are Idaho, Nevada and Puerto Rico.

[9] E.g. Colo. Const. Art. IX, §11.

[10] E.g. Del. Const. Art. X, §1.

[11] Okla. Const. Art. XIII, §4.

[12] Va. Const. Art. VIII, §3.

[13] Okla. Const. Art. XIII, §4.

[14] Nev. Const. Art. II, §2.

[15] Colo. Const. Art. IX, §11.

These are the only provisions in state constitutions which explicitly deal with compulsory attendance. There are, however, as we have noted, a number of provisions concerning education which appear in every state's constitution, which establish the general nature of the entire system within which the compulsory attendance requirement operates. A full-scale analysis of state constitutional provisions on education is beyond the scope of this study, but in order to place the compulsory attendance requirements, both those which are constitutional and those which are statutory, in proper perspective we will briefly review the other state constitutional articles on education.

State constitutional provisions on education, other than those on compulsory attendance, can be categorized generally into five major groups. Four of these groups can be conceptualized along a continuum of degree of commitment to a public education system. Ranging from strongest to weakest commitment, that continuum is as follows: provisions which require the establishment and maintenance of a public education system, provisions which set forth a state policy in favor of a public education system, hortatory provisions regarding the importance and desirability of education,[16] and provisions merely enabling the legislature to establish and maintain a public education system. The fifth category is composed of those few

---

[16]An example of what we call a statement of policy appears in Ill. Const. Art. X, §1: "A fundamental goal of the People of the State is the educational development of all persons to the limits of their (cont.)

provisions which explicitly grant - or deny - citizens a "right" to education.

In terms of the degree of commitment continuum, many jurisdictions' constitutions contain provisions which fall into more than one category, with the most common combination being some hortatory language regarding education paired with a requirement that the legislature establish and maintain a public school system. Thirteen constitutions[17] contain such a combination. A typical example of this combination is contained in the Michigan constitution which provides:

> Religion, morality and knowledge being necessary to good government and the happiness of mankind, schools and the means of education shall forever be encouraged.
>   The legislature shall maintain and support a system of free public elementary and secondary schools as defined by law.[18]

The overwhelming majority of jurisdictions have constitutional provisions expressly requiring the establishment and/or maintenance of a public education system. Only five states[19] lack such a provision and in three of those, courts have interpreted hortatory language or policy statements in ways that have rendered mandatory the establishment and/or maintenance of a public

---

[16] (cont.)capacities" while an example of "hortatory langauge" appears in Mich. Const. Art. VIII, §1: "Religion, morality and knowledge being necessary to good government and the happiness of mankind, schools and the means of education shall forever be encouraged."

[17] The constitutions of Arkansas, California, Idaho, Indiana, Maine, Michigan, Minnesota, North Carolina, North Dakota, Rhode Island, South Dakota, Texas and Vermont.

[18] Michigan Const. Art. VIII, §§1, 2.

[19] Alabama, Massachusetts, Mississippi, New Hampshire and Tennessee.

education system.[20] Only Alabama and Mississippi have constitutions which merely enable the legislature to maintain a public
system without any other provision or judicial interpretation
which transmutes the power into a duty.[21]

Four constitutions contain provisions which deal with a
"right" to education explicitly (as opposed to the argument
that, by requiring the establishment and maintenance of public
schools, the constitutions implicitly create such a right).
Three of the four contain an outright grant of such a right
although two of them are phrased rather strangely: North
Carolina's constitution provides that citizens have "a right to
the privilege" of education[22] while Wyoming's constitution provides that "the right of the citizens to opportunities for education should have practical recognition."[23] Obviously, neither
of these provisions are particularly strong statements. Only
Puerto Rico's provision reads in a manner one might expect of
a grant of a basic right:

> Every person has the right to an education
> which shall be directed to the full develop-
> ment of the human personality and to the
> strengthening of respect for human rights and
> fundamental freedoms.[24]

---

[20]See Cushing v. Newburyport, 10 Mass. (Metcalf) 508. (1845);
State v. Jackson, 71 N.H. 552, 53A. 1021 (1902); State v. Knoxville,
115 Tn. 175, 90 S.W. 289 (1905).

[21]See Ala. Const. Art. 14, §256 and Miss. Const. Art. VIII, §201.

[22]N.C. Const. Art. I, §15.

[23]Wyo. Const. Art. I, §23.

[24]Puerto Rico Const. Art. II, §5.

Alone among all the states, Alabama's constitution contains a provision expressly _denying_ citizens any right to education. After noting that it is "the policy of the state ... to foster and promote the education of its citizens" the Alabama constitution nevertheless goes on to declare "but nothing in this constitution shall be construed as creating or recognizing any right to education at public expense."[25]

Scattered throughout the state constitutional articles on education are a number of other provisions regarding the public school systems. Among these are provisions concerning the method of financing the system,[26] provisions requiring the system to be free from sectarian control,[27] provisions regarding the kinds of facilities which must be maintained,[28] provisions specifying that public education must be free,[29] and provisions specifying that it must be open to all children.[30]

As can be seen from this brief review, the nature and extent of education, unlike many other critically important processes or institutions in this country, is a matter which is the subject of rather extensive regulation within the constitutions of the states. The present system of compulsory attend-

---

[25] Ala. Const. Art. 14, §256.

[26] E.g. Conn. Const. Art. VIII, §2.

[27] E.g. N.Mex. Const. Art. XXI, §4.

[28] E.g. Ariz. Const. Art. XI, §1.

[29] E.g. So. Car. Const. Art. 11, §3.

[30] E.g. N.Y. Const. Art. XI, §1.

ance must be understood within the context of this broader,

intricate network, and proposals for major changes in compulsory

attendance must consider the full structure of this network

before reaching conclusions regarding the likely ramifications

of any substantial change in the compulsory attendance requirement.

9. STATE CHILD LABOR LAWS

Child labor is regulated by statute in every state.[1] Two
overriding concerns are reflected in state child labor laws:
the protection of the health and safety of the child and the promotion of education for the child. The purpose of this chapter
is to explore the child labor provisions of each state in order
to outline the general scheme of regulation and to understand
the principal variations among jurisdictions.

Child labor laws in most states regulate the employment of
persons under the state's age of majority, which age varies from
state to state although most states fix it at either eighteen or
twenty-one years. Since we are particularly interested in the
effect of child labor laws on children of compulsory school age,
most of the following analysis focuses on the rules affecting
children under the age of sixteen.

The very extensive statutory provisions in some states and
the great complexity of the provisions in most states have made
it necessary to simplify some of the provisions by omitting some
details in order to present an orderly and comprehensible comparison and analysis. In addition, except where noted, we deal only
with statutory provisions and not with regulations or case law.

Except in the broadest respect, there is no such entity as

---

[1]
  In this chapter and in the accompanying chart, Appendix E., the
term "state" is used to refer to the fifty states plus Puerto
Rico and the District of Columbia. In the interests of conserving space, the citations for all child labor statutes of all
jurisdictions are listed at the end of this chapter and are not
repeated in footnotes every time a jurisdiction is referred to
in the text.

the "typical" child labor statute. Child labor statutes may contain as few as five provisions, or as many as fifty. In over half the states, the statutes have at least twenty provisions and in many cases are buttressed by further details supplied in regulations. There is often some overlap between a state's education and child labor statutes, especially with respect to the issuance of work permits to children of compulsory school age. In general, however, a jurisdiction's child labor laws will usually contain provisions concerning minimum age for work, prohibited occupations, hours limitations, night work restrictions, requirements for the issuance of employment permits, regulation of "street trades", and provisions for enforcement, including a specification of penalties for violation. In this chapter we will examine the minimum age provisions, the permit procedure, the hours regulations and the enforcement procedures, to illustrate the similarities and differences among the states.

Child labor laws have been the subject of extensive reexamination and amendment in many states during the last decade.[2] In the past, the primary emphasis always has been on protecting the child from abuses. But recent trends in child labor laws appear to be taking a different tack. There is a new stress on orderly integration of minors into the working world which

---

[2]For a discussion of state child labor laws as they existed in 1965 see State Child Labor Standards (Washington: U.S. Government Printing Office, 1965), U.S. Department of Labor, Bulletin No. 158, Revised 1965.

has necessitated a certain easing of restrictions within the
framework of the basic safeguards contained in the statutes.[3]

I.   Minimum Age Provisions

Thirty-four states establish a minimum age for employment
of children during school hours. In twenty-two states,[4] sixteen
is established as the minimum age for employment during the
hours school is in session, while eight states[5] provide for a
minimum age of fourteen years. In two states, Maine and Washington, the minimum age at which a child may work when school
is in session is fifteen years, while New York sets the minimum
age at seventeen years. Wisconsin alone sets the minimum age
for work during school hours at eighteen years and it qualifies
this with an exception for children who have completed high
school.

Twenty-three states[6] also set a minimum age for work outside of school hours. All of these but Florida establish fourteen years as the minimum age. In Florida, twelve years is the

---

[3]The legislature of New Hampshire, for example, has declared it
is the policy of the state to foster the employment of young
people while at the same time providing the safeguards made
necessary by their age. See N.H. Rev. Stat. §276-A:1 (Supp.
1975). As another example, it is the policy of the state of
Utah to encourage growth and development of young people through
providing work opportunities while at the same time adopting reasonable safeguards to protect them from working hazards. See
Utah Code Ann., §34-23-1 (1974).

[4]Ala., Colo., Fla., Ga., Ha., Idaho, Iowa, Ky., La., Md., Mass.,
Miss., N.J., N.Y., N.C., Tenn., Utah, Va., Wash., Wis., Wyo., P.R.

[5]Ariz., Ind., Minn., Nev., N.M., N.D., Ore., S.D.

[6]Ala., Alas., Fla., Ha., Ill., Ga., Idaho, Iowa, Ky., La., Me.,
Md., Miss., N.J., N.Y., N.C., Tenn., Utah, Va., Wash., Wis.,
Wyo., P.R.

minimum age for work outside school hours.

While the thirty-four states mentioned above establish a minimum age by making reference to school hours, statutes in the remaining eighteen states[7] establish minimum ages for employment without referring to the hours that school is in session (although Alaska and Illinois do make reference to out-of-school hours). California and West Virginia, for example, set a general minimum age at sixteen years ("Sixteen in any gainful occupation at any time").[8] Six states[9] establish fourteen years as the general minimum age. Ten states[10] provide for a minimum age for employment in specific industries and occupations.

Many of the states establishing a minimum age for employment during school hours also set a separate minimum age limit for certain enumerated occupations. Most states also have statutory provisions prohibiting employment of persons under eighteen in certain types of industrial work or work generally labelled hazardous.

In the states that grant employment permits to minors of compulsory school age for work during school hours, the minimum

---

[7]Alas., Ark., Calif., Conn., Del., Ill., Kan., Mich., Mo., Mont., Neb., N.H., Okla., R.I., Tex., Vt., W.Va., D.C.

[8]Cal. Labor Code § 1290 (1971) and W. Va. Code § 21-6-1 (1973).

[9]Ark., Del., Kan., Mich., Mo., D.C.

[10]Alas., Conn., Ill., Mont., Neb., N.H., Okla., R.I., Tex., Vt.

age for employment, although set at sixteen by statute, may be
reduced, by special permit, to fourteen or fifteen years of age.
Further explanation of the permit procedure follows.

II. Employment Permits and Related Documents

A. Employment Permits

Most states require that persons under age sixteen
obtain an employment permit before they may be legally employed.
These employment permits, also referred to as "employment certificates", "work permits", "labor permits", "age and schooling
certificates", or "school leaving permits" usually require proof
of age,[11] proof of physical fitness for the job, and completion
of a specified school grade. In many states there are two types
of permits: one issued for work during school hours and the
other for work outside school hours.

Forty-four states[12] require that employment permits or
some type of permit with similar requirements[13] be obtained by
children who wish to work. Thirty-eight of these states require

---

[11]As proof of age, most states accept, in order of preference:
1) a birth certificate; 2) a baptismal record or bible record
of birth; 3) other documents such as a passport, immigration
certificate or life insurance policy in effect for over a year;
4) a physician's statement of the approximate physical age of
the child accompanied by the parents' affidavit that the child
is of legal minimum age.

[12]Ala., Ark., Calif., Colo., Conn., Del., Fla., Ga., Ha., Ill.,
Ind., Iowa, Kan., Ky., La., Me., Md., Mass., Mich., Minn., Mo.,
Neb., Nev., N.H., N.J., N.M., N.Y., N.C., N.D., Ohio, Okla., Ore.,
Penn., R.I., S.D., Tenn., Vt., Va., Wash., W.Va., Wis., Wyo., P.R.
D.C.

[13]Georgia and New Hampshire issue "age certificates", which require, in addition to proof of age, proof of physical fitness
and completion of specified grade.

that minors under sixteen who wish to work during school hours obtain a permit.[14] The others have varying requirements: New Hampshire requires merely an age certificate, and Wyoming an employer's statement. Louisiana requires permits for persons over sixteen to work during school hours, and under sixteen to work outside of school hours. New Jersey has permit requirements for persons over sixteen during school hours, and North Carolina and Rhode Island have provisions requiring permits for work out-side of school hours. Many also require minors under sixteen to obtain a permit to work outside of school hours. Several states also issue "street trade" permits that allow minors to engage in newspaper and magazine sales, shoeshining, and similar endeavors. Only six states[15] have no permit requirements at all.

The requirements for employment permits are basically the same everywhere: proof must be offered of age, of physical fitness and of completion of a specified school grade.[16] The only major difference lies in the nature of the school record requirement. In most states, in order for a child to be issued a permit to work during school hours, the child must have attained a minimum educational level, usually completion of a specified grade. Before an employment permit will be issued for work out-side of school hours, the child's attendance record is required as well as a statement by the child's teacher or school principal

---

[14]The exceptions are: La., N.H., N.J., N.C., R.I., and Wyo.

[15]Alas., Ariz., Idaho, Miss., S.C., Tex.

[16]See chart, Appendix E., for specific provisions of every jurisdiction.

that the child is capable of engaging in both school work and employment.[17]

To procure an employment permit to work during school hours, a child must be fourteen years of age or older in the majority of states which issue permits. In addition, in most of these states, the child must meet an educational requirement, have parental consent, have a letter from the potential employer and be found physically fit to perform the job.[18]

1. Age Requirement

As indicated above,[19] statutes in thirty-eight states provide for the issuance of permits to children under age sixteen for work during school hours. The majority of these states[20] specifically set fourteen as the minimum age at which a child can be issued a permit to work during school hours. Two states, Washington and Arkansas, require a minimum age of fifteen years, and five states[21] do not specify any minimum age for obtaining a permit to work during school hours.

---

[17]See chart, Appendix E,, for specific provisions of every jurisdiction.

[18]See chart, Appendix E., for specific provisions.

[19]See note 4, supra.

[20]Ala., Calif., Colo., Conn., Del., Fla., Ga., Ha., Ind., Iowa, Kan., Ky., Md., Mass., Mich., Minn., Mo., Neb., Nev., N.M., N.Y., N.D., Ohio, Okla., Ore., Penn., Tenn., Va., Wis., P.R., D.C.

[21]Ill., Me., S.D., Vt., W.Va.

2. Educational Achievement and School Record

Twenty-four[22] of the thirty-eight states which issue permits to a child of compulsory school age for work during school hours require achievement of some minimum educational level before a permit will be issued. Sixteen of them[23] require completion of the eighth grade. Georgia, Kentucky and Wisconsin require high school graduation. Ohio requires completion of a vocational training program. Massachusetts and Nebraska require completion of the sixth grade, and California completion of the seventh grade. Oklahoma, North Dakota and South Dakota require only literacy in the English language, but Indiana, Maine, Nebraska and the District of Columbia require literacy in addition to the grade level attainment. The other fourteen states[24] have no minimum education requirement, but several[25] of them require a school record containing information on the last grade completed. Permit requirements for Hawaii and Oregon are established by regulation, and some type of school record may be required.

Twenty-one states[26] require a school record before

---

[22]Ark., Calif., Conn., Del., Fla., Ga., Ind., Kan., Ky., Me., Mass., Minn., Neb., Nev., N.D., Ohio, Okla., Penn., S.D., Vt., Wash., W.Va., Wis., D.C.

[23]Ark., Calif., Conn., Del., Fla., Ind., Kan., Me., Minn., Nev., N.D., Penn., Vt., Wash., W.Va., D.C.

[24]Ala., Colo., Ha., Ill., Iowa, Md., Mich., Mo., N.M., N.Y., Ore., Tenn., Va., P.R.

[25]Colo., Ill., Md., Mich., Mo., N.Y., Tenn., P.R.

[26]Ala., Calif., Del., Ind., Kan., Ky., La., Md., Mass., Mich., Mo., Neb., N.J., N.C., N.D., Ohio, Okla., S.D., Tenn., W.Va., P.R.

an employment permit may be issued to a minor of compulsory school age for work outside school hours. The purpose of this permit is not to show that the child has completed a minimum educational requirement, but to give evidence that the child is regularly attending school and that working and going to school at the same time will not adversely affect the child's educational progress and general health.[27]

3. Parental Consent

Seventeen states[28] require parental consent before an employment permit may be issued to a minor. To fulfill this requirement, the parent must accompany the child when the permit application is made or must submit a written statement giving consent to employment of the child.

4. Physician's Statement

A physician's statement, or other evidence of the child's physical ability to perform the work for which the permit is issued, is required in about half of the states.[29] Iowa requires proof of physical fitness only for migrant labor by minors under age fourteen. New York and Ohio, which require a statement of physical fitness for all permits, will issue limited permits to minors with physical limitations which might affect

---

[27]See _Child Labor Laws_, U.S. Department of Labor, Bulletin No. 312, (Government Printing Office, Washington, D.C.) 1967.

[28]Ala., Calif., Colo., Del., Fla., Ill., Md., Mo., N.H., N.Y., Penn., Okla., Tenn., Va., W.Va., D.C., P.R.

[29]Ala., Calif., Fla., Ga., Ill., Ind., Ky., La., Md., Mass., Mich., Minn., Mo., N.H., N.J., N.M., N.Y., Ohio, Okla., Penn., Tenn., Vt., Va., P.R., D.C.

their performance in certain occupations.

5. Employer's Statement

An employer's statement regarding the work to be performed or a specification of employment is needed in twenty-nine states[30] before a permit of any type will be issued. Some indication of the number of daily and weekly hours to be worked and an approximation of the length of time of employment must be made in several states.[31] Fourteen[32] of the twenty-nine states which require employer's statements also have a minimum educational requirement to be met before a permit is issued to a child of compulsory school age for work during school hours and seven[33] also require a physician's statement as well.

6. Need for Income

In five states,[34] the child's need for income for personal or family support must be demonstrated before an employment permit will be granted.

7. Best Interest of the Child

Eight states[35] explicitly require that the decision whether or not to issue an employment permit to a minor for

---

[30]Ala., Calif., Colo., Del., Fla., Ga., Ha., Ill., Ind., Iowa, Kan., Ky., La., Mass., Mich., Mo., N.J., N.M., N.C., N.D., Ohio, Penn., Tenn., Va., Wis., W.Va., Wyo., P.R., D.C.

[31]Ky., La., Mass., Mich., Mo., N.J., N.C., Penn., Tenn., Va., P.R., D.C.

[32]Calif., Del., Fla., Ga., Ind., Kan., Ky., Mass., N.D., Ohio, Penn., W.Va., P.R., D.C.

[33]Calif., Fla., Ind., Ky., Ohio, Penn., P.R.

[34]Calif., Fla., Mich., N.M., Nev.

[35]Colo., Conn., Fla., Ill., Mass., Mo., Wash., W.Va.

work during school hours be made after considering the "best interests of the child". The factors that must be considered in determining if the work is in the best interests of the child are either set forth in the statute, or are implied by the language of related sections. Generally, these factors are the financial situation of the child and family, the school record, the child's physical health, the type of employment, the hours and degree of dangerousness of the work and the career possibilities of the job.

B. Age Certificates

Age certificates provide positive proof of a minor's age and were initially intended to ensure that no child under the minimum age was employed in a prohibited occupation. The primary concern reflected in age certificates is the health and safety of the child.

Four states, Georgia, Montana, New Hampshire and Utah, issue only age certificates. Twelve states[36] issue and require both age certificates and employment permits. In other states, employment permits serve the same function as age certificates. Generally, age certificates are not required of minors over age sixteen. Of the sixteen states which issue age certificates, all but five require them until age sixteen. In Alabama, they are required until the age of seventeen, and in Colorado, Illinois, Minnesota and West Virginia they are required

---

[36] Ala., Colo., Calif., Conn., Del., Fla., Ha., Ill., Ky., Minn., Ohio, W.Va.

until eighteen. Many states, including some that do not require age certificates, will issue them upon request for persons up to age twenty-one as proof of age for employment. In eight states,[37] the only requirement for issuance of an age certificate is proof of age. The requirements in the other eight states are similar to those for employment permits. In fact, four of these latter states[38] have requirements identical to those for employment permits.

C. Issuer

With a few exceptions, both age and employment permits are issued by local school officials. In North Carolina, local directors of social services issue permits according to regulations promulgated by the Department of Labor. In Hawaii, Montana, Oregon, Vermont, Wisconsin and Puerto Rico, employment permits are issued by the state labor department. Several states provide alternative issuing agents. District court judges in Nevada and Washington and juvenile court judges in Kansas, as well as school officials in all three states, have authority to issue employment and age permits. Probation officers in Kentucky may issue permits, as may the state employment service division in Iowa, and the state labor commissioner in Arkansas, Baltimore City (Maryland) and Orleans Parish (Louisiana).

---

[37]Colo., Conn., Del., Fla., Ha., Mont., Utah, W.Va.

[38]Ill., Ky., Minn., Ohio.

III.   Hours

   A.   Maximum Work Week in General

       Child labor laws generally limit the number of hours
per day and per week that minors may work. They also make special provisions for night work and for minors who work part-time
while attending school. Nearly half the states[39] limit to forty
per week the number of hours a child may work. Five states[40]
limit the total number of hours per week to forty-four. Nineteen
states[41] set the maximum number of hours for working minors at
forty-eight. Idaho allows minors under sixteen to work up to
fifty-four hours per week. Montana has no provisions relating
to hours and South Carolina's only hours provision relates to
work in cotton and woolen manufacturing establishments. Both
Montana and South Carolina, however, have strong minimum age
provisions that prohibit children under sixteen from working
during school hours at all, thus eliminating some of the need
for specific hours regulation.

   B.   Maximum Work Week for Those Attending School

       Twenty-nine[42] jurisdictions limit the number of hours

------

[39] Under sixteen: Ala., Ariz., Fla., Ga., Ha., Iowa, Kan., Ky.,
Md., Mo., N.Y., N.C., R.I., S.D., Utah, Wash., W.Va., Wis. Under
seventeen: Ind. Under eighteen: Alas., Colo., N.J., Tenn., Va., P.R.

[40] La., Miss., N.M., Ore., Penn. New Mexico's limitation applies
to minors under fourteen years of age.

[41] Under fifteen: Tex. Under sixteen: Ark., Calif., Conn., Del.,
Ill., Me., Mass., Minn., Neb., Nev., N.H., Okla., Vt., Wyo. (eight
hours/day). Under eighteen: Mich., N.D., Ohio, D.C.

[42] Ala., Alas., Ariz., Calif., Colo., Fla., Ga., Ha., Ill., Ind.,
Iowa, Ky., La., Me., Md., Mass., Mich., N.H., N.J., N.Y., N.C.,
N.D., Ohio, Penn., Tenn., Utah, Wash., Wis., P.R.

a child of school age may work while attending school; the other twenty-three limit the hours that children under sixteen may work while attending school. Six[43] of the twenty-nine which limit the working hours of school-age children continue this limitation up to age sixteen if the minor is still attending school. Maryland and Tennessee continue the limitation to age seventeen for those who are still attending school.

In ten[44] of the twenty-nine states, the maximum number of hours a minor may work while attending school is the difference between a fixed number and the number of hours the child spends in school. Four states[45] set this combined total at eight hours per day. Alaska and Ohio limit combined work and school to nine hours per day. Hawaii sets the combined total at ten hours. Michigan sets a combined total of forty-eight hours of school and work per week. In some states, the time spent in continuation school[46] by minors under age sixteen is counted as part of the time the minor is permitted to work. In Washington, one-half of the total school attendance hours are included in computing the maximum number of allowable work hours.

---

[43]Calif., Ky., Mich., Penn., Wis., P.R.

[44]Alas., Ga., Ha., Ill., Mich., N.J., N.C., Ohio., Wash., P.R.

[45]Ill., N.J., N.C., P.R.

[46]Although many statutes contain authority for the establishment of "continuation" or part-time schools for children who are employed, most of them neither require the establishment of such schools nor compel attendance by children. The states that do require attendance generally do so only when the child has not completed some minimum educational requirement.

The average number of hours of work allowed for minors who are still attending school is less than four hours per day and twenty-three and a half hours per week. The permitted hours per day range from three to eight. The number of permitted work hours per week range from eighteen to twenty-eight. Several states have neither daily nor weekly limitations.[47] Five states[48] have separate provisions for minors under age sixteen and minors over age sixteen; the maximum number of allowed work hours per week is significantly higher for school-attending minors over age sixteen than it is for those under age sixteen.[49]

C. Nightwork Restrictions

All states except Montana and Nevada restrict the night-time employment of minors. In forty-seven states, minors under sixteen are not permitted to work at night at all. In two other states, South Dakota and New Mexico, restrictions apply to those under age fourteen and in Texas to those under age fifteen.

Twenty-one states[50] prohibit child labor after 7:00 p.m. Other states' prohibitions range from 6:00 p.m. to 10:00

---

[47]Alas., Calif., Colo., Fla., Ga., La., Utah.

[48]Ky., Md., N.Y., Penn., Wis.

[49]In Pennsylvania, for example, minors under age sixteen attending school and working may work a maximum of eighteen hours per week; school attending minors over age sixteen may work twenty-eight hours per week.

[50]Alas., Ark., Del., Ha., Ill., Ind., Iowa, Ky., La., Md., Minn., Miss., Mo., N.Y., N.C., N.D., Penn., S.D., Vt., Wash., D.C.

p.m.[51] In most states,[52] minors may not begin work before 7:00

a.m., in twelve states[53] before 6:00 a.m. and in seven states[54]

before 5:00 a.m. Florida and Massachusetts prohibit employment

of minors before 6:30 a.m., and Puerto Rico forbids employment

of minors before 8:00 a.m.

Statutes in most states contain relaxed hours and

night work restrictions on days preceding non-school days and

during school vacations, thus indicating that the restrictions

on hours are related to the child's ability to function in

school.[55] The night work restrictions and hours limitations in

several states provide an extremely protective scheme for minors

under sixteen who both attend school and work. Of the twenty-

nine states[56] that place hour limitations on children under six-

teen who are both working and going to school, twenty-two[57]

---

[51]6:00 p.m.: Mass., N.J., Ohio, Okla., Ore., R.I., Va., P.R.;
8:00 p.m.: Ala., Fla., S.C., W.Va., Wis.; 9:00 p.m.: Ga., Idaho,
Me., Mich., N.H., N.M.; 9:30 p.m.: Ariz., Colo., Utah; 10:00 p.m.:
Calif., Conn., Kan., Neb., Tenn., Tex., Wyo.

[52]Ala., Ark., Ha., Ill., Iowa, Kan., Ky., Me., Md., Mich., Minn.,
Mo., N.H., N.J., N.M., N.Y., N.C., N.D., Ohio, Okla., Ore., Penn.,
Tenn., Va., Wash., Wis., D.C.

[53]Alas.,Ariz., Conn., Del., Ga., Idaho, Ind., La., Miss., Neb.,
R.I., Vt.

[54]Calif., Colo., S.C., Tex., Utah, W.Va., Wyo.

[55]See chart, Appendix E , for specific provisions.

[56]See note 44, supra.

[57]Three states have a ten hour night work restriction: Me., Mich.,
N.H.; Four states have an eleven hour period: Ala., Alas., Ill.,
Wis.; Ten have a twelve hour period: Ha., Ill., Iowa, Ky., Md.,
N.Y., N.C., N.D., Penn., Wash.; Massachusetts' night work restric-
tions extends for twelve-and-a-half hours; New Jersey and Ohio for
thirteen hours and in Puerto Rico for fourteen hours.

specify certain nighttime hours during which minors cannot work; these periods range in length from ten to fourteen hours. These states also significantly limit the number of daytime hours a school-attending child may work.[58]

In contrast, the hours provisions and nightwork restrictions of a few states[59] impose far fewer restrictions on minors who are both attending school and working. Four of these states[60] restrict night work for periods of only seven or eight hours, set no maximum number of hours a minor may work while attending school, and establish forty-eight hours as the maximum work week. The other two states, Idaho and South Carolina, allow minors under age sixteen to work up to fifty-four hours per week, prohibit night work of minors for a period of nine hours, and have no special provisions for school-attending child laborers.

IV.   States Not Issuing Permits

As noted earlier, six states[61] do not issue age or employment permits. In Arizona, Idaho and Texas, children under age sixteen are allowed to work during the hours school is in session. In Arizona, the minimum age for any gainful employment is set at age fourteen, by a constitutional provision. There are no statutory requirements to be met before a minor aged fourteen to sixteen may work during school hours. Idaho law provides that

---

[58]See previous section.

[59]Conn., Idaho, Neb., S.C., Tex., Wyo.

[60]Conn., Neb., Tex., Wyo.

[61]See note 15, supra.

children under age sixteen may work during school hours if they meet a literacy requirement. Texas, although it has no established employment permit system, does provide for exemptions from compulsory attendance by court order for children who are over fourteen years old and have completed the seventh grade, if they can establish their need for income, give proof of suitable employment, and produce a physician's statement of good health.[62] There are no statutory provisions in Alaska, Mississippi or South Carolina governing employment of children of compulsory school age during school hours. Alaska does provide for exemptions from the child labor laws but only under certain conditions and only for children aged sixteen and over. Mississippi requires that a parent's affidavit and a school certificate be presented to the employer before a child aged fourteen to sixteen may be employed. The school certificate must state the child's date of birth, the grade and last date of attendance, the name of the school and the name of the teacher.

V.   Enforcement

Generally, the child labor laws are enforced by the state labor departments. Exceptions to this pattern are: Idaho (probation officers and school trustees); Mississippi (the local sheriff); and the District of Columbia (the Department of School Attendance and Work Permits). Wyoming is the only state whose statutes create a Commissioner of Child Labor with power to

----

[62] Tex. Rev. Civ. Stat. Art. 5181(b) (Vernon's 1975 Supp.)

enforce the child labor laws. In most states labor and education officials have the major responsibility for applying and enforcing the laws. The labor departments set employment conditions and inspect places of business for violations of the law. Education officials issue the permits, often under regulations established by the labor department; monitor the child's progress at school; and, through the permit system, know where young people are working if they are not in school. Wisconsin has a Council on Child Labor that biennally reviews the law and administrative regulations and makes recommendations for changes.

VI. Conclusion

Several conclusions on child labor laws and on the interrelationship between child labor laws and compulsory school attendance can be drawn from this review of state child labor statutes.

1. Even though the details of the statutory scheme vary immensely from state to state, two principal concerns predominate throughout the provisions of every jurisdiction. The first is a concern for the education of the child, at least to a certain level; the second is a concern for the health and safety of the child.

In most states the issuance of employment permits is closely linked to the local educational system. Local school officials are the issuing agents and, in a majority of states, an examination of the child's school record is a prerequisite for issuance of a permit. A majority of the states also have

night work restrictions that are more stringent for days preceding school days than for days not preceding them or for
vacation periods. Twenty-nine states limit the number of hours
that a child attending school can work outside school hours. A
multitude of provisions appear directly aimed at ensuring that
a child's employment does not too severely interfere with his
or her education.

Evidence of a concern for the health and safety of
child workers is seen particularly in the hours provisions and
night work restrictions. Daily and weekly limits on the permissible work hours for children which are sufficiently stringent
to avoid health detriments exist in all but a few states. This
concern is further buttressed by permit provisions in many states
which require a physician's statement that the child is physically capable of performing the tasks necessary for the particular job.

This concern for the minor employee's safety is also
evidenced by the extensive lists of occupations declared too
hazardous to be engaged in at all by persons under a specified
age, usually eighteen.

2. As with all regulatory statutes, there are specifically authorized exceptions to the child labor laws of most
states. High school graduates are exempted from some minimum
age and maximum hours laws in many states, although generally
not from minimum age requirements for prohibited hazardous
occupations. More than half the states have provisions that

either relax restrictions or waive them entirely for minors
enrolled in vocational training or work-study programs. For
instance, persons enrolled in vocational training often are
allowed to work more hours while attending school, and the minimum age may be lowered for specific occupations if the minor
has received or is receiving training for work in that industry.

3. The child labor and compulsory attendance laws work
in harmony to keep most children under age sixteen in school.
Changes in compulsory attendance laws would require concomitant
changes in child labor laws in virtually every state. For
example, as noted above, thirty-four states define their minimum
age requirements for employment in terms of school attendance.
Also, a number of states have no hours provisions for children
under age sixteen, since their laws are premised on the fact
that children under age sixteen are prohibited from working
during school hours.

Several states recently have enacted legislation to
enable schools to offer year-round instruction on a rotating
enrollment basis, without altering pupil attendance standards.
Legislation of this type, leading to year-round school operation,
will necessitate re-examination of child labor laws developed
on the assumption that attendance hours in the state are uniform
for all school children.

4. From an analysis of the statutes it appears that all
but eleven states[63] allow children under age sixteen to be

---

[63] Alas., La., Miss., Mont., N.H., N.J., N.C., R.I., S.C., Utah,
Wyo.

employed during school hours. It must be emphasized, however, that the exemption of children of compulsory school age from school attendance to enable them to work is unusual.[64] The general rule is that the child must have attained the basic minimum age for employment and must attend school in accordance with the compulsory school attendance law. Issuance of an employment permit involves a screening process, and no child is issued a permit without meeting the requirements established by statute or regulation.

5. Even with regard to jurisdictions with very similar statutory provisions, the manner in which the child labor laws actually operate may vary considerably, depending upon the extent to which enforcement is seriously undertaken, and whether implementing regulations have been promulgated.

---

[64] Several states exempt from compulsory attendance those minors who are considered - usually without any precise standards - to be incapable of profiting from further school attendance. Kentucky, New York, Ohio and Virginia issue special employment permits. New Mexico, Pennsylvania and Washington require proof that the child is in such condition but do not issue special permits.

Statutory Provisions Concerning Child Labor in the Fifty
States and the District of Columbia and Puerto Rico, 1975

Alabama	Code of Alabama, T.26, §§343 to 375
Alaska	Alaska Statutes, §§23-10-330 to 23-10-370, Rules and Regulations issued by Commissioner of Labor
Arizona	Arizona Constitution, Art. 18, §2, Arizona Revised Statutes, §§23.107, 23.231 to 23.240
Arkansas	Arkansas Statutes, §§24.630, 81.609, 81.701 to 81.712
California	Deering's California Codes Labor, §§551, 554, 556, 1290 to 1311, 1390 to 1398; Education, §§12765, 12767 to 12795
Colorado	Colorado Revised Statutes, §§80-6-1 to 80-6-17
Connecticut	Connecticut General Statutes Annotated, §§22-13 to 22-16, 31-12 to 31-18, 31-22 to 31-25, 10-189 to 10-193
Delaware	Delaware Code Annotated, T.19, §§101, 501, 511 to 548, T.29, §8510(a)(1)
Florida	Florida Statutes Annotated, §§450.011 to 450.161, 232.07, 232.08
Georgia	Georgia Code Annotated, §§54.201, 54.205, 54.206, 54.301 to 54.318
Hawaii	Hawaii Revised Statutes, §§390-1 to 390-7
Idaho	Idaho Code Annotated, §§44-1107, 44-1301 to 44-1308
Illinois	Illinois Annotated Statutes, C.48, §§5, 31.1 to 31.22, 255, C.122, §26-1
Indiana	Indiana Code, §§20.8.1-4-1 to 20.8.1-4-31 (§§28-5351 to 28-5381)
Iowa	Iowa Code Annotated, §§92.1 to 92.14; Iowa Rules and Regulations Labor Bureau Rule 2.5 et seq.
Kansas	Kansas Statutes Annotated, §§38.601 to 38.612
Kentucky	Kentucky Revised Statutes, §§159.030, 339.210 to 339.450, 339.990, 337.370; Kentucky Administrative Regulations LAB 120 'Child Labor', Part IV and Part V
Louisiana	Louisiana Revised Statutes, §§23:151, 23:152, 23:161 to 23:170, 23:181 to 23:197, 23:211 to 23:218
Maine	Maine Revised Statutes, T.26, §§42, 438, 701, 702, 771 to 784
Maryland	Annotated Code of Maryland, Art. 100, §§4 to 16, 18 to 25, 35 to 39, 41 to 45, 47 to 51
Massachusetts	Massachusetts General Laws, C.149, §§1, 2, 53 to 105, C.76, §1
Michigan	Michigan Compiled Laws Annotated, §§409.1 to 409.30
Minnesota	Minnesota Statutes Annotated, §§181.31 to 181.51
Mississippi	Mississippi Code, §§71-1-17 to 71-1-31
Missouri	Vernon's Annotated Missouri Statutes, §§294.011 to 294.140
Montana	Revised Codes of Montana, C.10, §§201 to 210, C.41, §1113 to 1117

Nebraska	Revised Statutes of Nebraska, §§48.302 to 48.313
Nevada	Nevada Revised Statutes, §§607.160, 609.190 to 609.270, 392.090 to 392.110
New Hampshire	New Hampshire Revised Statutes Annotated, §§275:15, 275:17, 275:22, 275:25 to 275:27, 276-A:1 to 276-A:10
New Jersey	New Jersey Statutes Annotated, §§34:2-21.1 to 34:2-21.22, 34:2-21.56 to 34:2-21.64, 34:1A-6
New Mexico	New Mexico Statutes Annotated, §§59-6-1 to 59-6-15.1
New York	McKinney's Consolidated Laws of New York Annotated, Education Law §§3215 to 3231, 3234; Labor Law §§21, 130 to 140, 170 to 173
North Carolina	General Statutes of North Carolina, §§110-1 to 110-20
North Dakota	North Dakota Century Code, §§34-07-01 to 34-07-21
Ohio	Baldwin's Ohio Revised Code and Service, §§4101.02, 4109.01 to 4109.45, 4109.99, 3331.01, to 3331.17, 3331.99
Oklahoma	Oklahoma Statutes Annotated, T.40, §§1, 71 to 88
Oregon	Oregon Revised Statutes, §§651.050, 653.010 to 653.065, 653.305 to 653.340, 653.520; Oregon Administrative Regulations, Minimum Wage Order OAR 21-010 to 21-040
Pennsylvania	Purden's Pennsylvania Statutes Annotated, T.24, §§13-1330, 13-1391 to 13-1394, T.43, §§41 to 71, T.71, §567
Rhode Island	General Laws of Rhode Island, §§28-3-1 to 38-3-32
South Carolina	Code Laws of South Carolina, §§40-61, 40-161 to 40-166
South Dakota	South Dakota Compiled Laws, §§60-12-1 to 60-12-21
Tennessee	Tennessee Code Annotated, §§49-1710, 50-719, 50-726 to 50-738
Texas	Vernon's Texas Annotated Civil Statutes, Art. 5181a to Art. 5181h
Utah	Utah Code Annotated, §§34-23-1 to 34-23-13
Vermont	Vermont Statutes Annotated, T.21, §§6, 431 to 453
Virginia	Code of Virginia, §§40.1-78 to 40.1-116
Washington	Revised Code of Washington, §§26.28.060, 26.28.070, 28A.27.010, 28A.27.090, 28A.28.010 to 28A.28.060, 28A.28.130, 49.12.010 to 49.12.190, 49.28.010, 49.28.040, 49.28.070; Industrial Commission Order No. 49
West Virginia	West Virginia Code, §§21-6-1 to 21-6-10
Wisconsin	Wisconsin Statutes Annotated, §§103.19 to 103.31, 103.64 to 103.82; Wisconsin Administrative Code, §§Ind. 70.03, 70.05
Wyoming	Wyoming Statutes, §§27-218 to 27-234
District of Columbia	District of Columbia Code Encyclopedia, §§36.201 to 36.227, 36.301 to 36.303
Puerto Rico	Law of Puerto Rico Annotated, T.29, §§381, 431 to 456

10. FEDERAL CHILD LABOR LAW

In addition to extensive state laws regulating child labor, there are three major federal statutes with child labor provisions. These are the Fair Labor Standards Act,[1] the Walsh-Healy Public Contracts Act,[2] and the Sugar Act.[3] By their own terms and by the terms of regulations implementing them, the provisions of these statutes are superseded by state law wherever the relevant state law establishes a stricter standard than that prescribed in the federal statute.

The Walsh-Healy Public Contracts Act applies to manufacturers or dealers who contract to manufacture or supply materials valued in excess of $10,000 for the U.S. Government. This statute prohibits the employment of males under age sixteen and females under age eighteen in any work performed under such contracts.[4]

The Sugar Act provides for payment of benefits to growers of sugarbeets and sugarcane who comply with certain conditions.

---

[1] 29 U.S.C. §201 et seq. (Although the conventional citation form calls for the date of the most recently-published volume containing the cited statute to be indicated, we have, in this chapter, used instead the date of original enactment and of latest amendment, if any. The purpose of this is to give the reader some historical perspective concerning the development of federal child labor law.)

[2] 41 U.S.C. §35 et seq. (1936).

[3] 7 U.S.C. §601 et seq. (1933) (Agricultural Adjustment Act); 7 U.S.C. 1100 et seq. (1947, as amended 1971) (Sugar Act).

[4] 41 U.S.C. §35(d) (1936).

One of these conditions is that such growers not employ children under fourteen years of age for cultivation and harvesting of sugarbeets or sugarcane, and that they not employ children between fourteen and sixteen years of age in such work for more than eight hours per day.[5] During school hours, however, the higher standards set by the Fair Labor Standards Act are controlling.[6]

The Fair Labor Standards Act (FLSA) contains the most extensive federal child-labor provisions. It was enacted in 1938 to eliminate conditions found to be "detrimental to the maintenance of the minimum standards of living necessary for health, efficiency and general well-being of workers"[7] in industries engaged in interstate commerce or in the production of goods for interstate commerce.

In addition to its basic minimum wage, overtime and equal pay provisions, FLSA contains numerous provisions relating specifically to child labor. The child labor provisions of FLSA apply to any employer who employs any minor in interstate or foreign commerce or in the production of goods for such commerce, or in certain large enterprises (as defined in the act) engaged in interstate or foreign commerce or in the production of goods for such commerce; and to any producer,

---

[5] 7 U.S.C. §1131(a) (1947, as amended 1962).

[6] 29 C.F.R. §570.35 (1967). See also: "State Child Labor Standards", U.S. Department of Labor Bulletin #158 (Washington, D.C., Government Printing Office), 1965.

[7] 29 U.S.C. §202 (1938).(Congressional finding and declaration of policy.)

manufacturer, or dealer who ships goods or delivers goods for shipment in interstate or foreign commerce.[8]

I.   Age Standards and Age Certificates

The FLSA first defines "oppressive child labor" as the employment of children under the legal minimum age.[9] This legal minimum age is set at sixteen years for employment in any occupation other than a non-agricultural occupation declared hazardous.[10] There are no other restrictions. If not contrary to state or local law, young people of this age may be employed during school hours, for any number of hours, and during any periods of time.

For employment in non-agricultural occupations declared hazardous by the Secretary of Labor, the minimum age is eighteen years.[11] The minimum age for employment in hazardous agricultural occupations, and for employment in agriculture during the hours schools are in session in the district where the minor lives is set at sixteen years.[12] Fourteen is the minimum age set for employment in specified occupations outside of school hours, and under certain other specified conditions.[13]

---

[8]29 U.S.C. §212(a).(1938, as amended 1961).

[9]29 U.S.C. §203(e).(1938, as amended 1961).

[10]Id.

[11]Id., and 29 C.F.R. §§570.50-570.68.(1963 as amended).

[12]29 U.S.C. §213(c) (1) (1938 as amended 1974) and 29 C.F.R. §§570.70 and 570.71 (1970).

[13]29 U.S.C. §203 (1) (1938 as amended 1961) and 29 C.F.R. §§570.31-570.38 (1951).

A. Employment and Certification of Minors Sixteen
    Years or Over

The FLSA provides that "oppressive child labor shall
not be deemed to exist by virtue of the employment in any occupation of any person with respect to whom the employer shall
have on file an unexpired certificate issued and held pursuant
to regulations of the Secretary of Labor certifying that such
person is above the oppressive child labor age".[14]

Although employers are not actually required by the FLSA
to obtain age or employment certificates for any minors they may
employ, the statute offers a powerful incentive to do so because
possession of a certificate is conclusive evidence that the employer
is not acting in violation of the statute.

The certificate required may be either a federal age
certificate issued by a person authorized by the Wage and Hour
Division of the Department of Labor, or a state certificate
issued in conformity with federal regulations.[15] All but five
states[16] issue certificates acceptable under the FLSA as proof
that the minor employee is above the oppressive child-labor age.[17]

The federal certificate contains the name and address of
the minor to whom it is issued; the place and date of birth,

---

[14] 29 U.S.C. §203(1).(1938 as amended 1961).

[15] 29 C.F.R. §570.2(a) (1951).

[16] In Idaho, Miss., S.C., and Tex., only Federal Certificates of Age
are issued. In Alas.,special arrangements for proof of age are
made by regulation. See 29 C.F.R. §570.22 (1951).

[17] 29 C.F.R. §§570.22 (1951).

with a statement indicating the evidence on which this is based;[18] the minor's sex; name and address of parents or of the person standing in loco parentis; the name, address and industry of the employer;[19] and the signature of the issuing officer with the date and place of issuance.[20]

B. Employment of Minor Between Ages of Fourteen and Sixteen

The FLSA provides that the employment of minors between ages fourteen and sixteen under certain conditions regarding occupations, time periods, and other matters specified by the Secretary of Labor, shall not be deemed to constitute oppressive child labor, if the Secretary determines that such employment will not interfere with the minors' schooling or with their health or well-being.[21]

Regulations issued pursuant to this section specify in which occupations minors aged fourteen to sixteen may be employed and the hours and conditions under which they may work. Generally, minors between ages fourteen and sixteen may be employed as office workers, retail clerks, soda fountain or cafeteria workers and

---

[18]29 C.F.R. §570.4 (1951) provides that proof of age may be established by one of the following in order of preference: 1) a birth certificate issued by a registrar of vital statistics or officer charged with the duty of recording births; 2) A baptismal record or a record kept in a family Bible, or other documentary evidence such as a passport or life insurance policy; 3) A school record together with a sworn statement of the parent as to the minor's age and a certificate signed by a physician specifying what in his opinion is the physical age of the minor.

[19]This information need not appear on a certificate issued for employment in agriculture. 29 C.F.R §570.3 fn. 4. (1951).

[20]29 C.F.R. §570.3 (1951).

[21]29 U.S.C. §203 (1) (1938 as amended 1961).

service station attendants.[22] All of these occupations are subject to certain limitations, however, usually concerned with use
of mechanical equipment or heavy machinery.[23] The hours that
minors may work must be confined to periods outside school hours;
they may not work more than eight hours per day or forty hours
per week when school is in session. They may not work before
7 a.m. or after 7 p.m. except from June 1 to Labor Day when the
evening hour is 9 p.m.[24]

The regulations exempt from some provisions minors who
are enrolled in and employed pursuant to school-run work programs.
Minors enrolled in such work experience and career exploration
programs may work during school hours[25] and in any occupations
except manufacturing, mining, and occupations declared to be
hazardous.[26] Employment of these students must be confined to
twenty-three hours per week when school is in session and three
hours per day, any portion of which may be during school hours.[27]
Students must also receive school credit for such employment.[28]

---

[22] 29 C.F.R §570.34(a) (1962).

[23] 29 C.F.R. §570.33 (1962) and §570.34(b) (1962).

[24] 29 C.F.R. §570.35 (1967).

[25] 29 C.F.R. §570.35(a) (1974).

[26] 29 C.F.R. §570.35a(c) (1974). Students in such programs are also
subject to the job limitations imposed on all minors aged fourteen
to sixteen [see text at note 22, supra) unless granted a variation
by the Department of Labor 29 C.F.R §570.35a(c)(3)(1974)].

[27] 29 C.F.R. §570.35a(d)(1974).

[28] 29 C.F.R. §570.35a(b) (3) (ii) (1974).

Programs for providing work experience and career exploration must be submitted to the Department of Labor, and specifically approved as programs not constituting oppressive child labor.[29]

II. Hazardous Occupations

The Fair Labor Standards Act provides a minimum age of eighteen years for any non-agricultural occupation which the Secretary of Labor "shall find and by order declare" to be particularly hazardous for sixteen- and seventeen-year-old persons, or detrimental to their health and well-being."[30] Similarly, a sixteen year minimum age applies to any agricultural occupation that the Secretary of Labor finds and declares to be hazardous for the employment of children.[31]

Determination that an occupation is hazardous is made after an investigation by representatives of the Department of Labor.[32] Hazardous Occupation Orders are issued after public hearing and advice from committees composed of representatives of employers and employees of the industry and the public.[33] Once issued, the orders have the force of law, and a violation of their provisions constitutes a violation of the child labor provisions of FLSA.

---

[29] 29 C.F.R. §570.35a(b) (2) (1974).

[30] 29 U.S.C. §203(1)(1938, as amended 1961).

[31] Id.

[32] 29 C.F.R. §570.41 (1967).

[33] Id.

There are currently seventeen Hazardous Occupation Orders in effect. Occupations declared by such orders to be particularly hazardous for employment of minors aged sixteen to eighteen are occupations involving the use of power-driven machinery; occupations in mining, logging, wrecking and excavation work; meat packing and processing; brick and explosive manufacturing; and occupations involving exposure to radioactive materials.[34]

Agricultural occupations declared to be especially hazardous to children under age sixteen include those in which power-driven machinery is used, as well as those involving use of explosives or dangerous chemicals, and contact with certain animals.[35] Student-learners in agricultural occupations are exempted from the prohibitions against employment of minors under age sixteen in hazardous agricultural occupations if they are enrolled in a vocational education training program under a recognized state or local educational authority.[36] There are also exemptions to allow minors to operate farm machinery if they have completed such a vocational program, or are 4-H members who have completed a 4-H course in tractor operation.[37]

---

[34] 29 C.F.R. §570.51-570-68; Occupations Particularly Hazardous for the Employment of Minors, Orders #1-17. (1963).

[35] 29 C.F.R. §570.71 (1970).

[36] 29 C.F.R. §570.72(a) (1970).

[37] 29 C.F.R. §570.72(b)(1), (b)(3), (c)(1) and (c)(2)(1970).

III. Exemptions

The FLSA exempts from its child labor provisions several categories of child-laborers. Children under sixteen years of age employed by their parents in agriculture or in non-agricultural occupations other than manufacturing or mining occupations, or other than in occupations declared hazardous for minors under age eighteen, are exempt from the provisions of FLSA,[38] as are children under sixteen years of age who are employed by other than their parents in agriculture, if the occupation has not been declared hazardous and if the employment is outside the hours schools are in session in the district where the minor lives while working.[39] Also exempt are children employed as actors or performers in motion pictures, and employed in radio, or television productions;[40] children engaged in the delivery of newspapers to the consumer;[41] and homeworkers engaged in the making of wreaths composed principally of natural holly,

---

[38] 29 U.S.C. §203(1) (1938 as amended 1961) and 29 C.F.R. §570.126 (1951).

[39] 29 U.S.C. §213(c)(1) (1938 as amended 1974) and 29 C.F.R. §570.123 (1958).

[40] 29 U.S.C. §213(c)(3) (1938 as amended 1974) and 29 C.F.R. §570.125(1951).

[41] 29 U.S.C. §213(d) (1938 as amended 1974) and 29 C.F.R. §570.124(1951).

pine, cedar, or other evergreens (including the harvesting of
the evergreens).[42]

IV.   Enforcement

Any infringement of the child labor provisions of FLSA
constitutes a crime.[43] Penalties for wilful violations of the
act include a fine of up to $10,000, and/or imprisonment for up
to six months.[44]

The Secretary of Labor or his designated representatives
are charged with the duty of enforcing the provisions of the
act and are empowered to investigate and to gather data, to
enter and to inspect places of employment, to inspect and to
copy records, to question employees and to investigate other
matters as may be deemed necessary to insure enforcement.[45]
The Secretary is further authorized to utilize services of
state and local agencies charged with enforcement of state labor
laws, with the consent and cooperation of such state agencies.[46]

The act also requires employers to maintain records of
persons employed and to make reports to the Administrator of
the Department of Labor concerning employees, working conditions

---

[42] 29 U.S.C. §213(d) (1938 as amended 1974).

[43] 29 U.S.C. §215(a)(4) (1938).

[44] 29 U.S.C. §216(a) (1938, as amended 1974).

[45] 29 U.S.C. §211(a) (1938, as amended 1949) and 212(b).

[46] 29 U.S.C. §211(b) (1938, as amended 1949).

and other conditions of employment as required by the Secretary to enforce the act.[47]

The act does protect "innocent" purchasers from prosecution for violations committed by their suppliers by providing that any shipment of goods by a purchaser, who ships or delivers for shipment in interstate commerce goods acquired in good faith in reliance on a written assurance from the producer, manufacturer or dealer that the goods were produced in compliance with the child-labor provisions, and which he acquired for value without notice of any violation, shall not be deemed to be in violation of the act.[48]

V.   Relationship to Other Laws

The FLSA child-labor provisions state that no provision of the act relating to the employment of child labor shall justify noncompliance with any federal or state law establishing a higher standard.[49] Regulations interpreting the section further state that compliance with other child labor laws will not relieve any person of liability under FLSA, if the FLSA standard is higher; nor will compliance with FLSA relieve any person of liability under other laws that establish a higher child labor standard than those prescribed by the act.[50]

---

[47] 29 U.S.C. §215(a)(4) (1938).

[48] 29 U.S.C. §212 (1938, as amended 1967).

[49] 29 U.S.C. §218(a) (1938, as amended 1967).

[50] 29 C.F.R. §570.129 (1951).

11. THE RELATIONSHIP BETWEEN THE STATE SYSTEMS OF COMPULSORY ATTENDANCE AND THE UNITED STATES CONSTITUTION

Introduction

The purpose of this chapter is to analyze the relationship between the state compulsory school attendance systems and the United States Constitution. This analysis will focus primarily on landmark decisions of the United States Supreme Court in the area of elementary and secondary education. There will also be reference to decisions of the United States District Courts and Courts of Appeal in those areas of education law where the Supreme Court has not yet rendered a definitive decision. The analysis in this chapter will be the basis for the conclusions in that part of the next chapter relating to the federal constitutional implications of amending or repealing state compulsory attendance provisions.

I.   Federal Judicial Involvement in Education

Education has traditionally been a state responsibility in the division of authority between the federal government and the states. From a Constitutional[1] perspective, this is because education is not a responsibility specifically delegated to Congress nor prohibited to the states by the Constitution and, therefore, is a responsibility "reserved to the states respectively, or to

---

[1]Reference in this chapter to the "Constitution" shall mean the United States Constitution.

the people" by the provisions of the Tenth Amendment.[2]

Involvement of the federal courts in the area of education, nevertheless, has been extensive because of their jurisdiction over actions by states which violate rights guaranteed to individuals by the Constitution.[3] This jurisdiction has its origin in the Due Process and Equal Protection Clauses of the Fourteenth Amendment.[4] Both clauses direct their prohibitions against actions of the states rather than the federal government. The Due Process Clause, in addition, has been determined by the Supreme Court to include within its meaning certain of the first eight amendments to the Constitution, despite the fact that those amendments were originally considered to be directed only against the federal government.[5] Of particular importance for purposes of this analysis is that the Court[6] has determined that the provisions of the First Amendment are included within the meaning of

---

[2] The Tenth Amendment provides: "The powers not delegated to the United States by the Constitution, nor prohibited by it to the States, are reserved to the States respectively, or to the people."

[3] Cf. Koerner, J., Who Controls American Education, pp. 6-8, (1969).

[4] The Fourteenth Amendment provides, in relevant part: "No State shall...deprive any person of life, liberty or property, without due process of law; nor deny to any person within its jurisdiction the equal protection of the laws."

[5] E.g., included within the Due Process Clause has been the Fourth Amendment protection against "unreasonable searches and seizures" (Mapp v. Ohio, 367 U.S. 643 (1961), and the Sixth Amendment right to "the assistance of counsel in criminal cases" (Gideon v. Wainwright, 372 U.S. 335 (1963)).

[6] References to the "Court" or to the Supreme Court shall mean the Supreme Court of the United States.

the Due Process Clause.[7] Therefore, the words of the First
Amendment[8] apply to the states as well as to the federal government.

The great majority of the federal cases[9] relating
to compulsory attendance, specifically, and to elementary and
secondary education, generally, have been based upon the provisions of the Due Process and Equal Protection Clauses and on the
words of the First Amendment as applied to the states through
the Due Process Clause. It is this body of case law which will
be the basis for the following analysis.

II.   The Relationship Between Compulsory Attendance Laws and
        the Decisions of the Supreme Court and the Lower Federal
        Courts in the Area of Elementary and Secondary Education

Except for a small number of cases raising issues which
relate directly to the requirements of state compulsory attendance laws, the decisions of the Supreme Court and the lower
federal courts in the area of elementary and secondary education
rarely contain any reference to those laws. Occasionally, a
decision of the Court will mention a compulsory attendance statute, but then will leave to inference the precise relevance

----

[7]For incorporation of the Freedom of Speech clause, see Gitlow v.
New York, 268 U.S. 652 (1925), Whitney v. California, 275 U.S.
(1927) and Fiske v. Kansas, 274 U.S. 380 (1927); see Cantwell v.
Connecticut (1940) for incorporation of the Free Exercise Clause

[8]The First Amendment states that: "Congress shall make no law
respecting an establishment of religion, or prohibiting the free
exercise thereof; or abridging the freedom of speech, or of the
press; or the right of the people peaceably to assemble, and to
petition the Government for a redress of grievances."

[9]References to "federal case law" shall mean the totality of
cases decided by the Supreme Court and the lower federal courts.

of that statute to the holding in the case.

Because of this general lack of a clear statement of
the place of the compulsory attendance laws in the analytical
framework of federal cases relating to elementary and secondary
education, it is very difficult to classify those cases for purposes of this analysis. In addition, adding to this difficulty
in classification are the complex and difficult to reconcile
cases of the Court which address the issue of a "right to an
education". Nevertheless, the following analysis will suggest
a system of classification, which will encompass all of the
Supreme Court cases and certain lower federal court cases which
base their decisions in part, directly or by implication, on
the provisions of the compulsory attendance laws.

The federal cases relating to elementary and secondary
education can be divided into three categories for purposes
of this analysis. In the first, are those cases which primarily
and explicitly focus upon the compulsory attendance provisions
per se, i.e., those cases which challenge the basic requirement
of attendance at "school". In the second, are those cases which
address the issue of a "right to an education", through interpretation of the Due Process and Equal Protection Clauses of the
Fourteenth Amendment. Some of the cases in this second category
occasionally will make reference to compulsory attendance laws,
but in a manner which is unclear. In the third category are
those cases which decide issues concerning the substantive rights
of students within the public school system, outside of the
"right to an education" or to a certain quantity or quality of
education. The cases in this third category rarely mention the

compulsory attendance laws, although a few seem to rely on those
laws as a partial basis for their decisions.

A. Federal Cases Which Primarily and Explicitly Focus Upon the Compulsory Attendance Provisions, Per Se

The early cases in this category were brought by
persons seeking a Constitutionally-mandated flexibility in the
kind of learning arrangements permitted by the state to satisfy the
requirements of compulsory attendance. The most recent case was
brought by parents seeking an exemption from those requirements.[10]

1. Pierce v. Society of Sisters

The first decision of the Supreme Court to address
the issue of whether the Constitution required an expansion of
the alternative learning arrangements permitted by a compulsory
attendance law was Pierce v. Society of Sisters,[11] where the
Court held unconstitutional the compulsory attendance law of
Oregon which required parents of children between eight and
sixteen years to send their children to public school as the
exclusive manner of compliance with the law and which imposed a
criminal penalty on parents who failed to carry out this mandate.
The compulsory attendance law was challenged by the owners of
two private schools - one a parochial school and the other a
non-sectarian military academy. The Court agreed with the
private schools that the statute was unconstitutional because
it resulted in an "arbitrary, unreasonable and unlawful interference with their patrons and the consequent destruction of

---

[10] Wisconsin v. Yoder, 406 U.S. 205 (1972).

[11] 268 U.S. 510 (1925).

their business and property."[12]

Although parents who sent their children to the private schools or who wished to send their children to such schools were not parties to the suit, the Court considered their interests as an additional reason for the finding of a Constitutional violation. In language which is now famous, the Court said:

> The fundamental theory of liberty upon which all governments in this Union repose exludes any general powers of the state to standardize its children by forcing them to accept instruction from public teachers only. The child is not the mere creature of the state; those who nurture him and direct his destiny have the right, coupled with the high duty, to recognize and prepare him for additional obligations.[13]

The specific Constitutional basis on which the case was expressly decided was the general "substantive" requirement of the Due Process Clause of the Fourteenth Amendment which mandated that "rights" recognized by the Constitution, i.e., the rights in this case of the private schools and the parents, may not be abridged by state legislation which "has no reasonable relation to some purpose within the competency of the state.[14]

For purposes of this Constitutional analysis of state compulsory attendance laws, the Court held, in effect, that

---

[12] Id. at 536.

[13] Id. at 534.

[14] Id. Under the standard of "substantive due process" the Court recognized certain interests as being included in the phrase "life, liberty or property", even though those interests were not expressly provided for in the Constitution. Such interests in Pierce, for example were the interests of the parents in bringing up their children. Once recognizing such interests, the Court, applying the standard of substantive due process, held in effect, that those interests
(cont'd.)

it was "outside the competency of the state" for the state
to require attendance at public school as the sole means for
parents and children to satisfy the requirements of the compulsory attendance laws. Relating this holding to the earlier analysis
of state systems of compulsory attendance, the Court, by its ruling,
gave Constitutional status to the choice of a private school as
an alternative means to a public school for parents and children
to meet the requirement of compelled attendance. In conclusion,
the Court upheld the state's authority to compel attendance "at
school", but struck down the state's effort to limit parental
choice to "public school".

2. Farrington v. Tokushique

The holding in Pierce was applied in a subsequent
case, Farrington v. Tokushique,[15] where a state tried to avoid
the effect of Pierce not by prohibiting attendance at a private
school as a means of complying with the compulsory attendance
requirement, but by regulating the activities of the private
schools in such a manner and to such a degree that the schools
were effectively precluded from carrying out their purpose, i.e.,
to be alternative schools for Japanese-Americans who wanted their
children instructed in Japanese rather than in English. The
state regulations, implementing similar state legislation, provided that English had to be the language of instruction in most

---

[14] (cont.) could not be infringed without a "strong" showing by the
state. The standard is a vague one which has been replaced in modern
times by a variety of new standards including the "strict scrutiny"
test (in analyzing alleged violations of the Equal Protection Clause),
which will be discussed in a later part of this chapter.

[15] 273 U.S. 284 (1927)

grades and that the schools had to submit to extensive administrative requirements and financial levies.[16] In summing up the effect of the state statutes, the Court found that:

> They give affirmative direction concerning intimate and essential details of such schools, intrust their control to public officers, and deny both owners and patrons reasonable choice and discretion in respect of teachers, curriculum and textbooks. Enforcement of the act probably would destroy most, if not all, of them; and certainly it would deprive parents of fair opportunity to procure for their children instruction which they think is important and we cannot say is harmful.[17]

The Court cited _Pierce_ as the primary legal basis for its decision.[18] In relying on _Pierce_, the Court made it very clear that the private school attendance system mandated by _Pierce_ could not be evaded by state statutes and regulations which had the effect of transforming private schools into public schools or forcing the private schools to close their doors.

3. Wisconsin v. Yoder

The holdings in _Pierce_ and _Farrington_ laid the groundwork for the recent decision of the Court in _Wisconsin v. Yoder_.[19] Because of its importance in this analysis and because of its length and complexity, the _Yoder_ decision merits intensive analysis.

---

[16] _Id._ at 298.

[17] _Id._

[18] _Id._

[19] 406 U.S. 205 (1972).

In _Yoder_, the Court reviewed the cases of several Amish parents, who were convicted under a Wisconsin statute for failure to send their children to school in violation of the compulsory attendance law which mandated school attendance until age sixteen. The children, all between the ages of fourteen and fifteen, had completed eight grades of elementary school. They were not enrolled in a private school, nor were they attending any of the other learning arrangements which were permitted by Wisconsin law as alternatives to public school attendance.

The parents claimed, as a defense to the criminal charges, that the statute subjecting them to criminal penalties for failure to send their children to one of the learning arrangements permitted by the compulsory attendance law violated their right, guaranteed by the First Amendment to the Constitution, to freely practice their religion.[20] This Free Exercise claim was based upon the Amish religion and particularly the belief of the Amish that sending their children to high school would expose the parents to censure by the church community and would endanger the hopes for salvation of both the parents and children.[21]

Despite this defense, the parents were convicted by the Wisconsin trial court. Upon appeal, the Wisconsin Supreme Court reversed the convictions. The State of Wisconsin then appealed to the Supreme Court of the United States

---

[20]The First Amendment provides, in relevant part, that: "Congress shall make no law respecting an establishment of religion, or prohibiting the free exercise thereof..."

[21]406 U.S. at 209.

which upheld the claims of the parents and affirmed the decision
of the Wisconsin Supreme Court.

In rendering its decision, the United States
Supreme Court applied a two-step test originally articulated in
the case of <u>Sherbert v. Verner</u>.[22] First, the Court said it must
determine whether there was an infringement by the state of the
First Amendment right of individuals to practice their religion.
Second, if the Court found such an infringement, it would determine whether the infringement was justified by a compelling state
interest.[23]

In applying this two fold test, the Court recognized that Wisconsin had a "paramount responsibility"[24] to provide public education for its citizens; but, cautioned that this
state interest "is not totally free from a balancing process
when it impinges on fundamental rights and interests, such as
those specifically protected by the Free Exercise Clause of the
First Amendment, and the traditional interest of parents with
respect to the religious upbringing of their children."[25]

In applying the first part of the test, i.e.,
in determining whether there was an infringement of rights protected by the Free Exercise Clause, the Court examined at great
length the nature of the religious beliefs of the Amish and

---

[22]374 U.S. 398 (1963).

[23]406 U.S. 205 at 213-215.

[24]<u>Id</u>. at 213.

[25]<u>Id</u>. at 213, 214.

found that the parents sincerely believed "that their children's attendance at high school, public or private, was contrary to the Amish religion and way of life".[26] The Court was very careful to emphasize that in order for the claims of the plaintiff-parents to be sustained, those claims had to be clearly "rooted in religious belief"[27] and could not be based upon a personal or philosophical belief not of a traditional religious nature. Applying this standard, the Court found that the right being asserted was a "religious one" within the meaning of the Free Exercise Clause.[28] The Court concluded that compulsory high school attendance would substantially interfere with the religious development of Amish children and their integration into the Amish way of life and would, therefore, "gravely endanger, if not destroy that free exercise of [the Amish's] religious beliefs."[29]

The Court then had to decide whether the interest of Wisconsin in enforcing the compulsory attendance law as it applied to the secondary level was of sufficient weight to outbalance the infringement of the rights of the parents under the Free Exercise Clause. The state raised two primary arguments in support of its interest in enforcing its compulsory attendance law: 1) to prepare citizens to participate effectively in democratic government; and 2) to prepare citizens to be self-reliant

---

[26] Id. at 209.

[27] Id. at 215.

[28] Id. at 216.

[29] Id. at 219.

and self-sufficient members of society.[30] The Court accepted the
value of those interests, but found that they were being adequately
met by the Amish's own unique system of "education".[31]

The Court disposed of the first argument by deciding
that the difference between two more years of school beyond the
eighth grade and the "long established program of informal vocational education" of the Amish was so insignificant that any en-
croachment on the state's interest was negligible.[32] The Court
dealt with the second argument of the state by concluding that
"the Amish qualities of reliability, self-reliance, and dedication
to work" were sufficient to satisfy the interests of the state in
preparing its citizens to be self reliant and independent.[33]

As further justification for its holding, the
Court noted the common roots of compulsory attendance and child
labor laws, stating that the arbitrary sixteen year cut-off age
of the compulsory attendance law was the result of a desire to
keep persons under age sixteen out of the labor market. Accepting
the evidence that the Amish children would, as adults, live and
work in the Amish agrarian community, the Court concluded, from
a policy perspective, that "the Amish child...poses no threat
to adult laborers elsewhere; therefore the interest of Wisconsin

---

[30] Id. at 221.
[31] Id. at 222. In effect, the Court ruled that the Amish lifestyle,
in itself, was an acceptable form of education.
[32] Id.
[33] Id. at 224.

in compelling school attendance until age sixteen is somewhat less substantial for the Amish than for children generally."[34]

The final argument of the state in support of enforcing the compulsory attendance requirement against the Amish was that the children, themselves, had a right to an education independent of parental desires and that the state, therefore, under the doctrine of parens patriae, could require attendance at school despite the contrary wishes of the parents.[35] The Court disposed of this argument by a threefold response.

First, the Court refused to accept the proposition that the parents might be acting contrary to the best interests of their children. The Court indicated that such acceptance might result in the extension of this argument to all parental decisions about "any church schools short of college".[36] In this regard, the Court took notice of what it considered to be common knowledge, i.e. that parents of children between the ages of fourteen and sixteen do not generally consult with their children before placing them in a sectarian school.[37] Second, the Court cited Pierce v. Society of Sisters for the proposition that parents have a fundamental and overriding interest in guiding the religious development of their children.[38]

---

[34] Id. at 228-229

[35] Id. at 229.

[36] Id. at 232.

[37] Id.

[38] Id.

Third, the Court distinguished the case of Prince v. Massachusetts[39]
which held that the power of the parent "even when linked to a
free exercise claim, may be subject to limitation...if it appears
that parental decision will jeopardize the health or safety of the
child, or have a potential or significant social burden".[40]
The Court distinguished Prince on the grounds that the record
failed to support the state's claim that there was or would be
any impairment of the physical and mental health of the Amish children if they missed one or two additional years of compulsory
school attendance.[41]

      The Court concluded that the Free Exercise Clause
of the First Amendment, as applied to the states by the Due Process
Clause of the Fourteenth Amendment, prohibited Wisconsin from requiring the Amish parents to send their children either to a public
school or to a statutorily-permitted alternative to a public school.[42]
By so ruling, the Court permitted the Amish parents to raise
their children and prepare them for life in a manner not recognized by the Wisconsin compulsory attendance law.

      4. Commentary on Yoder, Farrington and Pierce

      From the perspective of this chapter, the decision
in Yoder is significant, most generally, as a recognition by the

---

[39] 321 U.S. 158 (1944)

[40] 406 U.S. 205 at 234.

[41] Id.

[42] Id. at 234.

Court that, in certain cases, i.e., those raising valid Free
Exercise claims under the First Amendment, the Constitution
requires not only that parents be permitted to enroll their
children in a private school, as mandated in Pierce and Farrington,
but that parents need not enroll their children in any statutorily
recognized educational program.

This conclusion, however, must be qualified by
the fact that the Court placed great emphasis on the evidence
that the Amish "way of life", in part, was tantamount to a high
quality vocational-education program, so that the children in
question would, in a sense, be continuing their education. This
finding by the Court casts some doubt on whether Yoder can be
read as granting anything more than a limited exemption from
a compulsory attendance requirement. In summary, the holding
in Yoder was so tailored to the facts in the trial record that
Yoder might not be a sufficient basis for a Free Exercise claim
for an exemption from compulsory attendance, absent substantial
supporting evidence to the effect that the lifestyle being presented
as an alternative to public school, was both intimately connected
to the religious beliefs of the claimants and was a form of
"education".

The holding in Yoder is also significant in its
references to Pierce, particularly with respect to providing
guidance to the modern meaning of Pierce. In its references to
Pierce, the Court, in Yoder, appears to treat Pierce as if it
were a case decided on the basis of the Free Exercise Clause of
the First Amendment. In Pierce, however, the Court specifically

stated that it was applying the traditional Fourteenth Amendment,
Due Process test of deciding whether the state statute bore a
reasonable relationship to some valid state purpose.[43] In addition, one of the appellees in Pierce was a private, non-sectarian
school (a military academy) and the Pierce Court clearly affirmed
the decision of the lower court with respect to this school as
well as to the sectarian school.[44] For these reasons, and
because Pierce was not expressly modified by Yoder, it
would appear that the Pierce decision, at a minimum, continues
to stand for the proposition that all parents, regardless of
whether their decision is based on religious grounds, have the
Constitutional right to send their children to private school.
As one recent commentator has pointed out, however, the modern
meaning of Pierce is far from clear.[45]

       Yoder, on the other hand, is clearly a Free
Exercise case. If one reads Pierce's holding to be that the
Constitution mandates parental choice of a private alternative
to public school, Yoder can be read to extend Pierce only to the
extent of creating a Constitutional exemption to compulsory attendance for the children of those parents who can establish a "valid"
religious claim, within the meaning of the Yoder requirements.
The validity of this religious claim will be determined by the

---

[43] Supra, note 14.

[44] Pierce at 534.

[45] For a highly interesting and provocative analysis of the modern
meaning of Pierce, see Arons, 46 Harv. Ed. Rev. 76 (February 19, 1976).

Court on a case by case basis with Yoder providing little in the way of general standards for decision. In conclusion, it is difficult to predict which future Free Exercise claim the Court will find to be "religious" rather than personal; and which the Court will find to outweigh the state's countervailing interest in compelling attendance at a public school or a statutorily recognized alternative to a public school.

B. Cases on Public Aid to Private Schools

Another line of Supreme Court cases which is related to the issues just discussed, are those cases which delineate the boundaries of permitted and prohibited public financial aid to private schools under the provisions of the Establishment Clause of the Fourteenth Amendment.[46] Those cases are directly related to Pierce, Farrington and Yoder in that the Establishment Clause cases address the practical question of the Constitutional limits of the state financial support which will be available to the parents who wish to exercise the choices provided by those three cases.

The Court has set forth a three part test for deciding whether a statute authorizing public aid to private schools violates the Establishment Clause.[47] First, the Court will determine whether the statute has a "valid secular purpose". Second, the Court will ask whether the "primary effect" is secular, or

---

[46] The Establishment Clause is that part of the First Amendment which provides that "Congress shall make no law respecting an establishment of religion ... "

[47] See Lemon v. Kurtzman, 403 U.S. 602 (1971).

is to advance or inhibit religion. Finally, the Court will determine whether the statute "fosters excessive entanglement between the state and religion."[48] If the determination in parts one or two is negative or in part three is affirmative, the statute will be declared unconstitutional.

In a recent case, Meek v. Pittenger,[49] the Court, in striking down Pennsylvania's "massive" system of aid to private schools, provided some guidance concerning the kinds of public aid which would, by their nature, meet the three requirements set forth above and, therefore, would be permissible under the Establishment Clause. The Court said:

> It is, of course, true that as part of general legislation made available to all students, a state may include church-related schools in programs providing bus transportation, school lunches, and public health facilities - secular and non-ideological services unrelated to the primary, religious oriented educational function of the private school. The indirect and incidental benefits to church related schools from those programs do not offend the Constitutional prohibition against establishment of religion ...[50]

In an earlier case,[51] the Court specifically addressed the validity of a New Jersey provision authorizing the payment by the state of bus fares of parochial school pupils as a part of a general program. Citing Pierce for the proposition that parents had the right to send their children to a religious

---

[48]Id. at 612-613.

[49]421 U.S. 349 (1975).

[50]Id. at 364-65.

[51]Everson v. Board of Education of Ewing Township, 330 U.S. 1 (1947).

school which met the secular educational requirements of the state,
the Court upheld the bus fare provision as a statute which
"does no more than provide a general program to help parents get
their children, regardless of their religion, safely to and
from accredited schools".[52]

However, in most cases raising the issue of the validity
under the Establishment Clause, of various types of state aid to private
schools, the Court has found the challenged statutes to be unconstitutional either because they had a primary effect of advancing
religion or they fostered an impermissible entanglement between the
state and religion.[53] In general, it is fair to conclude that the
Court has been very restrictive in allowing states to provide direct
or indirect financial aid to private, sectarian schools.

For purposes of this analysis, the cases under the
Establishment Clause make it clear that the rights of parents created
by Pierce, Farrington, and Yoder, will not be implemented through
substantial amounts of state aid to sectarian schools.

_____

[52] Id. at 18.

[53] E.g., see Committee for Public Education and Religious Liberty
v. Nyquist, 413 U.S. 756 (1973) (public funds for maintenance of
buildings held to advance religion because not restricted to buildings
for exclusively secular purposes); Levitt v. Committee for Public
Education and Religious Liberty, 413 U.S. 472 (1973), (payments to
religious schools for the costs of testing children held invalid
because it included payments for costs of administering tests written by teachers at religious schools); and Sloan v. Lemon, 413 U.S.
825 (1973) (held that a statute providing a tuition reimbursement
to parents for money they spent to send their children to religious
schools had a primary effect of advancing religion because it contained no way of limiting the reimbursement to that part of the
child's tuition which paid for secular education).

The Court has indicated that the Constitution requires neutrality in this area, neither favoring extensive amounts of state aid to sectarian schools, nor forbidding small amounts of indirect and incidental aid which are given as part of a general purpose program, the primary effect of which is non-religious.

C. Federal Cases Which Address the Issue of a Right to an Education

In this category of cases are those decisions of the Supreme Court and some decisions of the lower federal courts (in the area of special education), which analyze the content of a claimed Constitutional right to an education guaranteed by the Due Process and Equal Protection Clauses of the Fourteenth Amendment. The relevance of those cases to this analysis is that some of them rely, at least in part, on the existence of state compulsory attendance provisions, as a basis for determining whether there is a "right to an education" under the Constitution. In addition, these cases are included as a basis for clarifying the difference, which is often obscured, between an obligation to attend school and a right to an educational opportunity.

1. Cases under the Equal Protection Clause

a. Introduction

In order to understand the decisions of the Supreme Court and lower federal courts on claims brought on the basis of the Equal Protection Clause of the Fourteenth Amendment, it is necessary to be aware of the standards for judicial review under that Clause. These standards have been delineated in a series of Supreme Court opinions which will be discussed below.

It should be noted at the outset that it has been well established since the early decisions of the Court that not all cases where a class of persons receives unequal treatment from the state, constitute violations of the Equal Protection Clause. Rather, such violations have been found only where the interest involved is a very important one and where the Court has determined from the trial record that the state could not provide an adequate justification for its actions. In addition, the Court has decided that the nature of this justification is relative so that in certain cases of inequality, the state will be required to present "a more compelling justification" for its actions than in others.

In the ordinary case, the Court will only require the state to show that its challenged action is "rationally related to a legitimate state purpose". This test merely requires a showing that one or more specific and legally permissible state goals will be directly furthered as a result of the state's action.[54] When the Court applies this "rationality test", it normally upholds the state classification.

In certain other cases, however, the Court will apply a more rigorous test to the challenged state classi-

---

[54] Kotch v. Pilot Commissioners, 330 U.S. 552 (1947); Railway Express Agency v. New York, 336 U.S. 106 (1949).

fication. This test, known as the "strict scrutiny test",
will be applied to equal protection claims involving either a
"fundamental interest" or a "suspect classification". A "fundamental interest" is one (such as the right to travel interstate)
which the Court deems to be either expressly or implicitly protected by the Constitution.[55] A "suspect classification" is
involved if the class of persons receiving differential treatment is one that the Court has found to deserve special protection.[56]
For example, classifications based on race, national ancestry,
and status as an alien have been found by the Court to be "suspect".[57]

If the Court finds a "fundamental interest"
or a "suspect classification" to be involved, it will subject
the challenged state action to "strict scrutiny". This means
that the Court will require the state to prove that the challenged
action is "necessary to achieve a compelling state purpose" and
that such purpose cannot be achieved by another means which is
less discriminatory. Unlike the "rational basis test" which
the state can usually satisfy, application by the Court of the
standard of "strict scrutiny" will normally result in the action
of the state being declared in violation of the Equal Pro-

---

[55] Rodriguez v. San Antonio School District, 411 U.S. 1, 33-34 (1973).

[56] Id. at 20-22.

[57] Loving v. Virginia, 338 U.S. 1 (1967) (race); Yick Wo v. Hopkins, 118 U.S. 256 (1886) (nationanl ancestry); In re Griffiths, 413 U.S. 717 (1973) (status as an alien).

tection Clause.[58]

The implication of these equal protection standards is similar to that of the concept of "substantive due process" mentioned earlier,[59] in that by applying the various standards under the Equal Protection Clause, the Court, in effect, is giving recognition to certain "substantive" interests of individuals. It does this by requiring some form of policy justification from the state before permitting it to infringe upon those interests. The following analysis will examine the extent to which the Court has viewed "the right to an education" to be one of those substantive interests.

b. Brown v. Board of Education

In its landmark decision in Brown v. Board

---

[58]The practical application of these theoretical standards of review, unfortunately, is sometimes not as clear as the theory. The Court has, on occasion, under the rubric of the "rationality test", applied some stricter variation of that test. For example, the Court has sometimes said that the "rational basis" test requires that the challenged classification be rationally related to the purpose of the statute, and then invalidated a statute because, although the statute bore a rational relationship to a legitimate state purpose, the purpose was not the purpose for which the statute was enacted. (Eisenstadt v. Baird, 405 U.S. 438 (1972). At other times, the Court has required that the state prove not only that its action bears a rational relationship to a legitimate state purpose, but also, that the action will, in fact, further that purpose. (Reed v. Reed, 404 U.S. 71 (1974).

It is difficult to predict when the Court will apply these intermediate standards. As a general rule, however, the Court seems to apply them when it wants to strike down a statute, but is unwilling to hold that the interest involved is "fundamental" or that the classification being used is "suspect".

[59]Supra, note 14.

of Education,[60] the Court held that state statutes providing
for a public school system which was segregated on the basis of
race, violated the right of Black children to an equal educational opportunity guaranteed by the Equal Protection Clause of
the Fourteenth Amendment.[61] In so ruling, the Court made the
following, often quoted, statement about the importance of
education:

> Today, education is perhaps the most
> important function of state and local
> governments. Compulsory attendance laws
> and the great expenditures for education
> both demonstrate our recognition of the
> importance of education to our democratic
> society ... In these days it is doubtful
> than any child may reasonably be expected
> to succeed in life if he is denied the
> opportunity of an education.[62]
> (emphasis added)

The Court then concluded that "such an opportunity, where the
state has undertaken to provide it, must be made available to
all on equal terms"[63] and is effectively denied to Black children
by a state sanctioned, racially segregated public school
system.[64]

The importance of Brown for purposes of this
analysis is that it did not expressly hold that education was a
"fundamental right" under the Constitution, but rather, that

---

[60] 347 U.S. 483 (1954).

[61] Id. at 493, 495.

[62] Id.

[63] Id.

[64] Id.

education was a sufficiently important interest, as evidenced in part by compulsory attendance laws, that the Black plaintiffs were entitled to the application of the Equal Protection Clause. Thus, in terms of the preceding equal protection analysis, the Court did not state whether the primary basis for its finding of a violation of the Equal Protection Clause was the importance of education as a "fundamental right" or the existence of a classification based on race.

It should be noted, however, that it was not until after Brown that the sophisticated equal protection analysis described above, with its dual system of review, was regularly applied by the Court with the precision which was lacking in Brown. The decision in Brown, in itself, therefore, is inconclusive with respect to the issue of whether the Court considered education to be a "fundamental right" for purposes of equal protection analysis.

c. San Antonio Independent School District v. Rodriguez

In a recent decision, San Antonio Independent School District v. Rodriguez,[65] the Court discussed at some length, the status of education under the Constitution. Rodriguez was a class action brought on behalf of Texas school children who were members of poor families and minority group families residing in school districts having a low property tax base. The appellees (school children) challenged reliance by the

[65] 411 U.S. 1 (1973).

Texas school finance system on local property taxation. They
claimed that the system favored children from more affluent
families and violated the Equal Protection Clause because of
substantial interdistrict inequalities in per-pupil expendi-
ture resulting from the difference in value of assessable
property among school districts in Texas. The appellees
further asserted that because classifications based on wealth
are "suspect" and because education is a "fundamental interest",
the Court should apply the "strict scrutiny" test and require
Texas to demonstrate that its school finance system was "necessary" to the accomplishment of a "compelling state interest".[66]

The Court held that the "strict scrutiny" test was not
applicable for two reasons. First, the Court said that it could
find no definable, discriminated-against class. Therefore, the
Court did not reach the issue of whether wealth "was a suspect
classification" since, in the Court's view, there was no definable class of poor people who were being classified to their
disadvantage.[67] Second, the Court, in citing Brown v. Board of
Education as a case based upon a "suspect classification" (race),
held that education, although important enough to require the
application of the Equal Protection Clause, is not a "fundamental
interest", because it was neither explicitly nor implicitly

---

[66]Id. at 17.

[67]Id. at 22-25.

protected by the Constitution.[68]

The Court concluded, therefore, that the "strict scrutiny" standard did not apply and Texas was required only to demonstrate that its finance system bore a "rational relationship to a legitimate state purpose".[69] Applying this test, the Court concluded that the Texas school finance system encouraged local participation in and local control of the schools of each school district and that this goal of local participation and control constituted a "rational basis" for the system.[70] The Court, therefore, held that there was no violation of the Equal Protection Clause.[71]

d. Commentary on Brown and Rodriguez

In Brown, the Court found that education was a very important interest, as evidenced in part by the pervasiveness, throughout the nation, of compulsory attendance laws. Rodriguez, on the other hand, held that the mere importance of education under state law, although sufficient to require application of the Equal Protection Clause, was not sufficient for

---

[68]Id. at 37. The Court's opinion on this issue is rendered ambiguous by its dictum concerning the relationship of education to First Amendment rights where the Court said: "Even if it was conceded that some identifiable quantum of education is a constitutionally protected prerequisite to the meaningful exercise of either right (the right of free speech and the right to vote), we have no indication that the present levels of educational expenditures in Texas provide an education that falls short." The Court thus seemed to suggest that there might be merit to the claim of education as a fundamental right, if the alleged denial of an educational opportunity was total rather than comparative. Id. at 36.

[69]Id. at 44.

[70]Id. at 54-55.

[71]Id. at 55.

a finding that education was a Constitutional right. Such a finding, said the Rodriguez Court, could only be made if the Constitution contained an explicit or implicit reference to the importance
of education. The Court concluded that it could not find any such
reference in this case, but indicated in what appears to a contra-
dictory dictum that it might take a different view in a case where
there was a total denial of an educational opportunity.

On the issue of suspect classification, Brown clearly
stands for the proposition, which is now well accepted, that
classifications based on racial grounds are "suspect" under the
Equal Protection Clause. Rodriguez,however, did not reach the
issue of whether classifications on the basis of wealth or minority
status other than racial status are similarly "suspect". This
issue, therefore, remains unsolved.

In conclusion, for purposes of equal protection
analysis, it is clear that the mere existence of compulsory attendance laws does not elevate education to the level of a fundamental
interest. Such elevation, the Court has said, must have a
Constitutional rather than a state law basis.

2. Cases Under the Due Process Clause

    a. Introduction

The Due Process Clause of the Fourteenth Amendment provides that no state shall "deprive any person of life,
liberty or property, without due process of law". In the context
of this subsection, "due process" will be understood to refer to
"procedural rights" rather than to the substantive

rights discussed earlier.[72]   Procedurally, the Due Process Clause
requires the application of fair procedures before certain important interests of individuals can be denied by the state.
Some of the most basic traditional elements of procedural due
process are the right to notice of the proposed denial, the right
to a hearing on that proposed denial and the right to be represented by counsel once a denial of rights is being threatened.
As in the case of the Equal Protection Clause, the Due Process
Clause will be applied only where the interest threatened with
denial is of sufficient importance in the eyes of the Court.

The following discussion will touch upon the content of
these procedural protections, but it will mainly focus upon
the status of education as "liberty or property" under the Due
Process Clause, with particular reference to the relevance of
compulsory attendance laws to a determination of that status.
It will also compare education as a protected interest under the
Due Process Clause with the status of education in the context
of the Equal Protection Clause. Because the Supreme Court has
recently discussed these issues in the landmark case of Goss v.
Lopez,[73] this case will receive extended discussion and will
be the basis for the due process analysis.

b. Goss v. Lopez

In Goss, several students were suspended under
the authority of an Ohio statute that empowered the principal of
a public school to suspend a pupil for misconduct for not more

---

[72] See earlier discussion of "substantive due process" at note 14.

[73] 419 U.S. 565 (1975).

than ten days. While it required the principal to give written
notice of the reasons for the suspension to the student's parents or guardian or to the local Board of Education within
twenty-four hours of the suspension, the Ohio law provided for
no hearing before or after the suspension.[74] The students
filed suit in federal district court challenging the suspensions on the grounds that the lack of a hearing violated their
rights to procedural fairness guaranteed by the Due Process
Clause of the Fourteenth Amendment. The federal district court
ruled in favor of the students, and the administrators who
were enforcing the rule appealed to the Supreme Court.

The Court began its opinion first, by observing
that the Ohio Education Code required the state to provide a
free education to all children between the ages of six and twenty-
one.[75] The Court then noted that the Code also empowered the
principal of an Ohio public school to suspend a pupil for "misconduct" for up to ten days or to expel the student.[76]

The Court next addressed the argument of the appellants
(school administrators) that "because there is no constitutional
right to an education at public expense, the Due Process Clause
does not protect against explusions from the public school system".
The Court responded to this argument, based upon its recent decision in Rodriguez, by concluding that the "interests in liberty

---

[74]Id. at 567.

[75]Id.

[76]Id.

and property" protected by the Due Process Clause are different
from those considered in Rodriquez in that they are "not created
by the Constitution.[77] Rather they are created and their dimensions are defined by an independent source such as state statutes
or rules entitling the citizen to certain benefits. Board of
Regents v. Roth, 408 U.S. 564, 92 S.Ct. 2701, 2709, 33 L.Ed.
548 (1972)."[78] Referring back to the state statute giving
persons between the ages of six and twenty-one a right to a free
education, and to the state compulsory attendance law, the Court
held that the students had a "property right" within the meaning
of the Due Process Clause.[79] The Court then concluded by stating
that the state, having conferred this property right, could not
withdraw it for misconduct "without adherence to the minimum
procedures required by that clause".[80] This obligation of the
state, said the Court, exists despite the fact that "Ohio may not
be constitutionally obligated to establish and maintain a public
school system".[81]

The Court then responded to the argument of the appellants
that suspensions of less than ten days were so insubstantial that
they did not constitute the kind of "severe detriment or grievous

---

[77] Id. at 572-73.

[78] Id. at 573.

[79] Id. at 573.

[80] Id at 574.

[81] Id.

loss" which would entitle them to the protection of the Due
Process Clause. The Court rejected this argument quoting the
well-known statement in <u>Brown v. Board of Education</u> that "education is perhaps the most important function of state and
local governments."[82]

The Court indicated that the purpose of the Due Process
Clause, in the context of the case, however, was to protect a
student from an "unwarranted" suspension and not to "shield him
from suspensions properly imposed."[83] This qualification of its
decision was noted again at the end of its opinion where the
Court stated that if a child were suspended for more than ten
days or expelled "<u>for the remainder of the school term, or per-
manently</u>", (emphasis added) some more formal procedures might
be necessary than those required for short term suspensions.[84]
The Court, thus, made it clear that the kind of right involved
was not the right to an education, but the right to procedural
fairness if an educational opportunity was to be denied by school
officials.

The Court concluded its opinion by holding that the Due
Process Clause did not require the full panoply of traditional
procedural rights to be accorded to a student who was suspended
for a period of less than ten days.[85] The Court stated, however,

---

[82] <u>Id.</u> at 576.

[83] <u>Id.</u> at 579.

[84] <u>Id.</u> at 584.

[85] <u>Id.</u> at 583.

that certain minimum rights were required and that those rights
were the right to notice of the reason for the suspension and
to an opportunity to respond to that reason, both given prior
to the suspension except in emergency situations where they
could be given within a reasonable time after the suspensions.[86]

The opinion in <u>Goss</u> is particularly important in
the context of this analysis because it relied upon the Ohio
compulsory attendance law as a partial basis for its holding
that attendance at a public elementary or secondary school is
a "property right" within the meaning of the Due Process Clause.
This is one of the few times that the Supreme Court has cited a
compulsory attendance law so directly as a basis for conferring a
Constitutional right.

This conclusion must be qualified, however, by
the fact that the opinion in <u>Goss</u> is unclear regarding the degree
to which it relies on the compulsory attendance law for this
purpose, since the opinion also makes reference to Ohio's "right
to education" statute. Thus, it is difficult to determine if
the Court would have found an interest in "property"
to exist under the Due Process Clause, if the existence of such
an interest had been premised solely on the compulsory attendance
law, rather than on that law as well as the "right to education"
law.

3. <u>Mills, PARC and Rockefeller</u>

Both the "right to an education" within the

---

[86]<u>Id.</u> at 583-84.

substantive meaning discussed in Rodriguez and the "right to
an education" as an interest in liberty or property involving
the procedural protections of the Due Process Clause discussed
in Goss, were at issue in those cases involving the attempt by
public school officials to exclude children from school on the
basis of "mental, physical or emotional" disabilities. The
Supreme Court has not yet ruled on the nature of any "right to
education" within this context, but several opinions of federal
district courts have been reported. The earliest and best
known of these decisions were in the cases of Pennsylvania Association of Retarded Children (PARC) v. Commonwealth of Pennsylvania,[87] and Mills v. District of Columbia Board of Education.[88]
Plaintiffs in both cases filed suit challenging the exclusion of
handicapped children from a publicly-financed education, alleging
that such exclusion, based, in part, on the exemptions for physical, mental and emotional disability contained in the compulsory
attendance laws and other related statutes, violated the Due
Process and Equal Protection Clauses of the Fourteenth Amendment.

The Pennsylvania case was a class action brought on behalf
of all mentally retarded children in Pennsylvania challenging the
Pennsylvania statutes which permitted the exclusion from any
publicly-financed education of mentally retarded children who
were deemed uneducable or "unable to profit" from public school

---

[87]There were two separate orders in the PARC case; one at 334 F.
Supp. 1257 (E.D.Pa., 1971) PARC I); and one at 343 F. Supp. 279
(E.D.Pa., 1972) (PARC II).

[88]348 F. Supp. 866 (D.D.C. 1972).

attendance. The federal court did not formally "decide" the
Constitutional issues raised because the parties agreed on a
settlement which the Court approved.[89] The consent decree
stated that expert testimony in the case "indicated that all
mentally retarded persons are capable of benefitting from a
program of education and training".[90] It then said that
Pennsylvania, "having undertaken to provide a free public education to all of its children", could "not deny any mentally
retarded child access to a free public program of education
and training."[91] Finally, it required the application of extensive due process procedures before a handicapped child could be
placed or denied placement into an educational program.[92]

The second case, Mills v. District of Columbia Board of
Education,[93] was a class action brought on behalf of seven handicapped children of school age in the District of Columbia, seeking an injunction against the Board of Education to prevent it
from denying to them a publicly-financed education either in the
public schools or elsewhere. As in the Pennsylvania case, the
parties consented to the final decree, so the Court was not
required to "decide" the case.[94] The Court, however, did set

---

[89]The Court issued a "consent decree" which is an agreement of the
parties which has been approved by the court.

[90]334 F. Supp. 1257 at 1259.

[91]Id.

[92]343 F. Supp. at 303-306.

[93]348 F. Supp. 866 (D.D.C. 1972).

[94]Supra, note 89.

forth its legal basis for approving the order agreed to by the parties.[95]

First, the Court interpreted the relevant statutory provisions of the District of Columbia and the related rules and regulations to require some form of publicly-supported education for all children of compulsory attendance age.[96] Then the Court went on to conclude that if the equal protection requirements of the Fifth Amendment guaranteed to poor children an educational opportunity equal to that of more affluent children, as was found in a recent case in the District of Columbia,[97]

> A fortiori, the defendants' conduct here,
> denying plaintiffs and their class not just
> an equal publicly supported education but
> all publicly supported education while pro-
> viding such education to other children, is
> violative of the Due Process Clause.[98]

As in PARC, the consent decree contained elaborate proce-dures which had to be followed before a child could be transferred into or out of an educational placement. As in PARC, the Court based these protections on the requirements of the Due Process Clause of the Fourteenth Amendment.

In a case subsequent to both PARC and Mills, New York State Association for Retarded Children, Inc. v. Rockefeller,[99]

---

[95] 348 F. Supp. 866 at 874-876.

[96] Id. at 874.

[97] Id. at 874.

[98] Id.

[99] 357 F. Supp. 725 (1973).

however, a New York federal district court refused to find a
substantive Constitutional basis for the claims of institutionalized mentally retarded children who were being denied an
education. The Court, citing the decision of the Supreme
Court in San Antonio Independent School District v. Rodriguez,
concluded that:

> It would appear that if there is no consti-
> tutional infirmity in a system in which the
> state permits children of normal mental
> ability to receive a varying quality of edu-
> cation, a state is not constitutionally re-
> quired to provide the mentally retarded with
> a certain level of special education.[100]

The court went on to distinguish both Mills and PARC.
It found Mills inapplicable for three reasons: first, because
Hobson v. Hansen, on which it relied, was no longer viable with
respect to its holding on economic discrimination because of the
later Supreme Court decision in Rodriguez;[101] second, because
Mills was based on the District of Columbia Code and the board
of education regulations as well as on the Due Process Clause;[102]
and third, because the defendants in Mills had conceded that
they were under a duty to provide an educational opportunity to
the plaintiffs.[103] The Court distinguished the PARC case only
for this third reason. The Court then concluded that the "plaintiff's constitutional rights must rest on protection from harm

---

[100] Id. at 763.

[101] Id.

[102] Id.

[103] Id.

and not on a right to treatment or habilitation".[104]

a. Commentary on Mills, PARC and Rockefeller

The three cases just discussed provide a conflic-
ting and questionable basis on which to draw any clear conclusions
on the meaning of " a right to an education" within the context
of actions by public school officials who attempt to exclude children from school on the basis of "mental, physical or emotional" disabilities. Certainly, the prospect of exclusion from school for
whatever reason would seem to involve the procedural protections
outlined in Goss, and, in fact, the courts in both PARC and Mills
required extensive procedures to be applied.

The difficult question is whether the Court, in
light of its holding in Rodriguez would find that exclusion of a
child from school on the basis of a "mental, physical or emotional"
disability, required the application of the "strict scrutiny" standard under the Equal Protection Clause which the Court refused to
apply in Rodriguez.[105] This, of course, would depend on whether
the Court would find that a classification based on a "physical,
mental or emotional" disability was "suspect" or whether the Court
would find the denial of all education for reasons of "physical,
mental or emotional" disability was a denial of a fundamental right
protected by the Constitution.[106]

---

[104]Id. at 764.

[105]See note 69, supra.

[106]See discussion of this issue supra.

From the perspective of this analysis of compulsory attendance provisions, it is important to focus upon the role of the compulsory attendance laws and their exemptions for "physical, mental or emotional" disability to the ultimate outcome of those cases. This role is somewhat ambiguous in Mills but is clear in PARC.

In Mills, the Court began its opinion by quoting the provisions of the compulsory attendance law.[107] It then concluded that the existence of the compulsory attendance law imposed an obligation on the District of Columbia to provide an educational opportunity for all school age children. In this regard, the court said the following:

> The court need not belabor the fact that requiring parents to see that their children attend school under pain of criminal penalties presupposes that an educational opportunity will be made available to the children. The Board of Education is required to make such opportunity available.[108]

The court then, however, cited various rules of the board of education providing for the education of school age children in the District of Columbia and concluded, without stating the precise basis for this conclusion, that "the Board of Education has an obligation to provide whatever specialized instruction that will benefit the child." [109] Thus, the decision of the court is ambiguous with regard to the extent to which the compulsory attendance law was the basis for its conclusion that

---

[107] 348 F. Supp. at 866.

[108] Id. at 867.

[109] Id.

all school age children in the District of Columbia had the right to an educational opportunity.

In _PARC_, the place of the compulsory attendance law in the court's decision was clarified by the consent decree. The decree provided the following:

> The Attorney General agrees to issue an opinion declaring that Section 1326 (the compulsory attendance law) means only that parents of a child have a compulsory duty while the child is between eight and seventeen years of age to assure his attendance in a program of education and training; and section 1326 does not limit the ages between which a child must be granted access to a free, public program of education and training. Defendants are bound by Section 1301 of the School Code of 1949, 24 Stat. Sec. 13-1801 to provide free public education to all children six to twenty-one years of age.[110]

Thus, the consent decree made clear what was left ambiguous in _Mills_ - that the compulsory attendance law did not define a child's right to an education, but merely created an attendance obligation.

4. Federal Cases Which Concern the Substantive Rights of Students in the Public School System (Other Than the Right to Education, Itself).

The cases discussed in this part are those arising from the collision of the rights of students, primarily under the First Amendment, and the recognized authority of school administrators to maintain order and control in the public schools. These cases are relevant to the analysis of compulsory attendance laws first because some of them refer to the compulsory attendance laws as part of the articulated basis for their decisions;

---

[110]343 F. Supp. 279 at 309.

and second, because of the necessity in this analysis of ex-
ploring the possibility that if compulsory attendance provision were repealed, these cases would no longer arise.

    a. Meyer v. Nebraska

    In Meyer v. Nebraska,[111] the Court reviewed the
criminal conviction of a public school teacher who was convicted for teaching the German language to a ten-year-old child
in violation of a statute which made it a crime for any person
to teach any language other than English to children who have
not passed the eighth grade. In reversing the conviction, the
Court began by holding that "liberty" within the meaning of the
Due Process Clause encompassed "the right of the individual to
contract (and) to engage in any of the common occupations of
life . . ."[112] The Court concluded, therefore, that the right
of the convicted teacher to "engage in his occupation" was
within this meaning of "liberty" and could not constitutionally
be denied "by legislative action which is arbitrary or without
reasonable relation to some purpose within the competency of
the state to effect."[113]

    The Court made it clear that the issue involved was
not the "power of the state to compel attendance at some school
and to make reasonable regulations for all schools, including a
requirement that they shall give instruction in English . . ."[114]

---

[111] 262 U.S. 390 (1923).

[112] Id. at 399.

[113] Id. at 403.

[114] Id. at 402.

Nor, said the Court, was the issue the state's power to prescribe a curriculum for institutions which it supports..."[115]
Rather, the Court held that the issue was the reasonableness of
the state regulation and that, because there was no reasonable
basis shown on which the teaching of German could be prohibited,
the criminal "statute, as applied, is arbitrary and without reasonable relation to any end within the competency of the state..."[116]
The Court concluded, therefore, that the statute violated the
rights of the teacher under the Due Process Clause of the Fourteenth Amendment. By implication, the Court also concluded that
the absence of the compulsory attendance law would not have changed
the result in the case.

b. West Virginia State Board of Education v. Barnette

In a later case, West Virginia State Board of Education v. Barnette,[117] the West Virginia Board of Education required, pursuant to a state statute, that the salute to the flag
be "a regular part of the program of activities in the public
schools..." and that "all teachers and pupils shall be required
to participate in the salute honoring the nation, represented by
the flag". Several children who were Jehovah's Witnesses were suspended from school for refusing to salute the flag, and their parents
sought out an injunction in the federal district court against
the application of the statute and rule. The district court granted
the injunction and the Board of Education appealed to the Supreme
Court.

In affirming the decision of the district court, the

---

[115] Id.
[116] Id. at 403.
[117] 319 U.S. 624 (1943).

Supreme Court first ruled that the fact that "attendance is

not optional" was essential to the parents' case since if at-

tendance were optional, the case would come within the rule

of Hamilton v. Regents.[118] In restating its holding in Hamil-

ton, the Court said that:

> where a state, without compelling attendance,
> extends college facilities to pupils who volun-
> tarily enroll, it may prescribe military train-
> ing as part of the course without offense to the
> Constitution.[119]

The Court thus concluded that the fact of compelled attendance

at public school was critical to its ruling since what was

involved was the:

> validity of the asserted power (of the state)
> to force an American citizen publicly to
> profess any statement of belief or to engage
> in any ceremony of assent to one . . .[120]

In holding that the state's enforcement of the flag

salute requirement violated the First Amendment, the Court made

it clear that it was not basing its decision on the Free Exer-

cise Clause but, rather, on the freedom of speech protected by

the First Amendment.[121]

    c. Tinker v. Des Moines Independent School District

In a more recent case, Tinker v. Des Moines Indepen-

dent School District,[122] the Court struck down a school rule which

---

[118] Id. at 631.

[119] Id.

[120] Id. at 634.

[121] Id. at 634-635.

[122] 393 U.S. 503 (1969).

provided for the suspension of students who wore black arm
bands to school. The suspended student in this case wore a
black arm band to school as a protest against United States involvement in the Vietnam War.

The Court, in citing Meyer[123] and Barnette,[124] held
that teachers and students in public elementary and secondary
schools do not "shed their constitutional rights to freedom
of speech or expression at the schoolhouse gate."[125] In providing a guideline for types of "expression" which may not be
protected by the First Amendment, the Court said:

> The problem posed by the present case does
> not relate to regulations of the length of
> skirts or the type of clothing, to hair
> style, or deportment . . . It does not con-
> cern aggressive, disruptive action or even
> group demonstrations. Our problem involves
> direct, primary first amendment rights akin
> to "pure speech"[126]

In striking down the challenged rule, the Court
issued a broad statement concerning the authority of the public
schools in the area of speech:

> In our system, state-operated schools may
> not be enclaves of totalitarianism. School
> officials do not possess absolute authority
> over their students . . . In our system,

(cont.)

---

[123]See note 111.

[124]See note 117.

[125]393 U.S. 503 at 506.

[126]Id. at 507.

> students may not be regarded as closed
> circuit recipients of only that which the
> States choose to communicate. They made not
> be confined to the expression of those senti-
> ments that are officially praised. In the
> absence of a specific showing of constitu-
> tionally valid reasons to regulate their
> speech, students are entitled to freedom
> of expression of their views...[127]

The Court did not mention the compulsory attendance laws. It did,

however, cite the Barnette[128] case as one of the principal precedents

for its decision. It is reasonable to infer, therefore, that the

existence of compelled attendance at school played some part in

the Court's opinion.

d. Cases Involving Other Substantive Rights

In addition to the three cases just discussed, the

Court recently affirmed, without opinion,[129] the decision of a

lower federal court which held that it was Constitutional for a

public school system to administer corporal punishment to a stu-

dent, despite parental objection.[130] In another area, where the

Supreme Court has not ruled specifically on the rights of public

school students[131], the lower federal courts have issued conflicting

---

[127] Id. at 511.

[128] See note 117.

[129] The effect of an affirmance by the Supreme Court without an opinion indicates that the Court has approved of the result in the case
without necessarily concurring in the reasoning of the decision below.

[130] 96 S. Ct. 210 (1975). The decision of the lower court was in
Baker v. Owen, 395 F. Supp. 294 (D.C. M.D. N.C. 1975).

[131] See Richards v. Thurston, 304 F. Supp. 449 (D. Mass. 1967), aff'd.
424 F. 2d 1281 (1st Cir. 1970), which struck down a school rule
regulating hair style; but, see the recent contrary decision of the
Supreme Court relating to police: Kelley v. Johnson, 44 U.S.L.W.
4469 (4/5/76).

opinions on the regulation of hair style. In addition, federal courts have struck down exclusions of students from school for being pregnant[132] or for being a parent.[133] In none of these cases was the existence for the compulsory attendance law part of the expressed reason for the holding.

     e. Commentary on Meyer, Barnette, Tinker and the Other Cases Involving the Substantive Rights of Students in the Public Schools.

Of the cases discussed in this section, only in the Barnette case was the compulsory attendance statute part of the articulated basis for the holding of the Court. In Barnette, the Court strongly suggested that if it were not for the fact of compelled attendance the case might be decided the opposite way. One aspect of Barnette which is unclear is the exact nature of the compulsion. Since Barnette post-dated Pierce, it would appear that, from a legal perspective, attendance at public school could not have been compelled. It is unclear, therefore, why the Court assumed that attendance in public school was compelled unless the Court was taking notice of the fact that most parents do not have the financial means to send their children to an alternative to public school such as a private school.

III.   Conclusion

The opinions of the Supreme Court in Pierce, Tokushige and Yoder leave unclear the modern position of the Court with respect to the kind and degree of flexibility required by the Constitution in the learning arrangements authorized by state compulsory laws. The

---

[132] Ordway v. Hargraves, 323 F. Supp. 1155 (D.C., Mass. 1971).

[133] Perry v. Granada Independent School District, 300 F. Supp. 748 (N.D. Miss. 1969

first issue which requires clarification is the modern meaning of
Pierce. Specifically, since the Court has apparently repudiated the "substantive due process" standard applied in Pierce,
what modern standard will replace it? Will the rights of parents asserted in Pierce be viewed as having their basis in the
Due Process clause of the Fourteenth Amendment or in the First
Amendment? If the basis is the First Amendment, will it be viewed
as a case about the "free exercise" of religion or about "free speech"?

A related issue is the definition of what constitutes
a valid "free exercise claim" within the meaning of Yoder?
What will the Court consider to be a sincere and "deeply
rooted" religious belief deserving of an exemption from compulsory attendance? Will the Court find in some cases that, although the religious belief is "sincere" and "deeply rooted",
the lifestyle presented does not provide the kind of "education"
provided by that of the Amish, and that, therefore, an alternative learning arrangement is required before the Court can grant
a religious exemption from compulsory attendance? As the Court
answers these questions about Pierce and Yoder, the limits of
the Constitutionally mandated alternative learning arrangements
or exceptions under compulsory attendance laws will be rendered
clearer.

The extent of public aid which will be permitted by the
Constitution to enable parents to make the choice of private school
and other non-public school learning arrangements a reality for many
parents, is an issue which has been viewed by the Court as one

requiring it to maintain a neutral stance between the Establishment Clause, on the one hand, which requires a restrictive
approach, and the Free Exercise Clause, on the other hand,
which requires that children attending sectarian schools
not be totally deprived of the public benefits made available
to all children. So long as the issue of public aid to private
schools is viewed in this manner, i.e., as being an issue about
the state and religion, substantial amounts of public aid will
probably not be available to private schools. Thus, a practical
limit on parental choice of non-public school alternatives will
continue in effect.

In a different area of Constitutional law, the compulsory
attendance laws have received some attention in the current
discussion about the existence or non-existence of a Constitutional right to an education. For example, in analyzing the
status of education under the Equal Protection Clause, the
Court has said that the importance of education evidenced by
state laws requiring attendance and requiring public funding of
a public school system is irrelevant to the issue of whether
education is a "fundamental right" under the United States Constitution. The Court has said that the Constitution and not
state law must be the basis for deciding that issue.

On the other hand, in Goss, the Court has also said that
state laws providing for the right to attend school and requiring
attendance at school are very relevant in determining whether
education is a "liberty" or "property" right sufficient in
importance to involve the procedural protection of the Due

Process Clause, where, through the suspension process, a denial
of an educational opportunity is being threatened by the state.
It is unclear from the Court's opinion in Goss, however, whether
the existence of a state compulsory attendance law, absent a
"right to education" statute, would have been a sufficient
basis for the Court to find that education was an interest in
"liberty" or "property" of sufficient importance to involve
the application of the Due Process Clause. For this reason, the
importance of the compulsory attendance laws in the framework
of due process analysis is unclear.

Several lower federal courts have mentioned the compulsory
attendance laws in approving consent decrees providing for the
education of handicapped children. The decree in the PARC case
provides the clearest analysis by making the distinction between
the obligation to attend school, contained in the compulsory attendance law, and the state's duty to provide an educational
opportunity, concluding that such duty does not derive from the
compulsory attendance law, but does flow from "right to education"
statutes and the Equal Protection Clause of the Fourteenth Amendment. Thus, the court in PARC did not permit the Pennsylvania
school systems to limit their obligation to educate to children
within the age range contained in the compulsory attendance law.

The cases arising under the First Amendment and the cases
discussing other related substantive rights of students probably
would not have been decided differently in the absence of a compulsory attendance law. The one exception to this general rule is West
Virginia State Board of Education v. Barnette where the Court seemed

to consider the existence of the compulsory attendance law to be
a necessary condition for its finding of an infringement of First
Amendment rights. Presumably, this is because the complained of
violation, even though committed by the state, would have been
less serious, in the Court's view, if the children in question
could have had the option of leaving school.

This reasoning of the Court, however, seems to be completely at odds with all of its other decisions in the First
Amendment area, since in those cases the facts of state action
and of the infringement on free speech or the free exercise of
religion were sufficient for the Court to decide whether the
infringement was justified by a compelling state interest. Except in Barnette and in the Hamilton case cited in Barnette, the
Court has taken the position that absent a showing of a compelling
state interest, the infringement of First Amendment rights would
be struck down regardless of whether the person whose rights
were violated had the opportunity of asserting those rights
elsewhere. Thus, the reasoning in Barnette does not seem to
square with the usual standards of decision by the Court in
the First Amendment area. For this reason, the reference to compulsory attendance in Barnette is somewhat of an anomoly.

Putting aside the unusual reasoning of the Court in
Barnette, it is probably accurate to conclude that the reason
why compulsory attendance laws receive so little attention in
the decisions of the federal courts in the area of elementary
and secondary education is that these cases raise issues about

the denial of rights, while the compulsory attendance laws do not
confer any rights, but, instead, create an obligation on the
part of parents and children. It is not surprising, therefore,
that the principal cases discussing compulsory attendance are
those where the obligation is being challenged on the basis of
the denial of rights found in the First and Fourteenth Amendment.
It is almost nonsensical, on the other hand, to talk about the
"denial of an obligation" as violating any right.

Accepting this conclusion, it is also reasonable to
assume that there are two reasons why compulsory attendance
laws are mentioned at all in federal court decisions where the
constitutionality of those laws is not directly at issue. The
first is to stress the importance of education as a state function,
by presenting the cumulative effect of various state education
laws, including the compulsory attendance laws. This is particularly significant in a case such as Goss v. Lopez, where
the Court stressed that the right or privilege conferred by
the state had to be of a certain level of importance before it
would fall within the definition of "liberty" or "property".
protected by the Fourteenth Amendment.

The second reason is because the difference between the state
creating an obligation and the state conferring a right is
frequently blurred so that some courts use the terms "compulsory
attendance" and the "right to an education" synonomously. While
it is true that the fact of compelled attendance may have caused
policy makers to decide that the state should provide a publicly

financed educational opportunity to enable parents to satisfy that requirement, this decision is not legally required by the terms of compulsory attendance laws. This decision to provide a publicly financed educational opportunity for all children of certain ages is compelled in most jurisdictions by a state constitutional or statutory provision which requires the state to provide such an opportunity.

In conclusion, the existence of compulsory attendance laws has been a relatively minor factor in the articulated basis for the decisions of the Supreme Court and the lower federal courts in the area of elementary and secondary education, outside of these few cases where a compulsory attendance law, itself, was being challenged. The next chapter will discuss the implications of this conclusion in relation to possible amendment or repeal of compulsory attendance laws.

12. THE IMPLICATIONS OF PROPOSED CHANGES IN COMPULSORY ATTENDANCE LAWS

I.   Introduction

The preceding chapters have described the history and
current legal status of the various state systems of compulsory
attendance laws, the related state and federal systems of child
labor laws and the underlying constitutional bases of these systems. The principal conclusions of those chapters appear at the
end of each and, in summary form, in the Introduction to this
volume.

Throughout the history of the development of compulsory
attendance laws and currently, those laws have been the subject
of a substantial amount of criticism and the focus of various
proposals to modify the manner in which elementary and secondary
education has been provided in the United States. Some educational theorists consider the idea of compulsory attendance, in
itself, to be without any merit and, thus, propose repeal of compulsory attendance laws. Usually, such proposals are part of a
larger scheme to drastically reform elementary and secondary education. Other theorists and reformers focus upon the manner in
which the compulsory attendance laws limit the choice of an educational program or of an employment opportunity and propose that
those laws be amended to expand the educational and employment

choices of children and youth subject to their provisions.

This chapter will review the criticisms of and proposals for change in compulsory attendance laws made by both categories of educational reformers, the broader reform proposals of which those criticisms are a part, and the changes which are recommended as solutions to the perceived problems. The chapter will then discuss the changes in the legal structure which would be necessary to effectuate these recommendations. It will conclude with a commentary on the role of compulsory attendance laws in the debate over proposed reform of elementary and secondary education.

II.   Advocates of Repeal of Compulsory Attendance Laws

   A.   The Basic Criticisms

Aside from segregationists who advocate repeal of compulsory attendance laws as a way to avoid court-ordered racial integration,[1] the principal critics who seek repeal are educational theorists who find compulsory attendance laws to be a primary underpinning of an educationally bankrupt system of public elementary and secondary education.[2] A typical proponent of this point of

---

[1] See discussion in Chapter 2, supra.

[2] See, generally: Goodman, Paul, Compulsory Mis-Education, (N.Y., Horizon Press) 1964; Holt, John, Why Children Fail, (N.Y., Dell Publishing Co.) 1964; Postman, Neil, "My Ivan Illich Problem", Social Policy, January/February 1972, Vol. 3.

view is Judson Jerome:

> Compulsory education, like compulsory love, is a con-
> tradiction in terms. Where there is compulsion, a person
> can learn, but he learns mostly about compulsion rather
> than reading, writing or arithmetic. He learns to be do-
> cile or rebellious; he learns to sit still for long hours
> without thinking; he learns to fear or hate or be sicken-
> ingly dependent upon authority figures. Surely that ele-
> ment of education must go. If schools remain (be they
> "free" schools or traditional ones), the first business
> of the day should be to establish clearly and unequivo-
> cably that anyone is free to leave - the classroom, the
> school - whenever he wishes, and that there are real al-
> ternatives, places to go, things to do that are safe,
> stimulating, authorized.[3]

Most proposals for total reform of elementary and secondary education begin with some version of this position. Generally, these
reform proposals obscure the differences between compelled attendance, compelled course requirements and other compulsory features
of the public school system and simply oppose any form of compulsion. Thus, it is difficult to determine the position of this
group of educational reformers on each of the different aspects of
the compulsory system of education, or, for that matter, to determine if they even recognize that the different compulsory aspects
are separable, discrete entities unto themselves. Because these
reformers are generally viewed as among the most vociferous critics
of compulsory attendance, however, their views merit careful consideration.

Most of the critics who propose repeal of one or more of
the compulsory features of the public school system base their

---

[3]Jerome Judson, "After Illich, What?", Social Policy, March/April
1972, Vol. 3.

proposal on the proposition that schools have become totally irrelevant to the lives of today's young people.[4] In general terms, this
gap is characterized as one between,

> the older idea of education as social control and the
> newer idea of education as a liberator. In the last
> decade, the desire for liberation and for the develop-
> ment of healthy, integrated personalities has come into
> direct conflict with the older survival-oriented con-
> cept of education as credentials, reality principle and,
> an acculturation process.[5]

Critics claim that what is needed from educational systems
today is relevancy, environmental perspectives, personal growth,
freedom, and happiness; and what schools teach is vocational training, literacy, discipline, adaptation to cultural and social norms
and acculturation to the "heritage of a post-Renaissance Society".[6]

This view is echoed and re-echoed throughout the literature
over the past ten years. For example, Paul Goodman, in 1964, took
issue with what he termed the "mass superstitition" that "the schools
provide the best preparation for everybody for a complicated world;
are the logical haven for unemployed youth, can equalize opportunity
for the underprivileged, administer research in all fields and be
the indispensible mentor for creativity, business practice, social
work, mental hygiene, genuine literacy..."[7]

---

[4] See, e.g., Goodman, Paul, Compulsory Mis-Education, Chapter 1.

[5] Schwartz, Barry N., Ed. Affirmative Education, Chapter 1.

[6] Id., p. 2. Schwartz uses "post-Renaissance society" to refer to
society as affected by growth of cities, industrialization, the
Protestant Reformation, the invention of the cannon, etc., "a world
in which change is an ever-present feature". .

[7] Goodman, Paul, Compulsory Mis-Education, p. 10.

Goodman also criticizes the compulsory nature of the school
system, which he says follows logically if one adheres to the superstition.[8] That it is merely superstition, is evidenced, in his view,
by what happens to children forced to attend school. Because the
emphasis is on credentials, on grades and memorization of the
"right" answers, children lose their innate curiosity and desire
to learn and in the final analysis "[e]very kind of youth is hurt.
The bright, but unacademic can...perform; but the performance is
inauthentic and there is a pitiful loss of what they could be doing
with intelligence, grace and force. The average are anxious. The
slow are humiliated. But also the authentically scholarly are
ruined. Bribed and pampered, they forget the meaning of their
gifts."[9]

In 1970 a report commissioned by the Carnegie Corporation[10]
came to the same conclusions as Goodman. The three and a half
year study of the educational system in this country concluded
that not only do most schools fail to educate children adequately,
they are also "oppressive", "grim" and "joyless".[11] In its findings
about present schools, the report found that schools are preoccupied
with order, control and routine for the sake of routine, that students are subjugated by the schools; that by practicing systematic

---

[8] Id.

[9] Id., p. 181.

[10] Silberman, Charles E., Crisis in the Classroom, (N.Y., Random
House) 1970.

[11] Id.

repression, the schools create many of their own discipline problems;
and that they promote docility, passivity and conformity in their
students. Further, the report found that most classes are taught in
a uniform manner, without regard to individual students' interests
or abilities and that the curriculum is often "trivial" and "banal".[12]
The result of the system, in the view of both Goodman and the Carnegie Commission Report is to "destroy the students' curiosity along
with their ability - more serious, their desire - to think and act
for themselves".[13] This, the Commission charges, "denies students
sufficient ability to understand modern complexity and to translate
that understanding into action".[14]

Paulo Freire[15] describes the presently utilized method of
instructing students as the "banking concept of education"; that is,
"[e]ducation...becomes an act of depositing, in which students are
the depositories and the teacher is the depositor. Instead of com-
municating, the teacher issues communiques and makes deposits which
the students patiently receive, memorize and repeat".[16] The scope
of action of the student is, thus, limited to "receiving, filing
and storing the deposits;...in the last analysis, it is men themselves who are filed away through lack of creativity, transformation
and knowledge in this (at best) misguided system".[17] This concept

---

[12] Id.

[13] Id., p. 8.

[14] Id., p. 9.

[15] Friere, Paulo., The Pedagogy of the Oppressed, (N.Y., Herder and
Herder) 1970, Chapter 2.

[16] Id.

[17] Id.

projects onto students an absolute ignorance, "a characteristic of the ideology of oppression"[18] which negates education and knowledge as processes of inquiry.

In John Holt's view, this concept accounts for the destruction of the inborn desire and ability to learn that is obvious in very small children.[19] This destruction is accomplished by

> "encouraging and compelling [children] to work for petty
> and contemptible rewards - gold stars, or papers marked
> 100 and taped to the wall, or A's on report cards, or
> honor rolls or dean's list...in short, for the ignoble
> satisfaction of feeling that they are better than some-
> one else. We encourage them to feel that the end and aim
> of all they do in school is nothing more than to get a
> good mark on a test, or to impress someone with what they
> seem to know. We kill, not only their curiosity, but
> their feeling that it is a good and admirable thing to
> be curious."[20]

B. Proposals for "Affirmative Education"

The interest of the child, all critics agree, should be the basis of alternative systems and methods of education.[21] One alternative, perhaps one that could be classified as the most "conservative" among those advocating total reform of the system, is to continue the use of schools and classrooms, but to allow each child to satisfy his or her curiosity in his or her own way, develop abilities and talents, pursue interests and interact freely with the other children and adults in the school or classroom. This proposal has been advocated by the Carnegie Report, by Goodman, by Holt,

---

[18] Id.

[19] Holt, John, Why Children Fail, (N.Y., Dell Publishing Co.) 1964.

[20] Id.

[21] See generally Holt, J., Goodman P., Postman, Neil, and Friere, P.

and by many others as the least the system must do in order to provide a minimum level of meaningful education. Another common suggestion is for "classrooms-without-walls" - using an entire city's resources; e.g., museums, parks, theatres as the school and its people, businesses, factories, stores, etc. as the instructors.[22]

These proposed alternatives to the present system of schooling are classified by Barry Schwartz as proposals for "affirmative" education. Schwartz defines "affirmative" education as including the following five characteristics:

1) students and teachers find each other and learning emerges from mutual discoveries that are the result of their expanding relationship;

2) the core of the educational experience is not the curriculum or the reading material, but, rather, is the learning process itself;

3) the need for discipline, grades and other formal control mechanisms is an indication that this learning process is not occurring;

4) the learning process is related to real-life experience and its purpose is to increase the ability of the participants to solve real-life problems;

5) sincere emotional and intellectual interchange is the basis for the relationship between student and teacher.[23]

Achievement of the goals of "affirmative" education will result, according to its proponents, in education becoming a meaningful process, and in the realization by students of their full potential as "self-initiating learners".[24]

All of the proponents of such affirmative changes in the educational system are aware of the problems to be faced in

_____

[22]Goodman, Paul, p. 40-41.

[23]Schwartz, Barry N., _Affirmative Education_, p. 109.

[24]Rodgers, Carl, _Freedom to Learn_, (Columbus Ohio: Charles E. Merrill Publishing Co.) 1969.

implementing them: practical limitations such as the conservative
nature of schools and administrators, time allotments, class sizes,
as well as the challenge faced by the individual teachers to change
and adapt to a new method of "being".[25] Regardless of the difficulties, however, proponents contend that "affirmative" education is
essential to the achievement of a "decent society".[26]

C. The More Radical Critics

Some major educational critics and theoreticians believe
"affirmative" education is much too mild a prescription for the
"illness" which has overtaken our learning processes. Chief among
these advocates are Ivan Illich[27] and Everett Reimer,[28] both of
whom advocate outright abolition of schools themselves and total
decentralization of educational resources.

Illich's criticism of the educational system stems from
his theory that society has become over-institutionized and that
schools are at the center of the "over-institutionalization".
What schools do, according to Illich, is

> "school students to confuse process with substance.
> Once these become blurred, a new logic is assumed:
> the more treatment there is, the better are the
> results; or, escalation leads to success. The
> pupil is thereby 'schooled' to confuse teaching with
> learning, grade advancement with education, a diploma
> with competence, and fluency with the ability to say

---

[25] Schwartz, B.N., p. 161

[26] Id.

[27] Illich, Ivan, Deschooling Society, (N.Y., Harper and Row) 1970.

[28] Reimer, Everett, School is Dead: Alternatives to Education,
(N.Y., Doubleday) 1971.

something new. His imagination is 'schooled'
to accept service in place of value. Medical
treatment is mistaken for health care, social
work for the improvement of community life,
police protection for safety, military pose for
national security, the rat race for productive
work. Health, learning, dignity, independence,
and creative endeavor are defined as little
more than the performance of the institutions
which claim to serve these ends, and their
improvement is made to depend on allocating
more resources to the management of hospitals,
schools, and other agencies in question."[29]

A further problem with "schooling" for Illich is his

view that the "hidden curriculum" of schools serves to preserve

privilege and power for the schooled.[30] This "hidden curriculum"

"teaches all children that economically valuable knowledge is the

result of professional teaching and that social entitlements de-

pend on the rank achieved in a bureaucratic process. The hidden

curriculum transforms the explicit curriculum into a commodity

and makes its acquisition the securest form of wealth...school is

universally accepted as the avenue to greater power, to increased

legitimacy as a producer, and to further 'learning' resources."[31]

The key to liberating humanity from the control of these institu-

tions and from the hidden curriculum, is to "deschool" society.

To achieve this deschooling, Illich advocates the dein-

stitutionalization of schools, with a system of "learning webs"[32]

created in their place. These "learning webs" would allow the

---

[29]Illich, I., Deschooling Society, p. 1.

[30]Illich, I., "After Deschooling, What?", Social Policy, September/
October 1971.

[31]Id.

[32]Illich, I. Deschooling Society, Op. Cit., p. 105-150.

student to choose the subject area, the place, time and other persons with whom s/he wished to learn. Illich would set up four "networks", or learning exchanges that would contain all the resources needed for real learning. These four networks would consist of things, models, peers and elders: "[t]he child grows up in a world of things, surrounded by people who challenge him to argue, to compete, to cooperate and to understand, and if the child is lucky, s/he is exposed to confrontation or criticism by an experienced elder who really cares."[33]

The use of these "webs" Illich contends, will allow for self-motivated learning instead of [employment] of teachers to bribe or compel the students to find the time and the will to learn... and will give learners new links to the world instead of continuing to funnel all educational programs through the teacher.[34]

Illich concedes that "the rash and uncritical disestablishment of school could lead to a free-for-all, in the production or consumption of more vulgar learning, acquired for immediate utility or eventual prestige".[35] To avoid such a free-for-all, Illich stresses the need for certain minimal legal protections to insure freedom for education. In his view, these consist of "total prohibition of legislated attendance, the proscription of

---

[33] Id., p. 109.

[34] Id., p. 104.

[35] Illich, I., "After Deschooling, What?", p. 15.

any discrimination on the basis of prior attendance, and the trans-
fer of control over tax funds from benevolent institutions to the
individual person".[36]

Use of "learning webs", combined with his proposed legal
protections will, in his view, "provide all who want to learn with
access to available resources at any time in their lives; empower
all who want to share what they know to find those who want to learn
it from them; and finally, furnish all who want to present an issue
to the public with the opportunity to make their challenge known."[37]
Most importantly, Illich believes that his proposed system will result in the recognition of each person's freedom to determine the
course and structure of her/his own learning experience.[38]

Even though proposals such as those of Illich and Reimer
are not viewed by many critics to be workable solutions for the
problems of contemporary education, most critics are prepared to
use the theoretical underpinning of those proposals as a basis for
evaluating more practical innovations and experiments. Neil Postman
describes this process: "the Illich-Reimer proposals...can be
transformed into a series of questions whose answers can be used
as a measure of whether or not some specific innovation is moving
in the right direction. Will the innovation make resources more
widely available? Will it tend to deemphasize the importance of

---

[36] Id., p. 19.

[37] Id., p. 26.

[38] Id.

teaching as against learning? Will it tend to make students freer, and their learning less confused?"[39]

D. Summary

It is apparent from the foregoing discussion of the views of various critics of elementary and secondary education in the United States that, in general, they do not differentiate between the various aspects of the compulsory system of education such as, for example, between compulsory attendance, compulsory course requirements and activities requirements. Rather, these critics appear merely to condemn compulsion of any nature and to propose the abolition of all forms of it. Most of these critics either expressly state or clearly imply that any educational system which is based upon compelled attendance or on any other form of compulsion will inevitably be characterized by all the same faults which they find to exist in the current system of public elementary and secondary education.

III. Advocates of Amendment of Compulsory Attendance Laws

In the second major category of critics of compulsory attendance laws are those who do not seek repeal of those laws, but who are interested in amending these laws to achieve reform of the public school system or the development of alternatives to that system. In this category are educational reformers who seek to limit the exclusion of children from public school for reasons of "physical, mental or emotional disability", disciplinary reasons and other reasons which have been traditional bases for exclusion. Although

---

[39]Postman, N., "My Ivan Illich Problem".

the compulsory attendance laws do not generally authorize the
exclusion of students from schools, the exemptions specified in
those laws are frequently cited by school administrators for the
proposition that if a child is exempted from compulsory attendance,
the state does not have an obligation to provide an educational opportunity or its obligation is less than it would be if the child
were not exempted. Although this proposition is legally incorrect
since an exemption is merely a grant of permission to the child
for the child not to attend school or to the child's parents not to
require such attendance, reformers seeking inclusion of greater
numbers of children in the educational process must, nevertheless,
seek a narrowing or elimination of the various exemptions in order
to prevent such exemptions from being used as the "color of state
law" basis for exclusion. In addition, these same reformers seek
a clarification and expansion of state constitutional and statutory
provisions providing for a "right to a publicly financed education"
for all children so that the narrowing of the exemptions will be
rendered effective by the provision of an educational opportunity.

A sub-category of the reformers seeking amendment of compulsory attendance laws are those who believe that the number of
years of attendance required by these laws is excessive and that
children should be allowed to leave school at an earlier age than
that permitted, for reasons of employment, apprenticeship, vocational
training or for some other reason. Also in this sub-category of
reformers, but at the other end of the spectrum, are those who seek a
lowering of the minimum age of required attendance so that children

below the customary entry level age of five or six would be required to attend school. Persons advocating a lowering of the minimum age of attendance usually do so on the theory that the earlier the educational process begins, the more likely it will be that children will "suceed" in school.

Another sub-category of educational reformers seeking amendments in compulsory attendance laws are those who seek expansion of the learning arrangements, in addition to attendance at public school, which are permitted to satisfy the compulsory attendance requirement. Among these reformers, for example, are those who seek the addition of a "home study" alternative to a statute which previously permitted attendance only at a public or private school. Also, in this category of reformers are those who seek an expansion of "private" learning arrangements, both through changes in law and changes in the system of public financing of elementary and secondary education such as, for example, through state issuance of tuition vouchers to parents rather than, or in addition to, direct state funding of public schools.

The preceding discussion has summarized the principal proposals of the advocates of amendment of compulsory attendance laws. There are many other amendments which have been proposed which are variations on the main themes discussed above. The possibilities for amendment of compulsory attendance laws, are, in fact, virtually limitless since they range from the most minute to the most far-reaching. For purposes of our analysis, however, the proposed amendments which have been discussed are sufficiently illustrative to serve as a basis for the following analysis of the legal changes which are necessary to achieve repeal or amendment of compulsory attendance laws.

IV. The Legal Changes Required to Achieve Repeal or Amendment of Compulsory Attendance Laws

A. Introduction

The changes in the legal structure which would result from the proposals discussed in the preceding section for repeal or amendment of compulsory attendance laws fall into four general categories. In the first, and most obvious, are those changes which would be required in the primary compulsory attendance statutes, themselves, such as, for example, changes lowering the minimum or maximum ages of attendance which would require amendments to the compulsory attendance provisions establishing such ages.

In the second, are those changes which are in the nature of necessary conforming amendments to statutes whose provisions are directly keyed to compulsory attendance laws. An example of such a conforming amendment would be the repeal following repeal of a compulsory attendance law, of the statute providing for the hiring of attendance officers. Obviously, if the attendance requirement were removed, there would no longer be a need for the employees whose job it is to enforce that requirement.

In the third category are those statutory amendments which would be required in order to achieve the underlying purposes of the repeal or amendment of a compulsory attendance law. In this category, for example, might be an amendment lowering the minimum age for employment in a child labor law to correspond with a lower-ing of the maximum age for attendance in a compulsory attendance law. Such an amendment of a child labor law would be made where one purpose of amending the compulsory attendance law was to give young people the choice of working at an earlier age than that pre-viously permitted.

In the fourth category, are those amendments which would be required as the result of some of the practical effects of amend-ment or repeal of compulsory attendance laws. Thus, for example, if repeal of a compulsory attendance law were to result in an exo-dus from public school of large numbers of children, school financ-ing laws premised upon the number of school-attending pupils might have to be revised, so that the public schools would receive an adequate amount of funds to continue operating. Some of these potential practical effects will be alluded to in this part and will be discussed in greater detail in the next section.

A discussion of all of these types of statutory changes will provide the framework for the following analysis.

B. The Legal Changes Required To Achieve Repeal of Compulsory Attendance Laws

Although it is a matter of some speculation whether any state would actually repeal its compulsory attendance laws as part of a modern educational reform, the following discussion will con-sider the legal changes required to effectuate such a repeal since these changes are similar, in some respects, to the changes which would be required by various proposed amendments to compulsory

attendance laws and, will therefore, provide a useful framework for
a discussion of those amendments. In addition, although repeal of
compulsory attendance laws, at the present time, is probably a more
remote possibility than amendment of those laws, the preceding discussion has indicated that many critics already advocate repeal.
It is conceivable, therefore, that the issue of repeal may be one
which will be debated by state legislatures in the not-too-distant
future.

In order to facilitate an understanding of the ensuing
analysis, it is useful to define what is meant by repeal of compulsory attendance laws. By such repeal we mean the elimination of
the statutory obligation of children to attend "school" and of the
corresponding statutory obligation of their parents to require that
attendance. Repeal of a compulsory attendance law does not, in itself, necessitate any change in the manner in which education is
provided by the state. The only certain result of repeal is that
children who formerly would have been subject to the requirement
of compelled school attendance could, after repeal, choose not to
attend public school or any other educational program. The obfusca-
tion of this distinction between the elimination of the duty to
attend school and a reordering of the state system for providing
education has caused considerable confusion and, therefore, will be
discussed in more detail later in this chapter.

1. The reordering of state constitutional and statutory provisions as the result of repeal of the com-

pulsory attendance law

As indicated in the earlier chapter on state constitutional provisions concerning compulsory attendance, several states have consitutional provisions containing compulsory attendance requirements or requiring their state legislatures to enact such requirements.[42] In addition, the basic statutory attendance requirements mandating attendance at "school" of children between certain ages have spawned a complex network of state laws which define and enforce those requirements. In order for the basic attendance requirement to be repealed, those state constitutional provisions and that network of related laws would have to be substantially altered. The following discussion will summarize the specific nature of those alterations.

a. Changes in the state constitutions required by repeal

As indicated earlier, the great majority of state constitutional provisions relating to elementary and secondary education impose an obligation upon the state to provide a publicly-financed system of education, usually through the establishment of a public school system. A small number contain an additional provision requiring children to attend an educational program or requiring the legislature to enact such a compulsory attendance requirement.[43]

In those states with direct compulsory attendance requirements in their constitutions, mere repeal of the statutory compulsory attendance requirement would be ineffective in removing

---

[42] See discussion in Chapter 8, supra.

[43] Id.

the obligation to attend school. In those states with indirect
requirements obligating their legislatures to enact compulsory
attendance laws, repeal of the statutory compulsory attendance
requirement obviously would not be permitted until after a constitutional amendment removed the obligation on the legislature.
Thus, repeal of the statutory compulsory attendance requirements,
in states with either of these types of constitutional provisions,
could be effectuated only after amendment of the state constitution.

b. Changes in state statutes required by repeal

(1) Statutes which would have to be repealed

Repeal of the basic compulsory attendance
requirement would require repeal of all of the primary compulsory
attendance provisions defining and implementing the attendance
requirement, such as, for example, those relating to the permitted
learning arrangments authorized by that requirement, those specifying the exmeptions from the requirement and those concerning its
enforcement. In addition, conforming repeal of laws, such as
those establishing special schools for truants and creating the
position of truant officers, would be necessary since repeal of
compulsory attendance would obviate the need for enforcement of
the attendance requirements.

Similarly, the stautes relating to state
and local approval of private schools are frequently premised upon
the assumption that the private school will be one of the learning
arrangments, in addition to public school, which will be permitted
to be utilized by parents in satisfaction of the compulsory at-

tendance requirement. Thus, approval is frequently contingent on the private school demoinstrating that its offerings are "equivalent" to that of the public school. Since the requirement of "attendance at a public school or an equivialent learning arrangement" would be repealed, the requirement of equivalence, as well as the approval itself, would presumably no longer be necessary.

Of course states could continue to license and regulate private schools on other bases such as in the interest of protecting the public from fraud or where the private schools receive state or federal funds. Such bases for licensing and regulation, however, would probably be insufficient for requiring the course offerings of private schools to be equivalent to those of public schools, as is frequently required by compulsory attendance laws.

In short, then, all of the provisions which comprise the primary and secondary network of laws defining and implementing and enforcing the compulsory attendance requirement would have to be repealed. In addition, the provisions requiring course offerings at private schools would also have to be "equivalent" to those at public schools would also have to be repealed.

(2) Statutes which would require amendment in order to achieve the underlying purposes of repeal of a compulsory attendance law

Several tyoes of state statutes would have to be amended in order to achieve the underlying purposes of repeal of compulsory attendance laws. Unlike the amendments categorized above as "conforming" amendments, the amendments in this category are not literally necessitated by the very act of repeal, but their implementation would be necessary to the full realization of the underlying purpose sought to be achieved by the repeal.One principal example of such an amendment will be discussed in this part.

As indicated in the earlier chapter on state child labor laws,[44] those laws were enacted, in part, to encourage the attendance of children at school and, therefore, contain age restrictions which correspond closely to the age requirements of the compulsory attendance laws. Assuming that one of the reasons for repeal of the compulsory attendance laws would be to give young people more choice in governing their lives by allowing them to work rather than to attend school, repeal of a compulsory attendance law would necessitate then a rethinking and amendment of many of the age restrictions contained in child labor laws.

(3) Statutes which would not have to be repealed or amended

To emphasize the distinction, mentioned earlier, between repeal of the duty of children to attend school and revision of the state system for providing education, the following discussion will highlight two of the principal types of laws which would not require repeal or amendment solely as the result of repeal of compulsory attendance laws. It should be noted, however, that these laws might require amendment at a later stage, as the result of some of the effects of repeal of compulsory attendancce, such as, for example, the possibility that substantial numbers of children might decide not to attend public school, thereby necessitating amendment of school finances and other laws keyed to the level of pupil enrollment.

---

[44] See Chapter 3, supra.

(a) <u>Right to education laws</u>

State constitutional provisions requiring
the provision of a publicly financed educational opportunity for
all children would not have to be amended as the result of repeal
of compulsory attendance laws. In the same manner, no amendment
would be required in the few "right to education" statutes which
exist in the country, i.e., laws guaranteeing the right to a publicly financed education to children in a certain age range.[45]
Thus, children could be released from the obligation to attend
school and the states could still be obligated or could choose to
provide, as a matter of right, a publicly-financed educational
opportunity to those children who chose to attend school.

(b) <u>Statutes relating to the operation and</u>
<u>financing of public schools</u>

Repeal of compulsory attendance laws, in
itself, would not require any changes in the statutes governing
the manner in which the public school system is operated and financed. For example, the states could continue to require certain
courses to be taught in the public schools and to regulate the
certification of public school teachers. In addition, the states
could continue to utilize their existing systems for the financing of elementary and secondary education.

Obviously, if repeal of compulsory
attendance laws were to occur, it would not occur in a vacuum.
Presumably, one of the reasons for repeal would be to increase the

---

[45]See, e.g., Ohio Rev. Code s. 33.3.64.

freedom of children to choose work and/or to choose mechanisms
for learning other than those permitted by the present statutes.
If this presumption is accurate, the state would undoubtedly encourage these purposes by modifying the school finance laws to
allow some funds to go to children who opted out of the public
schools, but who required financial assistance to choose an alternative work or learning arrangement. Thus, some of the reasons
for repeal of compulsory attendance laws as well as some of the
indirect effects of such repeal, might well require amendment of
state laws which would not have had to be amended merely to effectuate the repeal, itself.

(4) Conclusion

In conclusion, the necessary legal reordering
required by repeal of compulsory attendance requirements would be
limited, primarily, to the repeal or amendment of those primary
state constitutional provisions and statutes which define and enforce that requirement. In addition, conforming repeal would be
required of those laws which implement and enforce the primary
provisions. Also, certain other related laws, such as those governing child labor, would require amendment, to the extent that repeal of the compulsory attendance laws was for the purpose of increasing the choice of learning and working opportunities for
children formerly subject to compulsory attendance.

On the other hand, mere repeal of compulsory
atendance laws, in itself, would not necessitate any changes in the
system of laws governing the establishment and provision of public

elementary and secondary education by the state. Later practical effects of repeal, however, might necessitate such changes, as we will discuss in a later part of this chapter.

  C. The Legal Changes Required by Amendment of the Statutes

   1. Amendments which expand or contract the attendance requirement

   In this category of possible amendments are the proposals of some reformers to alter the age requirements contained in the primary compulsory attendance laws or to modify the daily and hourly time requirements established primarily by regulation and occasionally by statute, to further define the meaning of the basic attendance requirement. Proposals to alter the age requirement include, for example, lowering the entering age so that children below the age of six would be required to attend school; lowering the leaving age so young people would have the option of leaving school at an earlier age that that permitted by the compulsory attendance law; and allowing young people to leave school upon reaching a certain level of proficiency, either to allow them to leave school at an earlier age than that permitted by the compulsory attendance law, or to ensure that they are literate when they graduate,even if that occurs at a later age than that which would have been permitted if the compulsory attendance law had not been amended.

   As in the case of possible repeal of compulsory attendance laws, but to a lesser degree, these proposals to alter the age requirements would necessitate changes in the primary state constitutional and statutory provisions which define and enforce

the compulsory attendance requirement. In addiiton, the laws relating to child labor would require conforming amendments, as
indicated earlier in the discussion of repeal, to the extent that
the amendment of the attendance laws was designed to give young
people greater opportunity to enter the job market.

The second type of change mentioned in the introduction to this sub-section refers to proposals, such as those
which would shorten the number of hours per day a child is in
school, or shorten the number of days per year that a child must
attend school. In general, these types of changes would not require amendment of the primary compulsory attendance provisions in
state consitutions or statutes, since these provisions usually do
not contain detailed time requirements. Most of this type of detail
appears in regulations of the state education departments, and it
is these regulations, therefore, which would have to be amended.

2. Amendments which reduce or increase the exemptions
   contained in the compulsory attendance laws

In this category of possible amendments are those,
for example, which would increase the opportunity of young people
to work rather than attend school by expanding the employment and
work-study exemptions; and, on the other end of the spectrum, those
which would include more children and youth within the compulsory
attendance requirement by narrowing the exemptions for "mental,
physical or emotional" disability, for marital or parental status,
for distance from school and for other conditions which, traditionally, have been the basis for exempting children and youth from
the attendance requirement.

Since these types of changes are specifically geared
to the exemption provisions contained in the primary compulsory
attendance laws, those primary provisions would require change.
In addition, as in the case of other types of amendments discussed
earlier, an expansion of the employment and work-study exemptions
would require conforming amendments of the child labor laws in
order to effectuate the purpose of such expansion. Otherwise, the
new choice granted by the expanded exemption might be nullified
by restrictive child labor provisions.

It should be emphasized, in conclusion, that the process of narrowing many of the existing exemptions, most notably
those for "mental, physical or emotional" disability, and for marital or parental status, has been and continues to be given greater
impetus by court decisions prohibiting public schools from excluding
students for those reasons.[46] These court decisions serve to emphasize the fact that public school systems may not infer the right
to exclude a student from the existence of an exemption in a compulsory attendance law. The existence of such an exemption merely
grants to the student qualifying for that exemption the choice not
to attend school.

3. Amendments which expand the permitted learning
   arrangements

In this category of suggested changes are proposals
to give greater choice to children and youth concerning the manner
in which they may satisfy the compulsory attendance requirement.
Examples of such proposals are those which would expressly permit
various "home study" arrangements, those which would clarify and

----

[46]See discussion in Chapter 11, supra.

expand the definition of a "private school", those which would remove or define broadly the "equivalency" requirement imposed on private schools and those which would generally liberalize the requirements for state or local approval of a "learning arrangement".

As in the case of exemptions, the <u>statutory</u> legal changes required to effectuate such expansion of the permitted learning arrangements would be relatively minor in degree, focusing on that part of the primary compulsory attendance law which specifies the permitted learning arrangments. Such legal changes, however, although small in a quantitative sense, would involve complex decisions of public policy concerning the extent and kind of non-public school learning arrangements which the state would be willing to permit. In addition, to the extent that the definitions of "private school" and of the "non-school" learning arrangements were expanded, conforming changes would probably have to be made in the various state and local regulations governing the approval and monitoring of such "private school" and "non-school" alternatives.

Also, as in the case of all of the other possible changes in compulsory attendance laws discussed in this chapter, corresponding changes would have to be made in the child labor laws in order to achieve the underlying purpose of the change in the attendance law. Again, this would be true in the situation where an expansion of the permitted learning arrangements was designed to give children and youth greater choice of employment and work/

study opportunities, in lieu of or in addition to public or private school attendance.

4. Conclusion

In conclusion, the various proposals to amend the compulsory attendance laws require a small number of amendments to the primary compulsory attendance provsions in state constitutions and statutes, as well as a large number of conforming amendments to state and local regulations. As in the case of repeal, amendment of compulsory attendance laws would also require corresponding changes in the child labor laws, to achieve one of the probable purposes of amendment of the attendance requirement, i.e., to increase the employment and work-study options of students.

V. Implications of Change

There are a number of potential implications which might result from the repeal or amendment of compulsory attendance laws and from the legal reordering which would be occasioned by such repeal or amendment. The most important of these implications will be discussed in this section.

A. Implications of Repeal or Amendment for the Public School System

1. In general

The preceding analysis makes it clear that neither repeal nor amendment of compulsory attendance laws would, in itself, necessitate any changes in the legal structure governing the establishment, operation and financing of the public school systems. Obviously, however, if repeal or amendment resulted in an exodus of students from the public schools, the manner in which an educational opportunity is provided by the state would have to be completely reconsidered. This reconsideration might very well result in decisions requiring changes in the laws governing the public school systems, such as, for example, a decision to provide tuition vouchers to potential school children and to allow them to choose the educational programs on which to spend those vouchers. Absent such indirect effects of repeal or amendment, however, the legal system governing the public schools would not require amendment.

2. The status of public school students

A review of the federal Constitutional case law relating to elementary and secondary education, indicates that, under current legal theory, the absence of compulsory attendance laws would probably not change the status, under the United States Constitution, of public school students with respect to their Constitutional rights. Thus, for example, even absent a compulsory attendance law, a state could not operate a school system which was segregated on the basis of race; nor could it suspend , without "due process of law", students who attended a public school system; nor could it abridge the First Amendment rights of students who chose to attend the public schools.

It is possible, however, that if a compulsory attendance law was repealed, a court might conclude, as did the Supreme Court in West Virginia State Board of Education v. Barnette (in dictum)[47], that the presence or absence of compulsion was a factor directly relevant to the issue of whether there was a violation of

---

[47]319 U.S. 624 (1943); see discussion in Chapter 11, supra.

a federal Constitutional right. In any event, the relevance of
the existence of a compulsory attendance law to the resolution of
such an issue would probably be made more explicit than it is in
current judicial opinions.

B. Implications of Repeal or Amendment for the Systems
   of Child Labor Laws

The previous section alluded to various changes in
child labor laws which would probably have to be made as the result of repeal or amendment of compulsory attendance provisions.
Obviously, any change in a compulsory attendance law which had the
effect of partially or completely freeing a young person from the
school attendance obligation would give that person the opportunity
to pursue some other endeavor. Traditionally, the principal endeavor which was considered an alternative to school was employment or apprenticeship, or some combination of the two. This alternative, however, would exist only in theory for many young people
who fall within the "protections" of the child labor laws.

Thus, policy makers would have to decide whether and
how child labor laws should be modified to actualize the new theoretical choice which would be provided to young people as the result of changes in the compulsory attendance laws. Most likely,
given the historical and legal connection between the systems of
compulsory attendance and child labor laws, the decision to change
the compulsory attendance law would be part of a larger policy decision which would include corresponding changes in the child labor
laws. Thus, these two systems which developed together and are

currently interconnected, would undoubtedly change together.

C. Implications of Repeal or Amendment on the Parent-
   Child Relationship

One effect of the repeal of compulsory attendance laws
and, to a lesser degree, of amendment of those laws is that the
decision of whether a child should attend school would no longer be
made by the state. Instead, it would be made by the parent and
child. To the extent that they are of the same opinion on this
decision, no immediate problem would be presented. If there is a
difference of opinion, however, important issues would be raised.

For example, whose decision would be the controlling
one? Would the basic common law rule of parental control prevail?
Would the child have an independent federal Constitutional right
to be the ultimate decision-maker, similar to the potential right
being considered by the Supreme Court[48] of children to be accorded
due process, in their own right, in cases where the parents wish to
commit them "voluntarily", to an institution for the mentally ill?
These questions are indicative of the fact that, under current law,
children have virtually no rights independent of their parents,
except for those few areas where the legislature has created such
a right. This point is bluntly stated in the Yoder opinion[49], and
is not contradicted by other Supreme Court decisions.

For purposes for this analysis, the question is whether
a body of law would develop to guarantee the right of children

---

[48]Bartley v. Kremens, 402 F. Supp. 1039 (E.D. Pa. 1975), Prob.
Juris. noted (44 U.S.L.W. 3531, 1976).

[49]406 U.S. 205 (1972); see discussion in Chapter 11, supra.

to decide to attend or not to attend school, in the face of parental opposition. In the absence of such case law, state legislators and other educational policy-makers would be required to decide, as a matter of public policy, whether and in what manner such a right should be established.

Important issues of policy which would require resolution, for example, are whether laws should be enacted allowing the state to intervene, as in abuse and neglect cases, where the interests of parent and child are adverse; and whether "right to education" provisions in constitutions and statutes should be amended, where they already exist, or added where they do not exist, to make it clear that the right to a publicly financed education is the child's right, independent of the rights of the parents.

D. Implications of Repeal or Amendment in the Area of
   Economic Discrimination

A separate issue concerning the matter of choice of attendance or non-attendance at schools might arise if large numbers of children of low-income families decided, after repeal of a compulsory attendance law or after an amendment which greatly reduced the attendance requirement, to seek employment. Conceivably, this could result in a situation where the public schools had a large disproportion, compared to the society as a whole, of children from middle and upper income families, with children from low-income families employed and not in school. Would this raise the issue of a wealth-based denial of an educational opportunity? For purposes of possible application of the Equal Protection Clause

of the Fourteenth Amendment to such a situation, would the state
be considered to be involved in such a "denial" of an educational
opportunity or would there be a finding of "no state action"? If
"state action" were found, would the Supreme Court find a "suspect
classification" to exist? Would there be a denial of an educational
opportunity or would the choice not to attend school be looked
upon as a free one uncoerced by the state? If a denial were found,
would the Court find that this type of denial, unlike that posited
in Rodriguez, involved the denial of a "fundamental right"? Would
an "intermediate" equal protection standard be applied to such a
denial?[50]

As in the situation concerning the parent-child relationship, current law provides few helpful precendents for a potential plaintiff raising the above issues. It is very conceivable,
however, that new legal theories would be accepted by courts to
prevent the development of the dichotomy between rich and poor hypo-
thesized above.

    E. Implications of Repeal or Amendment for the Development
      of Learning Arrangements in Addition to Public School
      Attendance

As indicated in the chapter on cases construing compulsory attendance provisions[51], although many states have restrictive

---

[50]See discussion of the "intermediate" standard in Chapter 11, supra.
[51]See Chapter 5, supra.

attitudes toward private school, particularly toward "non-school" alternatives to public school attendance, there is a substantial amount of leaway permitted in establishing such alternatives to public school. Increasing this leaway to allow more alternatives and to facilitate the establishment of such alternatives, would have some effect in expanding the educational choices of parents and children.

Nevertheless, this type of legal reform would probably be more limited in effect than one might suspect, absent corresponding changes in state financing systems to enable the new alternatives to be real choices for parents who could not otherwise afford them. Absent state funding directly to parents or to the alternatives, themselves, relatively few of such alternatives would probably ever be created. For parents who could afford to purchase an alternative education for their children, however, amendments to compulsory attendance laws which expanded and liberalized the requirements for non-public school attendance, would be very helpful in that they would encourage and facilitate the creation of new educational arrangements.

VI.   Summary of the Role of Compulsory Attendance Laws in the
       Debate over Reform of Elementary and Secondary Education

Critics of elementary and secondary education who seek fundamental reform of the system generally begin their proposals for reform with an attack upon the compulsory nature of the public school system. It is clear that mere repeal of compulsory attendance laws and of other directly related statutes which are designed to implement and enforce the attendance requirements, would only go part way in meeting the demands of these critics for the abolition of all forms of compulsion. In addition to repeal of the attendance laws, themselves, it would be necessary, in order to meet these demands, to repeal laws mandating a certain curriculum in the public schools and requiring participation in various school activities; and to repeal the rules and regulations which govern the daily lives of children in the public schools and, which, by their very nature contain many elements of compulsion. Repeal of the compulsory attendance law, in itself, therefore, would not result in the total elimination of compulsion.

On the other hand, amendment of the primary compulsory attendance laws and corresponding amendments to related laws would be of substantial significance to those critics who seek greater flexibility in the system and do not advocate fundamental reform. Many of these amendments, however, would have to be followed by changes in public policy relating to school finance and governance in order to have any practical effect. Thus, for example, an amendment expanding the alternative learning arrangements to public school permitted by a compulsory attendance law would be of limited significance unless public funds were made available to enable parents and children to afford such arrangements.

In conclusion, the requirements of compulsory attendance laws are significant in the debate over the quality and viability of public elementary and secondary education, but their significance is inversely proportional to the degree of reform of edu-

cation which is being proposed. Thus, for those seeking the most
fundamental reforms, repeal of compulsory attendance laws would
represent little more than a symbolic first step. On the other hand,
for those seeking greater flexibility in the system of elementary
and secondary education, amendment of compulsory attendance provisions would be of much greater significance. For many types of
such limited reform to be effective in fact as well as in theory,
however, such amendments would have to be accompanied by shifts
in public policy and major alterations in the system governing
public financing of elementary and secondary education in the
United States.

13. <u>BIBLIOGRAPHY</u>

Abbott, Edith, <u>Women in Industry: A Study in American Economic History</u>. 1910.

Abbott, Grace, <u>The Child and the State; Select Documents</u>, Vol. I 1938.

Alexander, K. and K.F. Jordan, <u>Legal Aspects of Educational Choice: Compulsory Attendance and Student Assignment</u>. 1973.

Arons, Stephen, "The Separation of School and State: <u>Pierce</u> Reconsidered", 46 <u>Harv. Ed. Rev</u>. 76. Feb. 1976.

Bender, John F., "Criticisms of Attendance Laws", <u>American School Board Journal</u> Vol. 76, 434. Feb. 1928.

Bentley, F.L., "Present Attendance Need", National League of Compulsory Education Officials, <u>Proceedings</u> of the twentieth annual convention, 1930, pp. 63-5.

_____, "School Attendance: A Factor of Social Welfare", in Ohio State Educational Conference, <u>Proceedings</u> of the 12th Annual Session, pp. 69-74.

Bland, Brown, and Towney, eds., <u>English Economic History: Select Documents</u>. 1914.

Brearley, H.C., "Should Schools Be Jails for Teenagers?", <u>American School Board Journal</u>, Vol. 140, No. 2:28-30. 1960.

Bremner, Robert H., <u>Children and Youth in America: A Documentary History</u>. 1970.

Brickman, William W. and Stanley Lehrer, <u>The Countdown on Segregated Education</u>. 1960.

Butts, R. Freeman and Lawrence A. Cremin, <u>A History of Education in American Culture</u>. 1953.

Carlile, A.B., "Compulsory Attendance Laws in the U.S., Historical Background", 4 <u>Educational Law & Administration</u> 35. April-October 1936.

Carpenter, W.W., "Is the Educational Utopia in Sight?", 8 <u>Nation's Schools</u>. September 1931.

Carroll, Mollie R., <u>Labor and Politics: The Attitude of the AFL Toward Legislation and Politics</u>. 1969.

Carter, E.J., "Do We Need a Strengthened Compulsory Education Law?", 26 <u>High School Journal</u> 18. January 1943.

Chambers, M.M., "Best Employment for American Youth", 17 Nation's Schools 39. February 1936.

"Changes Recommended in Child Labor and Compulsory Attendance Laws", 33 School and Community 9. January 1947.

Charters, W.W., "Sixteen-Year-Old Seventh-Grade Children", 8 Educational Research Bulletin 98. March 6, 1929.

Chatfield, G.H., "Place of the Agency for Enforcing Compulsory Education Laws in the School System." in National League of Compulsory Education Officials, Proceedings of the twentieth annual convention, pp. 26-8. 1930.

"Child Labor", 3 American Labor Legislation Review 364. 1913; 5 American Labor Legislation Review 694. 1915.

Child Labor Facts and Figures, U.S. Children's Bureau, Publication No. 197. 1930.

Child Labor Laws, U.S. Department of Labor, Wage and Labor Standards Administration, Bulletin No. 312. 1967.

"Child Labor Legislation", Book of the States, Vols. 1945-1973.

"Child Labor Legislation - Its Past, Present and Future", 7 Fordham L. Rev. 217. 1938.

Children's Defense Fund of the Washington Research Project, Inc., Children Out of School in America. 1974.

Commager, Henry Steele, "A Historian Looks at the High School", in Francis S. Chase and Harold Anderson, The High School in a New Era. 1958.

"Compulsory Attendance", U.S. Office of Education Library Division, Bibliography of Research Studies, pp. 244-5. 1930-31.

"Compulsory Attendance Laws", 25 Elementary School Journal 171. November 1924.

Compulsory School Attendance, North Carolina Dept. of Public Instruction. 1929.

"Compulsory School Attendance & Minimum Educational Requirements in the U.S.", U.S. Office of Education, Circular 440. 1955.

"Compulsory School Attendance Provisions Affecting Employment of Minors in the U.S., 1936", 44 Monthly Labor Review 356. February 1937.

"Compulsory Schooling", 6 International Bureau of Education Bulletin 51. April 1932.

DeBoer, Peter P. "Compulsory Attendance" in The Encyclopedia of Education, Lee C. Deighton, ed., Vol. 2. 1971.

_____, A History of the Early Compulsory School Attendance Legislation in the State of Illinois. 1968.

Deffenbaugh, W.S., <u>Compulsory Attendance Laws in the U.S.</u> 1914.

Deffenbaugh, Walter S. & Ward W. Keesecker, <u>Compulsory School Attendance Laws and Their Administration.</u> 1935.

_____, <u>Development of Compulsory School Attendance</u>, U.S. Office of Education. Bulletin No. 6. 1940.

DeYoung, Chris A., <u>Introduction to American Public Education.</u> 1950.

Dunlap, K., "Is Compulsory Education Justified?", 16 <u>American Mercury</u> 211. February 1929.

"Educational Progress in 1952-53: Compulsory Education", <u>International Yearbook of Education.</u> 1953.

Edwards, Netwon and Herman G. Richey, <u>The School in the American Social Order.</u> 1947.

"Enforcing School Attendance Laws", 76 <u>American School Board Journal</u> 68. March 1928.

Ensign, Forest Chester, <u>Compulsory School Attendance and Child Labor.</u> 1921.

Erickson, Donald A., "The Plain People v. the Common School", <u>Saturday Review</u>, Vol. 49, No. 46: pp. 85-7, 102-3. 1966.

Faust, H.F., "Compulsory Public Education" 29 <u>Current History</u> 140. September 1955.

Friere, Paulo, <u>The Pedagogy of the Oppressed.</u> 1970.

Fuller, Edgar and Jim B. Pearson, eds., <u>Education in the States</u>: Nationwide Development Since 1900. 1969.

Fuller, Raymond G., "Child Labor", <u>Encyclopedia of the Social Sciences</u>, Vol. III, p. 419, Erwin R.A. Seligman and Alvin Johnson, eds. 1937.

_____, <u>Child Labor and the Constitution.</u>

Garber, Leo O., "Four Big Educational Issues Dominate Court Cases", <u>Nation's Schools</u>, Vol. 73, No. 3, pp. 76ff. 1964.

_____, <u>The Law Governing Pupils.</u> 1962.

Gintis, Herbert, "Toward a Political Economy of Education: A Radical Critique of Ivan Illich's <u>Deschooling Society</u>", <u>Harvard Educational Review.</u> February 1972.

Glenn, A.L., "School or Work?", 36 <u>American Federationist</u> 1354. November 1929.

Goodman, Paul, <u>Compulsory Mis-Education.</u> 1964.

Goodman, R.C., "I Won't Send My Children to Public School", 132 <u>Collier's</u> 62. Nov. 13, 1953.

Hamilton, Robert R. and Paul R. Mort, The Law and Public Education. 1959.

Hand, William H., The Need of Compulsory Education in the South, Monograph IV, U.S. Bureau of Education Bulletin No. 2, 1914.

Herlihy, L.B., "What it Costs to Enforce Attendance Laws", 15 Nation's Schools 28. April 1935.

Holt, John, Why Children Fail, 1964.

Huber, L.W., "Compulsory Attendance and Indifferent Pupils", 35 Ohio Schools 8. February 1957.

Hutchinson, John Harrison, The Legal Basis of Public School Attendance in the U.S. 1941.

Illich, Ivan, "After Deschooling, What?", Social Policy. September/ October 1971.

_____, Deschooling Society. 1970.

Jackson, George Leroy, The Privilege of Education; A History of its Extension (1918).

Jennings, W.J., A History of Economic Progress in the United States (1926).

Jernegan, Marcus W., "The Beginnings of Public Education in New England", The School Review, Vol. 23, No. 5 pp. 319-30, May 1915; Vol. 23, No. 6 pp. 361-80, June 1915.

_____, "Compulsory and Free Education For Apprentices and Poor Children in Colonial New England", 5 Social Service Review 411, September 1931.

_____, "Compulsory Education in the American Colonies I," The School Review, Vol. 26, No. 10, December 1918.

_____, "Compulsory Education in the American Colonies II," The School Review, Vol. 27, No. 1, January 1919.

_____, "Compulsory Education in the Southern Colonies I", The School Review, Vol. 27, No. 6, pp. 405-25. June 1919.

_____, "Compulsory Education in the Southern Colonies II", The School Review, Vol. 28, No. 2, pp. 127-42. Feb. 1920.

_____, Laboring and Dependent Classes in Colonial America, 1607-1783. 1931.

Jerome, Judson, "After Illich, What", Social Policy, Vol. 3. March/ April 1972.

Johnson, Elizabeth Sands, "Child Labor Legislation", in Commons, et al., History of Labor in the United States, 1935.

Johnson, James A. et al., Introduction to the Foundations of American Education, 1969.

Keesecker, W.W., "Laws Relating to Compulsory Education," U.S. Bureau of Education. 1929.

Kennedy, F., "Compulsory Education, 6 to 60," 28 Saturday Review of Literature 22. November 10, 1945.

Kincaid, W.A., "School Census - A Basis for the Enforcement of Compulsory Education," 93 American School Board Journal 42. October 1936.

Koerner, J., Who Controls American Education? 1969.

Lawing, J.L., Standards for State and Local Compulsory School Attendance Service.

Laws of Ohio and Mass. Relating to Compulsory Education and Child Labor, Monograph V, U.S. Bureau of Education, No. 2 Bulletin 1914.

Liebler, C.C., "Court Decisions Affecting the Enforcement of Compulsory Education," 77 American School Board Journal 49. October 1928.

Lischka, C.N., "Constitutional Limitations of the Legislative Power to Compel Education," 27 Catholic Educational Review 18. January - April 1929.

Morse, H.N., "State Supervision of Compulsory Education," National League of Compulsory Education Officials, Proceedings of the 20th Annual Convention, pp. 61-2, 1930.

Munroe, Paul, ed., Cyclopedia of Education. 1911.

Murphy, Edgar G., Problems of the Present South. 1904.

National Industrial Conference Board, Inc., The Employment of Young Persons in the U.S. 1925.

Ogburn, W.F., The Progress and Uniformity of Child Labor Legislation. 1912.

Otey, Elizabeth, "The Beginnings of Child Labor Legislation in Certain States," U.S. Dept. of Labor Report 1910-1913.

"Our Legal School Age, How It Came to Be," 67 Wisconsin Journal of Education 364. April 1935.

Parkinson, W.D., "Limits of Compulsory School Attendance," 110 Journal of Education 381. November 4, 1929.

Pearl, Arthur, "The Case for Schooling America," Social Policy, Vol. 3. March/April 1972.

Postman, Neil, "My Ivan Illich Problem," Social Policy, Vol. 3. January/February 1972.

Proffitt, Maris M. and David Segel, "School Census, Compulsory Education, Child Labor: State Laws and Regulations," U.S. Office of Education Bulletin. 1945.

Reimer, Everett, School is Dead: Alternatives in Education. 1971.

Robson, A.H., The Education of Children Engaged in Industry in England, 1833-1876. 1931.

Rogers, Carl, Freedom to Learn. 1969.

Rosen, Sumner, "Taking Illich Seriously", Social Policy, Vol. 3. March/April 1972.

"School Attendance Laws; Age Limits, Term and Educational Requirements for Exemptions in the 48 States and the District of Columbia", 2 School Life 47. October 1935.

Schwartz, Barry N., ed., Affirmative Education.

Shaw, William B., "Compulsory Education in the U.S.", 3 Educational Review 444; 4:47-52, 129-141. 1892.

Silberman, Charles E., Crisis in the Classroom. 1970.

State Child Labor Standards, U.S. Department of Labor Bulletin No. 158. 1965.

"State Laws Relating to Compulsory Education", 29 School and Society 276. March 2, 1929.

Steinhilber, August and Carl J. Sokalowski, State Law on Compulsory Attendance, U.S. Dept. of H.E.W., Office of Education, Circular 793. 1966.

Stoops, E. et al., "Compulsory Education; Backgrounds and Issues", 33 Calif. Journal of Secondary Education 95. Feb. 1958.

"Symposium: Problems of Current School-Leaving Age Requirements", California Journal of Secondary Education, Vol. 33, No. 2. February 1958.

Trattner, W.T., Crusade for the Children: A History of the National Child Labor Committee and Child Labor Reform in America. 1970.

Umbeck, Nelda, State Legislation on School Attendance and Related Matters, School Census, and Child Labor, U.S. Dept of H.E.W. 1960.

"Validity of Public School Fees", 41 ALR 3d 753.

Waite, K.V., "High School Principal Looks at the School-Leaving Age Problems", 33 Calif. Journal of Secondary Education 126. February 1958.

Wood, Stephen B., Constitutional Politics in the Progressive Era. 1968.

APPENDIX A

BASIC REQUIREMENTS OF THE PRIMARY STATUTORY

REFERENCE OF THE COMPULSORY ATTENDANCE STATUTES

BASIC REQUIREMENTS OF THE PRIMARY STATUTORY REFERENCE[1]
OF THE COMPULSORY ATTENDANCE STATUTES

STATE and CITATION TO PRIMARY STATUTORY REFERENCE[2]	AGE SPAN OF ATTENDANCE[3]		RESPONSIBILITY FOR COMPLIANCE[4]		STATUTORY LANGUAGE[5]		
	Compelled	Permitted[3]	Parent	Child	Attendance Required	Instruction Required	Education Required
West Virginia §18-8-1	7 – 16	6, no upper limit ($18-2-5)	"attendance shall beginwith the 7th birthday"		Yes	No	No
Wisconsin §§40.77, 118.15	7 – 16 (18 if in a vocational school)	4 – 20, over 20 with school board permission.(Const. Art. 10, §3; 118.14)	Yes	No	Yes	No	No
Wyoming Educ. §21.1-48	7 – 16	6 – 21 Code §21.1-57	Yes	Yes	Yes	No	No

FOOTNOTES

1. Source: Analysis of state statutes.

2. In the interests of space, the citations are abbreviated. Unless otherwise noted, this citation applies to all columns.

3. Provisions which define "seven" or "six" as reaching that age by a particular date after the opening of school in September or at mid-term are common, as are allowances for the exercise of discretion by the board of education. Statutes are typically phrased to permit children over six to attend; where no upper age limit is set, this presumably permits all minors over six to attend.

4. Does not take into account language of the compulsory attendance law used elsewhere than in the primary reference statute, such as in separate truancy provisions.

5. Based on language in the primary statutory reference which compels a public school learning arrangement, not on language which permits (or exempts)alternative learning arrangements such as instruction in a private school or education by a certified teacher.

STATE and CITATION TO PRIMARY STATUTORY REFERENCE[2]	AGE SPAN OF ATTENDANCE[3]		RESPONSIBILITY FOR COMPLIANCE[4]		STATUTORY LANGUAGE[5]		
	Compelled	Permitted[3]	Parent	Child	Attendance Required	Instruction Required	Education Required
Alabama Tit. 52, 297	7 - 16	6 (Tit. 52, §298) No upper limit.	Yes	Yes	Yes	No	No
Alaska §14.30.010	7 - 16	6 - 19. (§14.03.070)	Yes	Yes	Yes	No	No
Arizona §15-321	8 - 16	6 - 21. (§15-302; Const. Art. XI, Sec. 6)	Yes	No	Yes	No	No
Arkansas Tit. 80-1502	7 - 15	6 - 21 (Tit. 80-1501, 80-1501.2)	Yes	No	Yes	No	No
California Educ. §12101	6 - 16	5 years 9 months. No upper limit. (§5301)	Yes	Yes	Yes	No	Yes. Child "subject to compulsory full-time education".
Colorado §123-20-5	7 - 16	6 - 21. (Const. Art. IX, §123-20-3)	Yes (§ 123-20 -9)	Yes	Yes	No	No

STATE and CITATION TO PRIMARY STATUTORY REFERENCE[2]	AGE SPAN OF ATTENDANCE[3]		RESPONSIBILITY FOR COMPLIANCE[4]		STATUTORY LANGUAGE[5]		
	Compelled	Permitted[3]	Parent	Child	Attendance Required	Instruction Required	Education Required
Connecticut §10-184	7 - 16	5, no upper limit. (§ 10-15)	Yes	No	Yes	"All parents and those who have care of children shall bring them up in some lawful and honest employment and instruct them or cause them to be instructed in (specified subjects.)"	No
Delaware Tit. 14, §2702	6 - 16	6 - 21 (Tit. 14, §202(a))	Yes	No	Yes	No	No
District of Columbia §31-201	7 - 16	Under rules of Board of Education	Yes	No	Yes	Yes	No
Florida §232.01	7 - 16	6, no upper limit (§232.01); 5, in systems with kindergartens (§232.04); 4, for public nursery schools (§232.04)	Yes	Yes	Yes "Pupils may be counted in attendance only if they are actually present at school or away from school on a school day and are engaged in an educational activity which constitutes a part of the school-approved instructional program for the pupil." (§232.022)		

STATE and CITATION TO PRIMARY STATUTORY REFERENCE[2]	AGE SPAN OF ATTENDANCE[3]		RESPONSIBILITY FOR COMPLIANCE[4]		STATUTORY LANGUAGE[5]		
	Compelled	Permitted[3]	Parent	Child	Attendance Required	Instruction Required	Education Required
Georgia §32-2104	7 - 16	6 - 19 (§32-937)	Yes	Yes	Yes	No	No
Hawaii §298-9	6 - 18	6, no upper limit (§§298-8)	Yes	Yes	Yes	No	No
Idaho §33-202	7 - 16	5 - 21 (§33-201)	Yes	No	Yes	Yes	No
Illinois Ch. 122, §26-1	7 - 16	6 - 21 (Ch. 122 §10-20.12)	Yes	No	Yes	No	No
Indiana §20-8.1-3-17	7 - 16	"Open to all children until they complete their course of study". (§20-8.1-2-2)	Yes	Yes	Yes	No	Yes (See also §20-8.1-3-1: "The legislative intent . . . is to provide an efficient and speedy means of insuring that children receive a proper education whenever it is reasonably possible.")

STATE and CITATION TO PRIMARY STATUTORY REFERENCE[2]	AGE SPAN OF ATTENDANCE[3]		RESPONSIBILITY FOR COMPLIANCE[4]		STATUTORY LANGUAGE[5]		
	Compelled	Permitted[3]	Parent	Child	Attendance Required	Instruction Required	Education Required
Iowa §299.1	7 - 16	5 - 21 (§282.1, 282.6)	Yes	No	Yes	No	No
Kansas §72-1111	7 - 16	6, no upper limit. 5, for kindergarten. (§72-1107)	Yes	No	Yes	No	No
Kentucky §159.010	7 - 16	6 - 21 (§158.030, 159.010)	Yes (See also §159.180)	No	Yes	No	No
Louisiana §17:221	7 - 15 (inclusive)	6, no upper limit (§17:222; Const. Art. 12, Sec. 1)	Yes	No	Yes	No	No
Maine Tit. 20, §911	7 - 17	6 - 20, 5 for kindergarten (Tit. 20 §859)	Yes	Yes	Yes	No	No
Maryland Art. 77, §92	6 - 16	5 - 20 (Art. 77, §73)	Yes	Yes	Yes	No	No
Massachusetts Ch. 76, §1	Established by the board of education (Ch. 76, §1)	every person may attend (ch. 76, §5)	Yes (Ch. 76, §2)	Yes	Yes	Yes	No

STATE and CITATION TO PRIMARY STATUTORY REFERENCE[2]	AGE SPAN OF ATTENDANCE[3]		RESPONSIBILITY FOR COMPLIANCE[4]		STATUTORY LANGUAGE[5]		
	Compelled	Permitted[3]	Parent	Child	Attendance Required	Instruction Required	Education Required
Michigan §340.731	6 - 16	5, no upper limit (§340.356, 340.357)	Yes	No	Yes	No	No
Minnesota §120.10	7 - 16	5 - 21 (§120.06)	Yes (§120.12)	Yes	Yes	No	No
Mississippi	No provision	6, no upper limit (§37-15-9)					
Missouri §167.031	7 - 16	5 - 20 (§160.051)	Yes	No	Yes	No	No
Montana §75-6303, 75-6304	7 - 16	6 - 21 (§75-6302, Const. Art. XI, §7)	Yes	No	Yes	Yes. Person responsible for the child shall cause it to be instructed in prescribed subjects in either public or private educational setting.	No

STATE and CITATION TO PRIMARY STATUTORY REFERENCE[2]	AGE SPAN OF ATTENDANCE[3]		RESPONSIBILITY FOR COMPLIANCE[4]		STATUTORY LANGUAGE[5]		
	Compelled	Permitted[3]	Parent	Child	Attendance Required	Instruction Required	Education Required
Nebraska §79-201	7 - 16	5 - 21 (§§79-802, 79-1001.01, Const. Art. VII, §6)	Yes	No	Yes	No	Yes
Nevada §392.040	7 - 17	6, no upper limit	Yes	No	Yes	No	No
New Hampshire §193:1	6 - 16	No provision	Yes (§193.2)	Yes	Yes	No	No
New Jersey §18A:38-25	6 - 16	5 - 20 (§18A:38-1) persons over 20 with permission of district board of education (§18A-38-4)	Yes	No	Yes	No	No
New Mexico §77-10-2	6 until attaining age of majority (18).	6 now, will be 5 in 1977. No upper limit (§77-11-2)	Yes	Yes	Yes	No	No
New York Educ. §3205(1)	6 - 16	5 - 21 (Educ. §3202(1))	Yes (Educ. §3212)	Yes	Yes. The child "shall attend upon full time instruction".	No	No

STATE and CITATION TO PRIMARY STATUTORY REFERENCE[2]	AGE SPAN OF ATTENDANCE[3]		RESPONSIBILITY FOR COMPLIANCE[4]		STATUTORY LANGUAGE[5]		
	Compelled	Permitted[3]	Parent	Child	Attendance Required	Instruction Required	Education Required
North Carolina §115-166	7 - 16	6, no upper limit (§§115-1, 115-162)	Yes	No	Yes	No	No
North Dakota §15-34.1-01	7 - 16	6 - 21 (§15-47-01)	Yes	No	Yes	No	No
Ohio §§3321.01, 3321.03, 3321.04	6 - 18 §3321.01	6 - 21 (§3313.64)	Yes	No	Yes	No	No
Oklahoma Tit. 70, §10-105	7 - 18	5 - 21 (Tit. 70, §1-114)	Yes	Yes	Yes	No	Yes. States that it is unlawful for the child to neglect or refuse "to receive an education".
Oregon §339.010	7 - 18	6 - 21 (§339.115)	Yes (§339.030)	Yes	Yes	No	No
Pennsylvania Tit.24, (§13-1326, 13-1327)	8 - 17	6 - 21 (§13-1301)	Yes	Yes	Yes	No	No

STATE and CITATION TO PRIMARY STATUTORY REFERENCE[2]	AGE SPAN OF ATTENDANCE[3]		RESPONSIBILITY FOR COMPLIANCE[4]		STATUTORY LANGUAGE[5]		
	Compelled	Permitted[3]	Parent	Child	Attendance Required	Instruction Required	Education Required
Puerto Rico Tit. 18, §80.	8 - 16	5 - 18 (T. 3, §141)	Yes	No	Yes	Yes "(Parent) shall cause such minor to be instructed in a public or private school and to attend regularly such school.	No
Rhode Island §16-19-1	7 - 16	No provision.	Yes	Yes	Yes	No	No
South Carolina §21-757	7 - 16 (inclusive)	6 - 21 (§21-752)	Yes	No	Yes	No	No
South Dakota §13-27-1	7 - 16	5 - 19 (over 21 with school board permission) (§13.28-1, §13.28-8)	Yes	No	Yes	No	No
Tennessee §49-1708	7 - 16 (inclusive)	6, no upper limit (§§49-1701, 49-1702)	Yes	No	Yes	No	No

STATE and CITATION TO PRIMARY STATUTORY REFERENCE[2]	AGE SPAN OF ATTENDANCE[3]		RESPONSIBILITY FOR COMPLIANCE[4]		STATUTORY LANGUAGE[5]		
	Compelled	Permitted[3]	Parent	Child	Attendance Required	Instruction Required	Education Required
Texas Tit.2, §21.032	7 - 17	5 - 21 (Tit. 2, §21.031)	No	Yes	Yes	No	No
Utah §53-24-1	6 - 18 (16 if 8th completed or is employed and attends part time)	5 - 18 (§53-4-7)	Yes	No	Yes	No	No
Vermont Tit. 16, §1121	7 - 16; children over 16 who are enrolled in a public school by parents also must attend. (Tit.16,§1122)	6 - 18 (Tit. 16, §1073)	Yes	No	Yes	No	Compulsory attendance is required unless the child receives "equivalent education" or has completed the 10th grade.
Virginia §22-275.1	6 - 17	6 no upper limit (§§22-218.1, 22-218.3)	Yes	Yes	Yes	Yes. § 22-275.6 requires a person having control of a child to cause the child to attend school or receive instruction as required by law.	No
Washington §28A.27.010	8 - 15 (18 if no reasonable proficiency in first 9 grades or unemployed.	6 - 21 (§28A.58.190)	Yes	No	Yes	No	No

APPENDIX B

PRIMARY LEARNING ARRANGEMENTS
WHICH MEET THE ATTENDANCE REQUIREMENTS
OF THE COMPULSORY ATTENDANCE STATUTES

Primary[1] Learning Arrangements
Which Meet the Attendance Requirements
of the Compulsory Attendance Statutes

State and Citation[2]	Public School	Non-Public School	Non-School
Alabama Tit. 52, §297	Yes	private, denomonational, parochial, certified by the department of education, and teaching courses required in the public schools (in English). (See also Tit. 52, §299).	instruction by a competent private tutor, teaching in English courses required in the public schools. Tit. 52, §300
Alaska 14.30.010	Yes	private with certified teachers providing an academic education comparable to that offered by public schools in the area	tutoring by certified personnel; enrolled in a full-time approved program of correspondence study
Arizona 15-321	Yes	regularly organized private, parochial school, taught by competent teachers	instruction at home by a competent teacher in subjects given in the public schools
Arkansas Tit. 80-1502	Yes	private, parochial, by certified teachers	no provision
California Educ. §12101	Yes "public full-time day school"	private school staffed by teachers capable of teaching the courses required in public schools. Educ. §12154	instruction by private tutor or other certified person, at least 3 hrs./day. Educ. §12155

[1]This chart addresses the distinction between permitted school and non-school learning arrangements. Statutory reference to hybrid arrangements such as special education and work-study programs or residential and truant schools are not included in this chart. SOURCE: Analysis of state statutes.

[2]In the interest of conserving space, the citations are abbreviated. Unless otherwise noted, this citation applies to all columns.

State and Citation[2]	Public School	Non-Public School	Non-School
Colorado §123-20-5	Yes	independent or parochial, and providing a "basic academic education" comparable to that provided in the public schools	instruction at home by a certified teacher; instruction under an established system of home study approved by the state board
Connecticut §10-184	Yes "public day school"	"equivalent instruction elsewhere in the studies taught in the public schools" "a school other than a public school". §10-188	
Delaware Tit. 14, §2702	Yes "free public school"	The child is not required to attend the public school if it can be shown by affidavit and by testing results that the child is receiving regular and thorough instruction similar to that received in the public schools. Tit. 14, §2703	
District of Columbia §31-201	Yes	private or parochial school where instruction is equivalent to that given in the public school	instructed privately if the instruction is equivalent to that given in the public school
Florida §§232.01, 232.02	Yes	parochial, denominational, private	tutoring at home in accord with state board regulations
Georgia §32-2104	Yes	private	no provision
Hawaii §298-9	Yes	private	home tutoring by a competent person; the instruction must be such as is approved by the superintendent

ate and tation[2]	Public School	Non-Public School	Non-School
daho §33-202	Yes	The parent "shall cause the child to be instructed in subjects commonly and usually taught in the public schools"	
		private, parochial	"otherwise [than in schools] comparably instructed"
llinois h.122, §26-1	Yes	private, parochial, having a curriculum corresponding to the public school curriculum	no provision
diana 0-8.1-3-17	Yes	"some other school taught in the English language and open to inspection by State attendance officer"	The parent must send a child to public school "unless the child is being provided with instruction equivalent to that given in the public school". §20-8.1-3-34
wa 299.1	Yes	"In lieu of such attendance such child may attend upon equivalent instruction by a certified teacher elsewhere".	
nsas 72-1111	Yes	private, denominational or parochial, if teacher is certified and competent	no provision
ntucky 159.010	Yes "regular public day school"	private or parochial day school approved by state board of education §159.030	no provision
uisiana 17:221	Yes	private day school, in regularly assigned classes.	no provision

State and Citation[2]	Public School	Non-Public School	Non-School
Maine Tit. 20, §911	Yes	private school equivalent to the public school instruction	equivalent instruction approved by the Commissioner
Maryland Art. 77, §92	Yes	regular and thorough instruction elsewhere in the studies usually taught in public schools	
Massachusetts Ch. 76, §1	Yes	some other day school approved by the school committee, as thorough and efficient as the public schools	instruction "otherwise" in a manner approved in advance by the superintendent or the school committee
Michigan §340.731 §340.732	Yes	private, parochial and denominational and comparable to school instruction	no provision
Minnesota §120.10	Yes	private with teaching in English by certified teachers	no provision
Missouri §167.031	Yes "some day school"	private, parochial or parish	regular daily home instruction during the usual school hours, at least "substantially" equivalent to the public school instruction.
Montana §75-6303 §75-6304	Yes	private institution in the subjects required to be taught in the public schools	supervised correspondence study or supervised home study under the transportation provisions (§75-7008(c) (d) and §75-7019(5)).
Nebraska §79-201	Yes	private, denominational, or parochial day school	no provision

ate and tation[2]	Public School	Non-Public School	Non-School
vada 392.040	Yes	some other school which some written evidence shows is providing instruction equivalent to that approved by the state board of education. §392.070	home instruction which some written evidence shows is equivalent to that approved by the state board of education §392.070.
w Hampshire 193:1	Yes	approved private school	no provision
w Jersey 18A:38-25	Yes	day school which gives instruction equivalent to that provided in public schools	instruction "elsewhere than at school", and equivalent to that given in public schools
Mexico 7-10-2	Yes	private school in approved courses	no provision
York uc. §3204(1) d (2)(e), 205(1)	Yes	"elsewhere" if instruction is equivalent to the public school instruction.	
th Carolina 15-166	Yes	"attend school" where teachers and curricula approved by State Board of Education	no provision
th Dakota 5-34.1-01, 5-34.1-03	Yes	parochial or private schools approved by County Superintendent of Schools.	no provision
o 321.04	"a school which conforms to the minimum standards prescribed by the state board of education"		home instruction by a person "qualified to teach the branches in which instruction is required"
homa . 70, -105	Yes Yes "some public, private or other school"		"other means of education...for the full term district schools are in session."

State and Citation[2]	Public School	Non-Public School	Non-School
Oregon §339.010	Yes	private or parochial school teaching subjects usually taught in public schools. §399.030	instruction by a parent or private teacher in the courses usually taught in the public schools. §399.030
Pennsylvania Tit. 24, §13-1327		"day school" meeting standards prescribed by the State Board of Education	instruction by a properly qualified approved private tutor
Puerto Rico Tit. 18, §80	Yes	private "other schools of recognized standing."	no provision
Rhode Island §16-19-1	Yes	private school equivalent to the public schools. §16-19-2	approved private instruction equivalent to that required in the public schools. §16-19-2
South Carolina §21-757	Yes	approved private, parochial or denominational	"other programs approved by the State Board of Education" "as substantially equivalent" to the instruction given in public schools. (see §21-757.3)
South Dakota §13-27-1	Yes	"non-public elementary school"	a child may be "otherwise instructed by a competent person" in the courses taught in the public schools. §13-27-3
Tennessee §49-1708	Yes	private day school	no provision
Texas Educ. §21.032	Yes	private or parochial which teaches a good citizenship course. §21.033	no provision

State and Citation[2]	Public School	Non-Public School	Non-School
Utah §53-24-1	Yes	regularly established private	home instruction in the branches prescribed by law
Vermont Tit. 16, §1121	Yes	A child need not attend public school if s/he is "otherwise being furnished with equivalent education"	
Virginia §22-275.1	Yes	private, denominational or parochial	home instruction by quali-fied tutor or teacher ap-proved by division superin-tendent
Washington §28A.27.010	Yes	approved private and/or parochial	no provision
West Virginia §18-8-1	Yes	approved private, parochial or other	instruction in home or other approved place by approved person
Wisconsin §118.15	Yes	private	"instruction elsewhere than at school", which is substantially equi-valent to public or private school instruc-tion
Wyoming Educ. §21.1-48	Yes	private	no provision

APPENDIX C

STATUTORY EXEMPTIONS FROM COMPULSORY ATTENDANCE
IN ADDITION TO THE PRIVATE SCHOOL EXEMPTION
FOR THE FIFTY STATES, THE DISTRICT OF COLUMBIA
AND PUERTO RICO

STATUTORY EXEMPTIONS FROM COMPULSORY ATTENDANCE IN ADDITION TO THE PRIVATE SCHOOL EXEMPTION[1] FOR THE FIFTY STATES AND THE DISTRICT OF COLUMBIA AND PUERTO RICO

State	Private Tutor or Home Instruction	Completion of Educational Requirement - Grade Levels	Mental, Emotional and/or Physical Disability	Distance - Lack of Transportation	Legal Employment Including Work Study or Vocational Employment	Expulsion or Suspension	Special Reasons Granted By Court or School Administration	Other Exemptions
Alabama	T.52, §297	12 T.52, §301(h)	T.52, §301(a)	T.52, §301(c)	T.52, §301(d)			
Alaska	§14.30.010(1)	12 §14.30.010(9)	§14.30.010(3)	§14.30.010(7)		§14.30.010(6)	§14.30.010(8)	§14.30.010(4) (court custody), §14.30.010(5) (temp. absence)
Arizona	§15-321(B)(1)	8 §15-321(B)(4)	§15-321(B)(3)		§15-321(B)(6) §15-321(B)(7)		§15-321(B)(5)	
Arkansas		8 §80-1504(b)	§80-1504(a)					80-1504(c) (to support widowed mother)
California	Educ §12155	12 §12601	Education §12152 §12156		Educ §12157, §12158, §12160 (vocational employment)	Educ §12103		Educ §12154.5 (mentally gifted & bi-lingual)
Colorado	§123-20-5(2)(j)	12 §123-20-5(2)(i)	§123-20-5(2)(d)		§123-20-5(2(f) §123-20-5(h) (work study)	§123-20-5(2)(e)	§123-20-5(b)	§123-20-5(2)(b)(temporary absence), §123-20-5(2)(g)(court custody)
Connecticut	Not specified, but see §10-184	8 §10-189	§10-190, §10-191		§10-184		§10-190	

State	Private Tutor or Home Instruction	Completion of Educational Requirement - Grade Level	Mental, Emotional and/or Physical Disability	Distance - Lack of Transportation	Legal Employment Including Work Study or Vocational Employment	Expulsion or Suspension	Special Reasons Granted By Court or School Administration	Other Exemptions
Delaware	Not specified, but see T.14,§2703		T.14;§2705, §2707					T.24,§2706 (temporary absence)
District of Columbia	§31-201	8 §31-202	§31-203		§31-202		§31-204	
Florida	§232.02(d)-		§232.06(1)	§232.06(2)	§232.06(3)	§232.26	§232.06(4)	§232.01(c)(1) (married or pregnant) §232.09 (financial inability)
Georgia		12 §32-2105	§32-2106(a)				§32-2106(b) §32-2104	§32-2119 (pages of Gen. Assembly) §32-2104 exams for military service
Hawaii	§298-9(2)	12 §298-9(5)	§298-9(1)		§298-9(3)	§298-11 §298-9	§298-9(4)	§298-15 (religious)
Idaho	Not specified, but see §33-202		§33-204			§33-205		
Illinois	Not specified, but see C.122,§26-1(1) C122§13-3	12	C.122,§26-1(2)		C.122,§26-1(3)			C.122,§26-1(2) (temporary absence) C.122,§26-1(4) (religious)
Indiana	Not specified, but see §20-81-3-17		§20-8.1-3-19		§20.8.1-4-3.0	§20-8.1-5-15		§20-8.1-3-18 (government service), §20-8.1-3-22 (religious)

State	Private Tutor or Home Instruction	Completion of Educational Requirement - Grade-Level	Mental, Emotional and/or Physical Disability	Distance - Lack of Transportation	Legal Employment Including Work Study or Vocational Employment	Expulsion or Suspension	Special Reasons Granted By Court or School Administration	Other Exemption
Iowa	§299.4	8 §299.2(2)	§299.5		§299.2(1)	§287.3	§299.2(3)	§299.2(4) (religious), §299.2(5)(college or prep school)
Kansas			72-1111					§72-1111 (religious)
Kentucky		12 §159.030(a)	§159.030 (c)		§339.290 §339.380			§159.035 4-H activities
Louisiana	but see 17:221		§17:226(1), :234	§17:226(2)		§17:416		§17:226(3) (temporary absence, religious included)
Maine	Not specified, but see T.20,§911	12 T.20,§911	T.20,§911		T.20,§911 (work study)			T.20,§911 (necessary absence) 20§1227 (religious Instru)
Maryland	Not specified, but see Art.77,§92		Art.77,§92			See Art. 77, §95		Art.77,§92 (necessary absence)
Massachusetts	Not specified, but see c.76,§1		c.76,§1		c.76,§1 149 §86			c.76,§1 (necessary absence) (religious)
Michigan	See 340.732(a)		§340.752 §340.771 §340.613	§340.732(c)		See §340.613		§340.732 (government service) (religious)

State	Private Tutor or Home Instruction	Completion of Educational Requirement - Grade Level	Mental, Emotional and/or Physical Disability	Distance - Lack of Transportation	Legal Employment Including Work Study or Vocational Employment	Expulsion or Suspension	Special Reasons Granted By Court or School Administration	Other Exemption
Minnesota	See §120.10 subdivision 1	9 §120.10 subdivision 3(2)	§120.10 subdivision 3(1)	§120.10 subdivision 3(4)				§120.10 subdivision 3(3) (religious)
Mississippi								
Missouri	§167.031	8 §167.051	§167.031 §167.041		§167.031(2) §167.051	§167.161		
Montana	§75-6303(3)	8 §75-6303	§75-6303(4)	See §75-7019(5)		§75-6304(3) §75-6311	§75-6303(5)	§75-6304(2) (necessary absence)
Nebraska	See §79-201	12 §79-201	§79-202		§79-202			§79-202 (necessary absence)
Nevada	§392.070	12 §392.060	§392.050	§392.080	§392.100, §392.110 (apprenticeship)	§392.030	§392.090	
New Hampshire		8 §193:1	§193:1	See §193:5	See §193:5	See §193:13	§193:5	
New Jersey	Not specified but see 8A:38-25		§18A:38-26		§18A:38-36	Not specified, but see §18A:38-26		
New Mexico		10 §77-10-2(3)	§77-10-2(5)		§77-10-6			§77-10-2(4) (under age 8) §77-10-2.1 (religious)

State	Private Tutor or Home Instruction	Completion of Educational Requirement - Grade Level	Mental, Emotional and/or Physical Disability	Distance - Lack of Transportation	Legal Employment Including Work Study or Vocational Employment	Expulsion or Suspension	Special Reasons Granted By Court or School Administration	Other Exemptions
New York	Educ. §3210 (2)	12 Education §3205(2)(a)	§3208	§3208 (3)	Education §3205(2)(b) §3206 §3215		§3210(2)(b), (d),(e)	Education §3210(b) (religious)
North Carolina	§115-116		§115-166 §115-172				§115-167 §115-171	§115-166 (temporary absence)
North Dakota	§15-34.1-03(1)	12 §15-34.1-03(2)	§15-34.1-03(4)		§15-34.1-03(3)			
Ohio	§3321.04(A)(2)	12 §3321.03	§3321.04(A)(1)		§3321.04(B) §3321.08 §3331.01			§3321.04, .05 §3321.05 (incapable of profiting substantially)
Oklahoma	T.70,§10-105	12 T.70,§10-105	T.70,§10-105(1)					T.70,§10-105(2) (necessary absence) §10-105(3) best interest of child over age 16.
Oregon	§339.030(6)	12 §339.010	§339.030(4)	§339.030(5)	§339.030(1)	§339.030(8)	§339.030(7), (9)	§339.030(1) (community college)
Pennsylvania	T.24,§13-1327	12 T.24,§13-1326	T.24,§13-1330 (2)	T.24,§13-1330 (5) but see 24§13-1331	T.24,§13-1330 (1),(3),(4)		24§13-1329	24§13-1330(2) "unable to profit further..."

State	Private Tutor or Home Instruction	Completion of Educational Requirement - Grade Level	Mental, Emotional and/or Physical Disability	Distance - Lack of Transportation	Legal Employment Including Work study or Vocational Employment	Expulsion or Suspension	Special Reasons Granted By Court or School Administration	Other Exemption
Puerto Rico	T.18, §80(2)		T.29, §452	T.18, §80(c)	T.29, §431 18, §491	T.18, §80(a)	T.18, §80(a)	
Rhode Island	§16-19-1		§16-19-1		See §16-19-5	§16-19-1	§16-19-1	
South Carolina	§21-757.3	12 §21-757.2(a)	§21-757.2(b)		§21-757.2(c)	See §21-771	§21-757.2(f)	§21-757.2(e) (married or pregnant)
South Dakota	§13-27-3	8 §13-27-1	§13-27-4, §13-27-5				§13-27-7 §13-27-2	§13-27-6 (illness in the family)
Tennessee		12 §49-1710(c)	§49-1710(a), (e)	§49-1710(b)	§50-703	§49-1710(e)	§49-1708	§49-1710(d) (temporary absence)
Texas	§21.033(1)	9 §21.033(4)	Education §21.033(2)		§21.033(4) (work study; vocational)	§21.033(5)		§21.035, §21.035(b) Jewish holidays. §21.033(3) temp. absence for remedial treatment
Utah	§53-24-1(b)(2)	12 §53-24-1(b)(1)	§53-24-1(b)(3)	§53-24-1(b)(4)	§53-24-1(a), §53-24-1(b)(5) (vocational)	§53-24-1(c)	§53-24-1(c)	
Vermont	Not specified, but see T.16,§1121	10 T.16,§1121(a)	T.16,§1121(a), §1124		T.16, §1123(c)		T.16§1122 T.16§1123	T.16,§1123(a) (temporary)
Virginia	§22-275.1		§22-275.3, §22-275.4	§22-275.3			§22-275.4 §22-275.4:1	§22-275.3 (contagious diseases)

State	Private Tutor or Home Instruction	Completion of Educational Requirement - Grade Level	Mental, Emotional and/or Physical Disability	Distance - Lack of Transportation	Legal Employment Including Work Study or Vocational Employment	Expulsion or Suspension	Special Reasons Granted By Court or School Administration	Other Exemptions
Washington		9 §28A.27.010	§28A.27.010		§28A.27.010 §28A.27.090		§28A.27.010	
West Virginia	§18-8-1 Exemption B	12 §18-8-1 Exemption F	§18-8-1 Exemption C	§18-8-1 Exemption D	§18-8-1. Exemption G	See §18-8-8		§18-8-1, Exemption F (hazardous conditions), Exemption H (illness), Exemption I (destitution), Exemption J (religious)
Wisconsin	§40.77(1)(c) §118.15(5)	12 §40.77(1)(b) §118.15(3)(a) (1)	§40.77(1)(b) §118.15(3)(a) (2)		§40.77(am)	118.15(3)(a) 3	§118.15(3)(a) (3)	§118.15(1)(d) (students in good standing)
Wyoming		8 §21.1-48	§21.1-48(a)			§21.1-48(c)	§21.1-48	

THIS PAGE WAS LEFT INTENTIONALLY BLANK

APPENDIX D

TRUANCY OFFENSES AND ENFORCEMENT PROVISIONS
IN THE FIFTY STATES, THE DISTRICT OF COLUMBIA
AND PUERTO RICO

OFFENSES DEFINED

STATE	PARENT		CHILD	
	FAILURE TO CAUSE TO ATTEND	OTHER	TRUANT	OTHER
Alabama	Yes T.52 Sec. 302	No	No	No
Alaska	Yes Sec. 14.30.020	No	No	No
Arizona	Yes Sec. 15-323	No	No	No
Arkansas	Yes Sec. 80-1508	No	No	All cases of non-attendance - not fault of parent as attested in writing Sec. 80-1512
California	Yes Sec. 12454	No	Yes - Any pupil subject to compulsory full time education, absent without valid excuse more than 3 days or tardy in excess of 30 minutes on each of more than 3 days in 1 school year. Sec.12401	Yes - Habitual truant. Any student reported as truant 3 or more times Sec. 12403
Colorado	Yes Sec.123-20-9	No	No	Neglect or refusal to obey court order to attend
Connecticut	Yes Sec.10-185	No	Yes Sec.10-184	No
Delaware	Yes T.14 Sec.2702	No	No	No

PROVISIONS FOR ENFORCEMENT
OF ATTENDANCE REQUIREMENTS

STATE	PROVIDES FOR ATTENDANCE OR TRUANT OFFICER	ALLOWS ARREST OF TRUANTS W/O WARRANT	REQUIRES NOTICE TO PARENTS TO COMPLY BEFORE COMPLAINT IS FILED
Alabama	Yes T.52 Sec.314	No T52 Sec.312 But can be taken into custody w/o warrant	Yes T52 Sec. 311 Must be written
Alaska	Yes Sec.14.30.050	No Must have warrant Sec.14.30.050	No provision
Arizona	Yes Sec.15-324	Yes Sec.15-325(B)(2)	No provision
Arkansas	Yes Sec.80-1511	No	Yes In person or in writing Sec.80-1511
California	Yes Sec.12351	Yes Sec.12405	No provision
Colorado	Yes Sec.123-20-8	No	Yes Sec.123-20-9(5) written
Connecticut	Yes Sec.10-199	Yes, habitual truants can be arrested. Any child can be stopped and if truant, taken to school Sec.10-200	No
Delaware	No But superintendent of schools is authorized to enforce statute T14 Sec.2711	No	Yes T14 Sec.2708

LIABILITIES AND CONSEQUENCES

STATE	WHO IS LIABLE FOR NON-ATTENDANCE PARENT AND/OR CHILD	PENALTIES - PARENT		
		CRIMINAL OR NOT CRIMINAL	FINE	IMPRISONMENT
Alabama	Parent, unless establishes that child was beyond parental control or that parent had no knowledge of absence T52 Sec. 303, 305	Criminal T52 Secs.302,311	Not more than $100	90 days at hard labor or both T52, Sec.302
Alaska	Both Sec.14.30.010	Criminal Sec.14.30.020	Not less than $50, more than $200 & costs of prosecution Sec.14.30.020	Until fine is paid or serve one day for each $2.00
Arizona	Both Sec.15-321	Criminal Sec.15-323	Not less than $5 or more than $300	Not less than 1 or more than 90 days or both Sec.15-323
Arkansas	Both Secs.80-1502 1512	Criminal Sec.80-1508	Not more than $10 for each offense each day = 1 offense Sec.1508	No
California	Both Sec.12101	Criminal Sec.12454	Not more than $25 first offense ------------- Not less than $25 or more than $250 subsequent offenses Sec.12454	Not more than 5 days ------------- Not less than 5 or more than 25 days or both
Colorado	Both Secs.123-20-5, 123-20-9	Not criminal	No	For contempt if parent does not comply with court order to cause child to attend Sec.123-20-9(5)
Connecticut	Both Sec.10-184	Criminal Sec.10-185	Not for more than $5 for each offense (1 wk absence = 1 offense) Sec.10-185	No
Delaware	Both Sec.27Q2	Criminal T.14 Sec.2709	Not less than $5 or more than $25 first offense ------------- Not less than $25 or more than $50 subsequent offenses T.14 Sec.2709	In default of payment, not more than 2 days ------------- Not more than 5 days

PENALTIES - CHILD

STATE	DECLARED DELINQUENT	CAN BE INSTITU-TIONALIZED	SPECIAL PLACE-MENT WITHIN SCHOOL SYSTEM
Alabama	Yes, if habitual truant and parent has filed state-ment of lack of control Sec.304	Yes T13 Sec.361	Truant schools T52, Sec.173
Alaska	No ,,Child in need of super-vision" Sec.47.10.290 Sec.47.10.010	Yes Sec.47.10. 080(j), but not in institution for delinquent children	No
Arizona	No "An incorrigible child" Sec.8-201(12)	Yes Sec.8-241(2) Dept. Correc. or private institution	No
Arkansas	Yes, if parent attests in writing that fault is child's Sec. 80-1512, 45-204	Yes Sec.80-1512 Sec.45-221	No
California	No, is a ward of the court Sec.601	Yes Sec.730, 727 Cannot be com-mitted to youth authority	Yes Opportunity schools Sec.6500, et seq.
Colorado	Yes Sec.123-20-9(6)(b) Sec.22-8-1(2)	Yes Sec.22-8-11	No
Connecticut	Yes Sec.17-53(a)	Yes Sec.17-68	No
Delaware	Yes T.14 Sec.2711	No, unless no special school available and child is found to be delinquent T.14 Sec.2711	Yes Special school T.14 Sec.203 T.14 Sec.2711

OFFENSES DEFINED

	PARENT		CHILD	
STATE	FAILURE TO CAUSE TO ATTEND	OTHER	TRUANT	OTHER
District of Columbia	Yes Sec.31-207	Failure to keep child in school regularly	No	Unlawful absence Absence of child between 7 & 16 for any reason other than those defined by the Board of Education as valid. Sec.31-204
Florida	Yes Sec.232.19(6)(a)	No	No	No
Georgia	Yes Sec.32-2104	No	No	No
Hawaii	Yes Sec.298-12	No	No	No
Idaho	Yes Sec.33-207	Knowingly allowing child to become an habitual truant Sec.33-207	No	Yes, habitual truant-any pupil who has repeatedly violated attendance regulations, or whose parents have refused to provide instruction as provided in Secs.33-202 and 33-206
Illinois	Yes Sec.122-26-10	Inducing absence Sec.122-26-11	No	No

PROVISIONS FOR ENFORCEMENT
OF ATTENDANCE REQUIREMENTS

STATE	PROVIDES FOR ATTENDANCE OR TRUANT OFFICER	ALLOWS ARREST OF TRUANTS WITHOUT A WARRANT	REQUIRES NOTICE TO PARENTS TO COMPLY BEFORE COMPLAINT IS FILED
District of Columbia	Yes Sec.31-212	No	No
Florida	Yes T.15 Sec.232.17	No, but attendance officer authorized to "find" truant child and return such child to parent or principal Sec.232.17(d)	Yes 15 Sec.232.17(c) written
Georgia	Yes Sec.32-2110	No	Yes Sec.32-2115
Hawaii	No, but department of education is authorized to enforce statute Sec.298-13		No
Idaho	No, but Board of Trustees is authorized to enforce statute Sec.33-205,6	No	Yes Sec.33-205, 6
Illinois	Yes Sec.122-3-13	No	Yes Sec.122-26-7 written

LIABILITIES AND CONSEQUENCES

STATE	WHO IS LIABLE FOR NON-ATTENDANCE PARENT AND/OR CHILD	PENALTIES - PARENT		
		CRIMINAL OR NOT CRIMINAL	FINE	IMPRISONMENT
District of Columbia	Both Sec.13-201	Criminal Sec.31-207	$10 for each offense or both (2 days absence = 1 offense) Sec.31-207	5 days
Florida	Both Sec.232.19(6)	Criminal Sec.232.19(6)a	Not more than $500 (2nd degree misdemeanor) Sec.775.083	Not more than or 60 days Sec.775.082
Georgia	Both C Secs.32-2104, 2115	Criminal Sec.32-9914	Not more than $100 or both Sec.32-9914	Not more than or 30 days
Hawaii	Parent Secs.298-9, 12	Criminal Sec.298-12	Not less than $5 or more than $50 or Sec.298-12	2 months
Idaho	Both Secs.33-202,206	Criminal Secs.16-1817, 33-207	Not more than $300 or both Sec.18-113	Not more than or 6 months
Illinois	Both Secs.26-1, 34-121	Criminal Sec.122-26-10	Not more than $500 Sec.1005-9-1	Not more than or 30 days Sec.1005-8-3

PENALTIES - CHILD

STATE	DECLARED DELINQUENT	CAN BE INSTITUTIONAL	SPECIAL PLACEMENT WITHIN SCHOOL SYSTEM
District of Columbia	No, is a "child in need of supervision" Sec.16-2320	Yes, but not in facility for delinquent children Sec.16-2820	No
Florida	No, "incorrigible and a menace to the school"	Yes, if adjudicated in need of supervision more than once Sec.39.11(1)	No
Georgia	Yes Sec.32-2115	Yes Sec.32-2115	No
Hawaii	No Sec.571-11	No	No
Idaho	No, habitual truant Sec.16-1803	Yes Sec.16-1814 Same as if delinquent	No
Illinois	No "minor in need of supervision" Sec.37-702-3	Yes Secs.37-705-2, 705-7	Yes parental or truant schools Sec.34-117

OFFENSES DEFINED

STATE	PARENT		CHILD	
	FAILURE TO CAUSE TO ATTEND	OTHER	TRUANT	OTHER
Indiana	Yes Sec.20.8.1-3-33	No	No	No
Iowa	Yes Sec.299.6	No	Any child between 7 & 16, in proper physical & mental condition who fails to attend school regularly w/o reasonable excuse Sec.299.8	No
Kansas	Yes	Contributing to truancy Sec.38-830	A child who being by law required to attend school habitually absents himself or herself therefrom. Sec.38-802	
Kentucky	Yes Sec.159.180	No	Any child absent without valid excuse for more than 3 days or tardy more than 3 days Sec.159.150	Habitual truant-any child reported a truant more than 3 times Sec.159.150
Louisiana	Yes Sec.17.221	Inducing absence Sec.17.221.1	No	A child shall be considered habitually absent when the condition continues to exist after all reasonable efforts by the principal have failed to correct the condition. Sec.17.233
Maine	Yes T.20 Sec.911	No	No	Habitual truancy and wilful absence from school w/o sufficient excuse or failure to attend without excuse for 5 day sessions in any 6 mo. period T.20 Sec.914

PROVISIONS FOR ENFORCEMENT
OF ATTENDANCE REQUIREMENTS

STATE	PROVIDES ATTENDANCE OR TRUANT OFFICER	ALLOWS ARREST OF TRUANTS WITHOUT A WARRANT	REQUIRES NOTICE TO PARENTS TO COMPLY BEFORE COMPLAINT IS FILED
Indiana	Yes Sec.20-8.1-3-4	Yes	Yes By phone if possible by mail in any case. Secs.28-5334,5337 (20-8.1-3.28) (20-8.1-3.33)
Iowa	Yes Sec.299.10	Yes Sec.299.11	No
Kansas	Yes Sec.72-1113	No	No
Kentucky	Yes Sec.159.180	No	Yes Sec.159.180 written
Louisiana	Yes Sec.17:228.9	No	Yes Sec.17:233 Written or in person
Maine	Yes T.20 Sec.913	Yes T.20 Sec.913	No

LIABILITIES AND CONSEQUENCES

STATE	WHO IS LIABLE FOR NON-ATTENDANCE PARENT AND/OR CHILD	PENALTIES - PARENT		
		CRIMINAL OR NOT CRIMINAL	FINE	IMPRISONMENT
Indiana	Parent, unless not a party to the violation Sec.20-8.1-3-33	Criminal Sec.20-8.1-3-37	Not more than $500	Not more than 6 months
			or both Sec.20-8.1-3-37	
Iowa	Both Secs.299.1,8	Criminal Sec.299.11	Not less than $5 or more than $20 for each offense Sec.299.6	No
Kansas	Both Sec.72-1111	Criminal Sec.38-830	Not more than $1,000 or or both Sec.38-830	1 year
Kentucky	Both Secs.159.010, .180, .990	Criminal Sec.159.990	Not more than $10 (first offense) Not more than $20 (subsequent offenses) Sec.159.990	No
Louisiana	Both Secs.17:221, 233	Criminal Sec.17:221	Not more than $10 for each offense	Not more than 10 days for each offense
			or both 1 day's absence = 1 offense Sec.17:221	
Maine	Both 20 Sec.911	Criminal 20 Sec.911	Not more than $25 or for each offense 20 Sec. 911	Not more than 30 days

LIABILITIES AND CONSEQUENCES

PENALTIES - CHILD

STATE	DECLARED DELINQUENT	CAN BE INSTITUTIONALIZED	SPECIAL PLACEMENT WITHIN SCHOOL SYSTEM
Indiana	Yes Sec.20.8.1-3-31 "confirmed truant"	Yes Secs.20-8.1-3-31, 31-5-7-15	No
Iowa	No Sec.232.2	No	Yes Truant schools Sec.299.9
Kansas	No	Yes, but not in state training school or state industrial school Sec.38-826	No
Kentucky	No "habitual truancy" Sec.208.020	Yes Sec.208.200	Yes truant schools Sec.159.190
Louisiana	No, is a "child in need of supervision" Sec.13:1569	Yes Sec.13:1580 same as delinquent child	No
Maine	No "juvenile offender" 15 Sec.2552	Yes 15 Sec.2611	No

OFFENSES DEFINED

| | PARENT | | CHILD | |
STATE	FAILURE TO CAUSE TO ATTEND	OTHER	TRUANT	OTHER
Maryland	Yes 77 Sec.92(b)	Inducing absence 77 Sec.92(c)	No	Absence without lawful excuse or irregular in attendance 77 Sec.94
Massachusetts	Yes 76 Sec.2	Inducing absence 76 Sec.4	No	No
Michigan	Yes Sec.340.740	No	No	No
Minnesota	Yes Sec.127.20	Inducing absence Sec.127.20	No	No
Mississippi	-	-	-	-
Missouri	Yes Sec.167.061	No	No	No

PROVISIONS FOR ENFORCEMENT
OF ATTENDANCE REQUIREMENTS

STATE	PROVIDES FOR ATTENDANCE OR TRUANT OFFICER	ALLOWS ARREST OF TRUANTS WITHOUT A WARRANT	REQUIRES NOTICE TO PARENTS TO COMPLY BEFORE COMPLAINT IS FILED
Maryland	Yes 77 Sec.68(h)	No	No
Massachusetts	Yes 76 Sec.19	No Truants can be 'apprehended' and taken to school 76 Sec.20	No
Michigan	Yes Sec.340.733	No	Yes Sec.340.742 written
Minnesota	Yes Sec.120.14	Yes Sec.120.14	Yes Sec.120.14
Mississippi	Yes Sec.37.9.5	-	-
Missouri	Yes Sec.167.071	Yes Sec.167.071	Yes Sec.167.081 written

LIABILITIES AND CONSEQUENCES

| STATE | WHO IS LIABLE FOR NON-ATTENDANCE PARENT AND/OR CHILD | PENALTIES - PARENT | | |
		CRIMINAL OR NOT CRIMINAL	FINE	IMPRISONMENT
Maryland	Both 77 Sec.92	Criminal 77 Sec.92(b)	Not more than $50 for each offense 77 Sec.92	No
Massachusetts	Both 76 Secs.1 & 2	Criminal 76 Sec.2	Not more than $200 76 Sec.4	No
Michigan	Both	Criminal Secs.340.740	Not less than $5 or more than $50 or both Sec.340.740	Not less than 2 or more than 90 days
Minnesota	Both Secs.120.10,12,15	Criminal Sec.127.20	Not more than $50	Not more than or 30 days Sec.127.20
Mississippi	-	-	-	-
Missouri	Both	Criminal	Not less than $5 or more than $25 or both Sec.167.061	Not less than 2 or more than 10 days

LIABILITIES AND CONSEQUENCES

PENALTIES - CHILD

STATE	DECLARED DELINQUENT	CAN BE INSTITUTIONALIZED	SPECIAL PLACEMENT WITHIN SCHOOL SYSTEM
Maryland	No, is a "child in need of supervision" CJ Sec.3-801	No, unless also found to be delinquent CJ Sec.3-831	Yes truant school 77 Sec.93
Massachusetts	No, is a "child in need of services" 119 Sec.21	Yes, but not to facility maintained for delinquents 119 Sec.39	No
Michigan	No "juvenile disorderly person" Sec.340.746	Yes Sec.712A.18 Same as for delinquent child	Yes Ungraded school Sec.340.746
Minnesota	Yes Sec.260.015	Yes Sec.260.185	Yes Ungraded school Sec.120.15
Mississippi	-	-	-
Missouri	No Sec.211.031	No	Yes Truant schools Sec.167.091

OFFENSES DEFINED

| STATE | PARENT | | CHILD | |
	FAILURE TO CAUSE TO ATTEND	OTHER	TRUANT	OTHER
Montana	Yes Sec.75-6304	No	No	No
Nebraska	Yes Sec.79-216	No	No	No
Nevada	Yes Sec.392.210	Abetting truancy Sec.392.220	Any child absent from school without valid excuse acceptable to teacher or principal. Sec.392.130	Habitual truant, any child deemed a truant 3 or more times within a school year. Sec.392.140
New Hampshire	Yes Sec.193:2	No	No	No
New Jersey	Yes Sec.18A:38-31	No	Repeated absence from school by child between 6 and 16. Sec.18A:38-27	No
New Mexico	Yes Sec.77-10-7	No	No	No

PROVISIONS FOR ENFORCEMENT
OF ATTENDANCE REQUIREMENTS

STATE	PROVIDES FOR ATTENDANCE OR TRUANT OFFICER	ALLOWS ARREST OF TRUANTS WITHOUT A WARRANT	REQUIRES NOTICE TO PARENTS TO COMPLY BEFORE COMPLAINT IS FILED
Montana	Yes Sec.75-6305	Yes Sec.75-6306	Yes Sec.75-6307 written
Nebraska	Yes Sec.79-210	No, but atten- dance officer is vested with "po- lice power" and must do every- thing in his power to compel truant to attend some school. Sec.79-210,211	Yes Sec.79-211 written
Nevada	Yes Sec.392.150	Yes Sec.392.160	Yes Sec.392.130
New Hampshire	Yes Sec.189:34	Yes Sec.189:36	No
New Jersey	Yes Sec.18A:38-32	Yes Sec.18A:38-29	Yes Sec.18A:38-29 written
New Mexico	Yes Sec.77-10-7	No	Yes Sec.77-10-7 written

LIABILITIES AND CONSEQUENCES

STATE	WHO IS LIABLE FOR NON-ATTENDANCE PARENT AND/OR CHILD	PENALTIES - PARENT		
		CRIMINAL OR NOT CRIMINAL	FINE	IMPRISONMENT
Montana	Both Secs.75-6303, 6306	Criminal Sec.75-6307	Not less than $10 or more than $20 or $100 bond with sureties	Not less than 10 or more than 30 days for failure to pay fine or post bond Sec.75-6307
Nebraska	Both Secs.79-201,211	Criminal Sec.79-216	Not less than $5 or more than $100	Not more than 90 days or both Sec.79-216
Nevada	Both Sec.392.040	Criminal Sec.392.210	Not more than $500	Not more than 6 months or both Sec.193.150
New Hampshire	Both Sec.193:172	No "Violation" Sec.193.7	Not more than $100 Sec.651:2(iv)(a)	Not more than 3 months Sec.625:8 or both Sec.651:2(iv)
New Jersey	Both Secs.18A:38-25, -27	Criminal Sec.18A:38-31	Not more than $5-first offense Not more than $25 each subsequent offense Sec.18A:38-31	No
New Mexico	Both Sec.77-10-2	Criminal Sec.77-10-7	Not more than $100	Not more than 6 months or both Sec.40A-29-4

LIABILITIES AND CONSEQUENCES

PENALTIES - CHILD

STATE	DECLARED DELINQUENT	CAN BE INSTITUTIONALIZED	SPECIAL PLACEMENT WITHIN SCHOOL SYSTEM
Montana	No Is a "child in need of supervision." Sec.10-1203	Yes But not in a detention facility. Sec.10-1222(d)	No
Nebraska	No "in need of special supervision" Sec.43-201(5)	Yes But not to Dept. of Correctional Services Sec.43-210.01	Yes Special schools Sec.79-212
Nevada	No Sec.62.040	Yes same as if a delinquent Sec.62.200	No
New Hampshire	Yes Sec.169:2(II)	Yes state industrial school Sec.193:17	No
New Jersey	No Sec.2A:4-43 is a "child in need of supervision"	Yes But not to facility for delinquent children Sec.2A:4-62	No
New Mexico	No is a "child in need of supervision" Sec.13-14-3	Yes But not to facility for delinquent children Sec.13-14-31	No

OFFENSES DEFINED

	PARENT		CHILD	
STATE	FAILURE TO CAUSE TO ATTEND	OTHER	TRUANT	OTHER
New York	Yes Art 65, Sec.3233	No	No	School Delinquent a child who is irregular in attendance or habitually truant Art.65 Sec.3214(1)
North Carolina	Yes Sec.115.169	No	No	No
North Dakota	Yes Sec.15-34.1-05	No	No	No
Ohio	Yes Sec.3321.38	No	No	No
Oklahoma	Yes 70 Sec.10-105	No	No	No
Oregon	Yes Sec.339.990	No	No	Irregular Attendance - 8 unexcused half-day absences in any 4 week period during which school is in session. Sec.339.065

PROVISIONS FOR ENFORCEMENT
OF ATTENDANCE REQUIREMENTS

STATE	PROVIDES FOR ATTENDANCE OR TRUANT OFFICER	ALLOWS ARREST OF TRUANTS WITHOUT A WARRANT	REQUIRES NOTICE TO PARENTS TO COMPLY BEFORE COMPLAINT IS FILED
New York	Yes Sec.3213	Yes Sec.3213(2)(a)	Yes Sec.3213
North Carolina	Yes Sec.115-168	No	Yes Sec.115-168 written
North Dakota	Yes Sec.15-34.1-04	No	No
Ohio	Yes Secs.3321.14,15	No Can be "taken into custody" and returned to school. Sec.3321.17	Yes Sec.3321.19
Oklahoma	Yes 70 Sec.10-101	No	Yes 70 Sec.10-106 written
Oregon	Yes Sec.332.040,505	No	Yes Sec.339.080 written

LIABILITIES AND CONSEQUENCES

STATE	WHO IS LIABLE FOR NON-ATTENDANCE PARENT AND/OR CHILD	CRIMINAL OR NOT CRIMINAL	FINE	IMPRISONMENT
New York	Both Act.65,Sec.3213	Criminal Sec.3233	Not more than $10 Not more than $50	10 days or (first offense) 30 days or or both Sec. 3323
North Carolina	Both Secs.115-166, 7A-278	Criminal Sec.115-169	Not more than $50	Not more than or 30 days or both Sec.115-169
North Dakota	Both Sec.15.34.1-01	Criminal Sec.15.34.1-05	Not more than $100-1st of-fense. Not more than $200-subse-quent offense Sec.15.34.1-05	No
Ohio	Both Sec.3321.03	Criminal Sec.3321.38, .99	Not less than $5 or more than $20	For failure to pay fine - not less than 10 or more than 30 days Sec.3321.99
Oklahoma	Both 70 Sec.10-105	Criminal 70 Sec.10-105B	Not more than $50	Not more than 10 or days or both 70 Sec.10-105B
Oregon	Parent Secs.339.010,020	Criminal Sec.339.990	Not more than $100	Not more than or30 days or both

LIABILITIES AND CONSEQUENCES

PENALTIES - CHILD

STATE	DECLARED DELINQUENT	CAN BE INSTITUTIONALIZED	SPECIAL PLACE-MENT WITHIN SCHOOL SYSTEM
New York	No is "person" in need of super-vision" Act.7,Sec.712(b)	Yes But not to faci-lity for delin-quents Secs.454,756	Yes parental schools Sec.3214
North Carolina	No "undisciplined child" Sec.7A-278	No Sec.7A-286(4)	No
North Dakota	No "unruly child" Sec.27-20-01	Yes - except not in state train-ing or industrial school Sec.27-20-32	No
Ohio	No is an "unruly child" Sec.2151.022	No unless other forms of rehab-ilitation prove futile. Sec.2151.354	No
Oklahoma	No 10 Sec.1101 "child in need supervision"	Yes 10 Sec.1116 same as for delinquent	No
Oregon	No Sec.419.476(1)(b)	No	No

OFFENSES DEFINED

| STATE | PARENT | | CHILD | |
	FAILURE TO CAUSE TO ATTEND	OTHER	TRUANT	OTHER
Pennsylvania	Yes 24 Sec.13-1333	No	No	Unlawful absence-absence 3 days or their equivalent without lawful excuse 24 Sec.13-1354
Puerto Rico	Yes T18 Sec.80(g)	No	No	No
Rhode Island	Yes Sec.16-19-1	No	No	Habitual truant-every child required to attend school who wilfully and habitually absents himself therefrom. Sec.16-19-6
South Carolina	Yes Sec.21-757.1	No	No	No
South Dakota	Yes Sec.13-27-11	Interfering with attendance Sec.13-27-18	No	Child in need of supervision-any child of compulsory school age who habitually absents himself without legal excuse. Sec.26-8-9
Tennessee	Yes Sec.49-1735	No	No	Habitual absentee-Any child who habitually and unlawfully absents himself from school. Sec.49-1726

PROVISIONS FOR ENFORCEMENT
OF ATTENDANCE REQUIREMENTS

STATE	PROVIDES FOR ATTENDANCE OR TRUANT OFFICER	ALLOWS ARREST OF TRUANTS WITHOUT A WARRANT	REQUIRES NOTICE TO PARENTS TO COMPLY BEFORE COMPLAINT IS FILED
Pennsylvania	Yes 24 Sec.13-1341	Yes 24 Sec.13-1341	Yes 24 Sec.13-1341
Puerto Rico	No-But provides that statute be enforced by municipal authorities. T.18 Sec.80(f)	No	No
Rhode Island	Yes Sec.16-19-3	No	No
South Carolina	Yes Sec.21-761	No	Yes Sec.21-766
South Dakota	Yes Sec.13-27-14	No Sec.13-27-19 can be apprehended and taken to school	Yes Sec.13-27-16
Tennessee	Yes Sec.49-1711	No	Yes Sec.49-1718 written

LIABILITIES AND CONSEQUENCES

STATE	WHO IS LIABLE FOR NON-ATTENDANCE PARENT AND/OR CHILD	PENALTIES - PARENT		
		CRIMINAL OR NOT CRIMINAL	FINE	IMPRISONMENT
Pennsylvania	Both 24 Sec.13-1327, -1338	Criminal 24 Sec.13-1333	Not more than $2-1st offense Not more than $5 each subsequent offense + costs 24 Sec.13-1333	In default of payment-not more than 5 days
Puerto Rico	Parent T.18 Sec.80	Criminal 18 Sec.80(g)	1st offense- public reprimand 2nd offense- not more than $5 3rd offense- not more than $10 18 Sec.80(g)	No
Rhode Island	Both Sec.16-19-1	Criminal Sec.16-19-1	Not more than $20 Sec.16-19-1	No
South Carolina	Both Secs.21-757, 757.5 757.6	Criminal Sec.21-757.1	Not more than $50	Not more than or 30 days Sec.21-757.1
South Dakota	Both Secs.13-27-1, 26-8-9	Criminal Sec.13-27-11	Not less than $10 or more than $50 (first offense) Not less than $25 or more than $100 (subsequent offenses) or both Sec.13-27-11	Not more than 30 days or (first offense) Not more than 30 days or
Tennessee	Both Secs.48-1708, 1726	Criminal Sec.49-1723	Not less than $2 or more than $10 (first offense) Not less than $5 or more than $20 (subsequent offenses) Sec.49-1735	No

LIABILITIES AND CONSEQUENCES

PENALTIES - CHILD

STATE	DECLARED DELINQUENT	CAN BE INSTITUTIONALIZED	SPECIAL PLACE-MENT WITHIN SCHOOL SYSTEM
Pennsylvania	No 11 Sec.50-102 is a "deprived child"	Yes But not to facilities for delinquent children 11 Sec.50-321	YES truant schools 24 Sec.5-502
Puerto Rico	No T34 Sec.2002	No T34 Sec.2010	No
Rhode Island	No is a "wayward child" Sec.16-19-6, 14-1-3	Yes to a training school Sec.14-1-36	No
South Carolina	Yes-if truant without parent's knowledge or consent Sec.21-757.6	No Sec.15-1095.20 unless also delinquent	No
South Dakota	No "child in need of supervision" Sec.26-8-9	Yes Sec.26-8-40.1 But not to facility for delinquent children	No
Tennessee	No "disorderly juvenile person" Sec.49-1727	No	Yes truancy school Sec.49-1727

OFFENSES DEFINED

STATE	PARENT		CHILD	
	FAILURE TO CAUSE TO ATTEND	OTHER	TRUANT	OTHER
Texas	Yes Sec.4.25(a)	No	No	No
Utah	Yes Sec.53-24-3	No	No	Incorrigible child - any child between 8 and 18 who in defiance of parents or teacher is habitually truant. Sec.53-25-1
Vermont	Yes T16 Sec.1127	No	No	No
Virginia	Yes Secs.22-275.6,7	Inducing absence Sec.22-275.10	No	No
Washington	Yes Sec.28A.27.100	No	No	Habitual truant- one who absents himself frequent- ly from the school he is re- required to attend. Sec.28A.27.070
West Virginia	Yes Sec.18-8-2	Inducing absence Sec.18-8-7	No	No

PROVISIONS FOR ENFORCEMENT
OF ATTENDANCE REQUIREMENTS

STATE	PROVIDES FOR ATTENDANCE OR TRUANT OFFICER	ALLOWS ARREST OF TRUANTS WITHOUT A WARRANT	REQUIRES NOTICE TO PARENTS TO COMPLY BEFORE COMPLAINT IS FILED
Texas	Yes Sec.21.036	No - must have a warrant or permission of parent.	Yes Sec.4.25 written
Utah	Yes Sec.53-24-2	No	No
Vermont	Yes T.16 Sec.1125	No, but children of school age may be stopped, and if truant, returned to school. T.16 Sec.1128	Yes T.16 Sec.1127 written
Virginia	Yes Sec.22.275.16	No	Yes Sec.22.275.10
Washington	Yes Sec.28A.27.040	Yes Sec.28A.27.070	No
West Virginia	Yes Sec.18-8-3	Yes Sec.18-8-4	Yes Sec.18-8-4 written

LIABILITIES AND CONSEQUENCES

STATE	WHO IS LIABLE FOR NON-ATTENDANCE PARENT AND/OR CHILD	PENALTIES - PARENT		
		CRIMINAL OR NOT CRIMINAL	FINE	IMPRISONMENT
Texas	Parent - unless proves inability to compel child to attend Sec.4.25(b)	Criminal Sec.4.25	Not less than $5 or more than $25 (first offense) Not less than $10 or more than $50 (second offense) Not less than $25 or more than $100 each subsequent offense Sec.4.25	No
Utah	Both Secs.53-24-1, 53-25-1	Criminal Sec.53-24-3	Not more than $299 or Sec.76-3-301 or both Sec.76-3-201	Not more than 6 months Sec.76-3-204
Vermont	Parents T.16 Sec.1121,27	Criminal T.16 Sec.1127	Not less than $5 or more than $25 T.16 Sec.1127	No
Virginia	Both Sec.22-275.1	Criminal Sec.22-275.7	Not more than $1,000 or or both Sec.18.1-9	Not more than 12 months
Washington	Both Secs.28A.27.010, 13.12.040	Criminal Sec.28A.24.100	Not more than $25 Sec.28A.27.100	No
West Virginia	Parents Sec.18-8-3	Criminal Sec.18-8-2	Not less than $3 or more than $20 + costs of prosecution or Sec.18-8-2	Not less than 5 or more than 20 days

LIABILITIES AND CONSEQUENCES

PENALTIES - CHILD

STATE	DECLARED DELINQUENT	CAN BE INSTITUTIONALIZED	SPECIAL PLACE-MENT WITHIN SCHOOL SYSTEM
Texas	No in need of super-vision Sec.51.03(b)(2)	Yes But not to Texas Youth Council Sec.54.04(d)	Yes juvenile Training School S4.25
Utah	No "incorrigible" Sec.53-25-1	No	Yes Special schools Sec.53-26-1
Vermont	No T.33 Sec.631	No	No
Virginia	No Sec.16-1-158	Yes But not to state board of correc-tion Sec.16-1-178	No
Washington	No Sec.13.04.010	No	Yes Truant Schools Secs.13.04.075, 13.12.040
West Virginia	Yes Sec.49-5-1	Yes Sec.49-5-1	No

OFFENSES DEFINED

| | PARENT | | | CHILD |
STATE	FAILURE TO CAUSE TO ATTEND	OTHER	TRUANT	OTHER
Wisconsin	Yes Sec.40.77(3)	No	Any absence of one or more days during which the teacher or principal has not been notified in writing of the legal cause by parent - or - intermittent attendance for the purpose of defeating purpose of Sec.40.77(1) Sec.40.78(1)	No
Wyoming	Yes Sec.21.1-51	No	No	Unexcused absence - absence of any child re-required to attend school when such absence is not excused to the satisfaction of the Board of Trustees by parent. 21.1-47(a) Habitual truant- any child with 5 or more unexcused absences in any 1 school year Sec.21.1-47(b)

PROVISIONS FOR ENFORCEMENT
OF ATTENDANCE REQUIREMENTS

STATE	PROVIDES FOR ATTENDANCE OR TRUANT OFFICER	ALLOWS ARREST OF TRUANTS WITHOUT A WARRANT	REQUIRES NOTICE TO PARENTS TO COMPLY BEFORE COMPLAINT IS FILED
Wisconsin	Yes Sec.40.78(4)	Yes Sec.40.78(7)(c)	Yes Sec.40.78(7)(a) written
Wyoming	Yes Sec.21.1-49	No	Yes Sec.21.1-50 written

LIABILITIES AND CONSEQUENCES

STATE	WHO IS LIABLE FOR NON-ATTENDANCE PARENT AND/OR CHILD	PENALTIES - PARENT		
		CRIMINAL OR NOT CRIMINAL	FINE	IMPRISONMENT
Wisconsin	Both Sec.40.77	Criminal Sec.40.78(7)(b)	Not less than $5 or more than $50	Not more than 3 months
			or both Sec.40.77(3)	
Wyoming	Both Sec.21.1-48	Criminal Sec.21.1-51	Not less than $5 or more than $25	Not more than 10 days
			or both Sec.21.1-51	

LIABILITIES AND CONSEQUENCES

PENALTIES - CHILD

STATE	DECLARED DELINQUENT	CAN BE INSTITUTIONALIZED	SPECIAL PLACE-MENT WITHIN SCHOOL SYSTEM
Wisconsin	No is a "child in need of super-vision" Sec.48.12	Yes Sec.48.345	No
Wyoming	No is a "child in need of super-vision" Sec.14.115-2	Yes Sec.14.115-30 same as for delinquent child	No

APPENDIX E

CHILD LABOR LAWS AND OTHER STATUTORY PROVISIONS
CONCERNING EMPLOYMENT OF CHILDREN
OF COMPULSORY SCHOOL AGE

NOTES TO CHILD LABOR CHART
APPENDIX E

1. Except where otherwise noted, this chart only specifies child labor standards contained in the state statutes. Several states have administrative regulations concerning child labor that should be consulted for additional child labor requirements.

2. Some age limits noted in Column (1), "Minimum Age...," extend beyond the compulsory school attendance age.

3. The minimum age provisions for hazardous and prohibited occupations are not listed on this chart for every state.

   A few states have minimum age provisions for street trades, i.e. occupations such as newspaper and magazine sales and shoeshining. The minimum age for street trades is lower than that for other occupations and nightwork restrictions are often less stringent. School attendance is not waived for street trades. Most states either exclude street trades from coverage of the child labor laws or do not specifically mention them. Regulations, if any, are established by municipal ordinance.

4. Requirements for issuance of a permit:

   a) <u>Proof of Age</u>. As proof of age most states accept, in order of preference: i) a birth certificate; ii) a baptismal certificate or a Bible record of birth; iii) other documents, for example, a passport, immigration certificate, or life insurance policy in effect for over one year; iv) a physician's statement approximating the physical age of the child and an affidavit from the child's parent that the child is of the legal minimum age.

   b) <u>Parental Accompaniment</u>. The parent accompanies the child when application for a permit is made.

   c) <u>Employer's Statement</u>. A letter from the employer containing a promise of employment and a description of the job. Several states require information on the number of hours per day and per week and the starting and ending time of work.

   d) <u>School Record</u>. In most states, a statement from the principal of the school which the minor last attended. It contains information on attendance and the child's general schooling record. Of primary concern for the issuance of permits for work during school hours is the child's grade level. The attendance record is often required before an employment permit for outside school hours is issued.

   e) <u>Physician's Statement</u>. A letter from the school physician or an approved physician regarding the child's general health and ability to perform the work required for the job.

CHILD LABOR LAWS AND OTHER STATUTORY PROVISIONS[1] CONCERNING

EMPLOYMENT OF CHILDREN OF COMPULSORY SCHOOL ATTENDANCE AGE[2]

State	Minimum Age at Which a Child May Work (in a specified occupations[3] and/or at specified times)	Maximum Work Time Permitted at Indicated Ages	Issuance of Employment Permits	Requirements for Issuance[4] of Employment Permits - Types of Permits Specified	Permitted Age for Issuance of Permits for Work During School Hours	Minimum Education Requirement for Employment Permit for Work During School Hours	Nightwork Prohibited for Minors of Ages Indicated and for Hours Specified	Enforcement Agency
Ala.	16 (gainful employment during school hours; in manufacturing or mechanical establishment, or cannery) 14 (gainful employment outside school hours) 12 (for boys during school vacations, employed in business offices, mercantile establishments, or dairies, or as caddies) (T.26, §§ 343, 354)	Under 16: 8 hours/day 40 hours/week 6 days/week 4 hours/school day 28 hours/school week (T.26, §§ 344, 357)	Local public school official (T.26, § 355)	Requirements: 1) parental accompaniment; 2) letter from employer; 3) school record only for work outside school hours; 4) physician's statement Types of Permits: 1) regular; 2) outside school hours, 14 or 15; 3) special-boys, 12-14 during school vacations (T.26, §§ 355, 356, 357, 363)	14 to 16 (T.26, §§ 354, 355)	None specified, but recommendation of superintendent of education required. (T.26, § 354)	Under 16: 8 p.m. to 7 a.m. (T.26, § 344)	Department of Industrial Relations (T.26, § 344)
Alas.	16 (manufacturing and processing operations, building contraction, restaurants) 14 (any occupation outside school hours except for the above) (§23.10.340)	Under 18: 8 hours/day 20 hours/week 6 days/week, except during public school vacations for 16-18, provided employment accords with prevailing hours in the industry (§23.10.350(1)) Under 16: 9 combined hours of work and school on schoolday, 23 work hours in school week. (§23.10.340(a))	Exemption-Commissioner of Labor (§23.10.345) No permits.	No permit provision.	No provision.	No provision.	Under 16: 7 p.m. to 6 a.m. (§23.10.340(a))	Department of Labor (§23.10.360)

State	Minimum Age at Which a Child May Work (in specified occupations[3] and/or at specified times)	Maximum Work Time Permitted at Indicated Ages	Issuance of Employment Permits	Requirements for Issuance of Employment Permits - Types of Permits Specified	Permitted Age for Issuance of Permits for Work During School Hours	Minimum Education Requirement for Employment Permit for Work During School Hours	Nightwork Prohibited for Minors of Ages Indicated and for Hours Specified	Enforcement Agency
Ariz.	14 (gainful occupation during school hours) (Ariz. Const. Art. 18, 2) 16 (manufacturing, mining, processing occupations, public messenger service, etc.) 10 (newspaper sales on street) (§§23.232, 23.234)	Under 16: 8 hours/day 40 hours/week Under 16 enrolled in school: 3 hours/day on school days 18 hours/week during school week (§23.231 et seq.)	No permits	No permit provision.	No provision	No provision	Under 16: 9:30 p.m. to 6 a.m. (§23.233)	Industrial Commission (§§23.107, 23.240)
Ark.	14 (any remunerative occupation except during school vacation; child under 14 may be employed by parent in occupation controlled by parent. (§81.701)	Under 16: 8 hours/day 48 hours/week 6 days/week (§81.706) 16 to 18: 10 hours/day 54 hours/week 6 days/week (§81.707)	State Labor Commissioner or local public school official (§81.708)	None, except proof of age (§§81.708, 81.709)	Children 7 to 15 whose services are necessary to support widowed mother. (§80.1504)	8 grades (s.80.1504(b))	Under 16: 7 p.m. (9 p.m. before non-schoolday) to 6 a.m. (§81.706) 16 to 18: 10 p.m. before schoolday to 6 a.m. (§81.707)	Department of Labor (§81.712)
Calif.	16 (manufacturing establishment or other place of labor at any time, except as provided by law). (Labor §1290. See also Labor §§1292, 1294)	Under 18: 8 hours/day 48 hours/week (Labor §1391) Under 18 required to attend school: 4 hours/schoolday (Education §§12769, 12774)	Local public school official (Education §12767)	Generally: 1) parental accompaniment; 2) school record; 3) employer statement; 4) physician's statement. Part-time: 12 to 18, regular school vacations; 12 to 18, completion of 7th grade and outside school hours; 14 to 17, high school or vocational student. Full-time: 14 to 16 (Education §§12777, 12778) See also: Column 5, "Age for Issuance. . ."	14 to 16, if earnings of minor are needed for support. (Education §12776)	Elementary school. (Education §12776) Compulsory part-time school attendance also required.	Under 18: 10 p.m. (12:30 a.m. before non-schoolday) to 5 a.m. (Labor §1391)	Division of Labor Law Enforcement (Labor §1398)

State	Minimum Age at Which a Child May Work (in 3 specified occupations[3] and/or at specified times)	Maximum Work Time Permitted at Indicated Ages	Issuance of Employment Permits	Requirements for Issuance[4] of Employment Permits - Types of Permits Specified	Permitted Age for Issuance of Permits for Work During School Hours	Minimum Education Requirement for Employment Permit for Work During School Hours	Nightwork Prohibited for Minors of Ages Indicated and for Hours Specified	Enforcement Agency
Colo.	16 (on school days and during school hours) (§80-6-5, but see: Column 5, "Permitted Age for Issuance . . .")	Under 18: 8 hours/day 40 hours/week Under 16: 6 hours/schoolday (§80-6-5)	Local public school official (§§80-6-11, 80-6-13)	Exemption from provisions of child labor laws, if director determines that it is in the best interest of child (§80-6-4) School release: 1) specification of employment position; 2) parental consent; 3) 30-day limit; 4) limited school attendance (§80-7-13)	14 to 16 (§80-6-13)	None specified.	Under 16: 9:30 P.m. to 5 a.m. before schoolday (§80-6-5 et seq.)	Director of Division of Labor (§80-6-15)
Conn.	16 (general manufacturing; mechanical, mercantile, theatrical industry; restaurants; bowling alleys; shoeshining establishments; or barbershops) 14 (agriculture) (§§22-13, 31-23)	Under 18: 9 hours/day 48 hours/week (§31-18) Under 18 in stores and 14 to 16 in agriculture: 8 hours/day 48 hours/week 6 days/week (§§31-12, 22-13)	State Board of Education (§31-23)	During school hours: finding by state board of education that this is in best interest of child. (§10-189)	14 to 16 (§10-189)	8 grades. (§10-189)	Under 18: 10 p.m. to 6 a.m. 16 to 18: 11 p.m. (midnight if not attending school) to 6 a.m. in dining rooms before non-schoolday and during vacation (§31-18)	Labor Department (§31-22) Commissioner of Agriculture (§22-15, provisions specifically related to agriculture)
DeL.	14 (work in connection with any establishment or occupation) (T.19, §511)	Under 16: 8 hours/day 48 hours/week 6 days/week (T.19, §515)	Local public school official (T.19, §544)	A)General - entire year: 1)parental accompaniment; 2) school record; 3) statement of employer. (T.19, 541(a), 543, 545) B)Provisional - outside of school hours: 1)parental accompaniment; 2) principal's statement of capability to both work and go to school. (T.19, §§ 543, 546)	14 to 16 (T.19, §542(b))	8 grades. (T.19, § 545)	Under 16: 7 p.m. (9 p.m. in stores on Friday, Saturday, and vacation) to 6 a.m.	Division of Industrial Affairs Department of Labor (T.29, § 8510(a)(1))

State	Minimum Age at Which a Child May Work (in specified occupations3 and/or at specified times)	Maximum Work Time Permitted at Indicated Ages	Issuance of Employment Permits	Requirements for Issuance4 of Employment Permits - Types of Permits Specified	Permitted Age for Issuance of Permits for Work During School Hours	Minimum Education Requirement for Employment Permit - for Work During School Hours	Nightwork Prohibited for Minors of Ages Indicated and for Hours Specified	Enforcement Agency
Fla.	16 (during school hours) 12 (any gainful occupation if exempted from school or on vacation) (§450.021)	Under 16: 8 hours/day 40 hours/week 6 days/week 3 hours/school day before beginning of a school day) (§450.081)	Local public school official (§232.07)	Types: A) Regular: ages 14 to 16 during school hours: 1) parental accompaniment; 2) statement re: need for child's earnings; 3) employer's statement; 4) school record; 5) physician's statement (§§232.07, 450.111(1)) B) Special: ages 12 to 16 during out of school hours: same as above, except school record not required (§450.111(2))	14 to 16, but 12 to 15 only if in best interests of child. (§232.07)	8th grade (§232.07)	Under 16: 8 p.m. (10 p.m. before non-schoolday) to 6:30 a.m. 16 to 18: 10 p.m. to 5 a.m.	Division of Labor (§450.121)
Ga.	16 (during school hours; and in mill, factory, laundry, manufacturing establishment or workshop) 14 (any gainful occupation) (§§54.301, 43.302, 54.309)	Under 16: 8 hours/day 40 hours/week 4 hours/schoolday Age 16 and over: 60 hours/week in cotton & woolen factories (§§54-201, 54-308)	Local public school official (§54-310) Age permits only.	No employment certificates issued, but see §§54.311, 54.313, re age certificates requiring statement of employer and proof of physical fitness for child 14 to 16.	14 to 16 (§54.309)	High School (§54.309)	Under 16: 9 p.m. to 6 a.m. (§54.305)	Labor Department (§54.316)
Haw.	18 (any gainful occupation 16 (during school hours if excused from attendance) 14 (outside school hours) (§390.2)	Under 16: 8 hours/day 40 hours/week 6 days/week 10 hours combined work and school on schoolday (§390.2)	Director of Labor and Industrial Relations (§390.6)	Consideration of nature of employment. Form and conditions for issuance prescribed by Director, Division of Labor (§§390.2(c), 390.3)	14 to 16 (§390.2(c))	No provision	Under 16: 7 p.m. (8 p.m. June 1 through day before Labor Day) to 7 a.m.	Director of Labor and Industrial Relations (§390.6)

State	Minimum Age at Which a Child May Work (in specified occupations[3] and/or at specified times)	Maximum Work Time Permitted at Indicated Ages	Issuance of Employment Permits	Requirements for Issuance of Employment Permits – Types of Permits Specified	Permitted Age for Issuance of Permits for Work During School Hours	Minimum Education Requirement for Employment Permit for Work During School Hours	Nightwork Prohibited for Minors of Ages Indicated and for Hours Specified	Enforcement Agency
Id.	16 (during school hours) 14 (outside of school hours in mine, factory, workshop, mercantile establishment, store, telephone or telegraph office, laundry, restaurant, hotel apartment house or messenger service.) 12 (regular school vacations) (§§44.1301, 44.1302)	Under 16: 9 hours/day 54 hours/week (§34.1304)	No permits	No permit provision	No permit provision for child under 16 allowed to work if she meets literacy requirements (§§44.1302, 13.1901)	Can read and write simple English sentences (§§44.1302, 13.1901)	Under 16: 9 p.m. to 6 a.m.	Probation officers and school trustees (§44.1308)
Ill.	16 (theatre, concert hall, place of amusement, mercantile establishment, store, office, hotel, manufacturing establishment, mill, cannery, factory, workshop, restaurants, exception below situations) 14 (outside of school hours, but not in hazardous or dangerous factory work) 10 (agricultural work) (c. 48, §31.1)	Under 16: 8 hours/day 48 hours/week 6 days/week Under 16 attending school: 3 hours/schoolday 8 hours combined school and work/schoolday (c. 48, §31.3)	Local public school officials. (c. 48, §31.11)	Under 16: 1) in best interests of child; 2) parental accompaniment; 3) employer's statement; 4) physician's statement; 5) school record for work outside school hours (c. 48, §§ 31.9-31.12)	Under 16: Any child necessarily or lawfully employed according to provisions of the law (c. 122, § 36.1)	No provision, but must attend part-time continuation school at least 8 hours/week (c. 122, § 26.1)	Under 16: 7 p.m. to 7 a.m.	Department of Labor (c. 48, § 31.7)
Ind.	14 (during school hours and in any gainful occupation) 10 (in farm labor) (§20.8.1-4-21)	Under 17 – except minors of 16 not attending school: 8 hours/day 40 hours/week 6 days/week Minors of 16 attending school: 9 hours/day & 48 hours/week, before non-schoolday and during summer vacation Under 16: 3 hours/schoolday 23 hours/school week	Local public school officials. (c.48, 31.11) (s.20 8-1-4-4)	1) physician's statement; 2) proof of schooling; 3) employer's statement 20.8.1-4-1. 20.8.1-4-8 to 20.8.1-4-11)	14 to 16 (§20.8.1-4-1)	8 grades (§20.8.1-4-10)	Under 16: 7 p.m. (9 9.m. before schoolday) to 6 a.m. Minors of 16 attending school: 10 p.m. (midnight before nonschoolday and during summer vacation) to 6 a.m. (§20.8.1-4-20)	Division of Labor (§20.8.1-4-29)

State	Minimum Age at Which a Child May Work (in specified occupations[3] and/or at specified times)	Maximum Work Time Permitted at Indicated Ages	Issuance of Employment Permits	Requirements for Issuance[4] of Employment Permits - Types of Permits Specified	Permitted Age for Issuance of Permits for Work During School Hours	Minimum Education Requirement for Employment Permit for Work During School Hours	Nightwork Prohibited for Minors of Ages Indicated and for Hours Specified	Enforcement Agency
Ia.	16 (during school hours and in manufacturing, mining, processing workshops, public messenger service) 14 (any occupation except street trades and migratory labor) (§§92.3, 92.4, 92.6)	Under 16: 8 hours/day 40 hours/week 4 hours/schoolday 28 hours/schoolweek	Local public school official or state employment service division (§92.11)	Employer's statement (§§92.10, 92.11) For migrant labor if child under 14: physician's statement also required. (§92.12)	14 to 16 (§§92.3, 92.10)	No provision	Under 16: 7 p.m. (9 p.m. June 1 through Labor Day) to 7 a.m. (§92.7)	Labor Commissioner (§92.22)
Kan.	14 (in any occupation or trade or in any business or service) (§38.601)	Under 16: 8 hours/day 40 hours/week (§38.603)	Local public school official or judge of juvenile court (§38.606)	1) employer's statement; 2) school record) (§§38.604, 38.606)	14 to 16 (§§38.601, 38.604)	Elementary School (§38.606)	Under 16: 10 p.m. before school-day to 7 a.m.	Labor Commissioner (§38.611)
Ken.	16 (during school hours) 14 (at any gainful occupation except employment program supervised and sponsored by school and approved by Department of Education) (§§339.220, 339.230)	Under 16: 8 hours/day & 40 hours/week on non-schoolweeks 3 hours/day & 18 hours/week on schooldays/schoolweeks. 16 to 18 attending school: 4 hours/schoolday, 8 hours/Friday & non-schooldays 32 hours/schoolweek 16 to 18 not attending school: 10 hours/day 60 hours/week 6 days/week (Kentucky Administrative Regulations, LAB 120, Part IV A,B,C; Part V)	Local public school officials or probation officers (§339.300)	Types: 1) General: ages 16-18, completed high school, any period of time; 2) Vacation: ages 14-16, outside school hours; 3) School supervised; 4) Special: ages 14-15 excused from compulsory school attendance during entire year. Requirements: 1) Employer's statement; 2) physician's statement; 3) school record except for special permit. (§§339.280, 339.340)	14 to 16 (§339.230(1)(a))	High School (§§159.030(a), 339,230 (1)(c))	Under 16: 7 p.m. (9 p.m. June 1 through Labor Day) to 7 a.m. 16 to 18 attending school: 10 p.m. (midnight on Friday, Saturday, and during vacation) to 6 a.m. 16 to 18 not attending school: Midnight to 6 a.m.	Department of Labor (§339.450)

State	Minimum Age at Which a Child May Work (in specified occupations[3] and/or at specified times)	Maximum Work Time Permitted at Indicated Ages	Issuance of Employment Permits	Requirements for Issuance[4] of Employment Permits - Types of Permits Specified	Permitted Age for Issuance of Permits for Work During School Hours	Minimum Education Requirement for Employment Permit for Work During School Hours	Nightwork Prohibited for Minors of Ages Indicated and for Hours Specified	Enforcement Agency
La.	16 (any gainful occupation during school hours) 14 (outside school hours) (§§23.162, 23.163, 23.166)	Under 17: 8 hours/day 44 hours/week 6 days/week (§§23.211, 23.215) Under 16: 3 hours/schoolday (§23.214)	Commissioner of Labor, Orleans Parish; local public school official elsewhere (§23.183)	Types: 1) During school hours and over age 16: employer's statement s.23:184) 2) Outside school hours and under age 16: a)employer's statement; b)physician's tatement; c) school record. ss.23:184-23:186, 23:189)	16 (by implication from statutes)	No provision	Boys under 16 and girls under 17: 7 p.m. to 6 a.m. Boys of 16 and girls of 17 if attending school: 10 p.m. to 6 a.m. (§23.215)	Commissioner of Labor (§23.152)
Me.	16 (manufacturing or mechanical establishment, hotel, roominghouse, dry-cleaning establishment, bakery, bowling alley, poolroom, place of amusement, laundry) 15 (during school hours, except child employed under supervision of parents) 14 (eating place, automatic laundry, retail establishment where frozen foods are manufactured, sporting or overnight camp, mercantile establishment) (T.26, §§ 771, 773)	Under 16: 8 hours/day 48 hours/week 6 days/week Under 16 enrolled in school: 4 hours/schoolday 28 hours/schoolweek (T.26, §774)	Local public school officials (T.26, §§ 775,776)	Types: 1) Full-time, under age 16: school record 2) Part-time and vacation, under age 16: school record (T.25, § 775)	Under 16 (T.26, § 775)	Elementary School, can read and write simple English sentences (T.26, § 775)	Under 16: 9 p.m. to 7 a.m.	Bureau of Labor and Industry (T.26, §42)

State	Minimum Age at Which a Child May Work (in specified occupations[3] and/or at specified times)	Maximum Work Time Permitted at Indicated Ages	Issuance of Employment Permits	Requirements for Issuance[4] of Employment Permits - Types of Permits Specified	Permitted Age for Issuance of Permits for Work During School Hours	Minimum Education Requirement for Employment Permit for Work During School Hours	Nightwork Prohibited for Minors of Ages Indicated and for Hours Specified	Enforcement Agency
Md.	16 (during school hours) 16 (manufacturing, mechanical or processing occupations, except office work) 14 (any gainful occupation) (Art. 100, §§ 5-7; see also: §§ 61, 62)	Under 16: 8 hours/day 40 hours/week 6 days/week 16 to 18 not enrolled in school: 9 hours/day 48 hours/week 6 days/week Under 16 attending school: 3 hours/schoolday 23 hours/schoolweek & when school in session 5 or more days 16 and 17 attending school: 5 hours/schoolday & 30 hours/school week when school in session 5 or more days 8 hours/non-school-days and 40 hours/non-school-week when school in session less than 5 days.	In Baltimore city - Commissioner of Labor & Industry; In counties - local public school officials (Art. 100, § 23(d))	1) parental accompaniment; 2) school record; 3) physician's statement (Art. 100, §§ 23, 24; see also: school and work coordination plan, Art. 100, §39)	14 to 16 (Art. 100, § 23 (d))	No provision	Under 16: 7 P.m. (9 p.m. June 1 through September 1) to 7 a.m. 16 to 18 attending school: 11 P.m. to 6 a.m. (Art. 100, §§ 20(a), 20(b))	Commissioner of Labor, factory inspectors, supervisors or pupil personnel and other authorized inspectors (Art. 100, §§ 23(d), 35)
Mass.	16 (when school in session) 16 (factory, workshop, manufacturing or mechanical establishment) (c. 149, § 60; see also: §§ 61, 62)	Under 14 in farmwork: 4 hours/day 24 hours/week (c. 48, § 56) Under 16: 8 hours/day 48 hours/week 6 days/week (c. 48, § 65) 16 to 18: 9 hours/day 48 hours/week 6 days/week (c. 48, § 67) Time spent in continuation school part of time permitted to work. (c. 48, § 65)	Local public school official (c. 48, § 87)	Full-time & limited employment - school not in session, ages 14-16: 1) school record; 2) employer's statement; 3) physician's statement (c. 149, §§ 86, 87, 88) Specified Occupations, 16-18: school record (c. 149, § 95)	14 to 16 (c. 149, § 86)	6 grades (c. 76, § 1)	Under 16: 6 p.m. to 6:30 a.m. (c. 48, § 65) 16 to 18 10 p.m. (midnight in restaurants on Friday, Saturday and vacations) to 6 a.m. (c. 48, §66)	Department of Labor (c. 48, § 2)

State	Minimum Age at Which a Child May Work (in specified occupations and/or at specified times)	Maximum Work Time Permitted at Indicated Ages	Issuance of Employment Permits	Requirements for Issuance of Employment Permits - Types of Permits Specified	Permitted Age for Issuance of Permits for Work During School Hours	Minimum Education Requirement for Employment Permit for Work During School Hours	Nightwork Prohibited for Minors of Ages Indicated and for Hours Specified	Enforcement Agency
Mich.	14 (any gainful occupation) (This minimum age results from the fact that permits are required for employment of minors under 18 and no permit may be issued to a minor under 14: §409.3)	Under 18: 10 hours/day 48 hours/week 6 days/week, average of 8 hours/day (§409.17) 48 combined hours of work and school/schoolweek (§409.18)	Local public school official (s.409.3)	Full-time and limited employment outside school hours: 1) employer's statement; 2) physical fitness; 3) attendance and standing in school work; 4) need for income (§§409.3-409.5)	14 to 18 (§§409.3, 409.5)	No provision	Under 16: 9 p.m. to 7 a.m. (§409.17) 16 to 18 attending school: 10:30 p.m. to 6 a.m. 16 to 18 not attending school: 11:30 p.m. to 6 a.m. Girls under 18: 6 p.m. to 6 a.m. in factories. (§409.18)	Department of Labor (§409.25)
Minn.	14 (when public school in session) 14 (factory, mill, workshop, mine, construction) (§181.31)	Under 16: 8 hours/day 48 hours/week (§181.37)	Local public school official (§181.33)	During time public school is in session, 14 to 16: 1) school record; 2) physician's statement (§§181.32, 181.34)	14 to 16 (§181.32)	Common schools (§181.34)	Under 16: 7 p.m. to 7 a.m.	Department of Labor and Industry (§181.39)
Miss.	16 (when school attendance required) 14 (in mill, cannery, factory or manufacturing establishment) (§§71-1-17, 71-1-19)	Under 16: 8 hours/day 44 hours/week 16 and over: 10 hours/day, in mills factories & other specified establishments (§71-1-21)	No permits	No permit provision, but see: §71-1-19 requiring school certificate with affidavit of parent as proof of age as condition of employment	No provision	No provision	Under 16: 7 p.m. to 6 a.m.	Sheriff (§71-1-23)
Mo.	14 (any gainful occupation at any time) (§294.024)	Under 16: 8 hours/day 40 hours/week 6 days/week (s.294.030)	Local public school official (§294.045)	Full-time & part-time (non-school hours), 14 to 16: 1)consent of parent; 2)employer's statement; 3)physician's statement; 4)school record; 5)determined to be in best interest of child. (§§294.027 294.031, 294.054 (2))	14 to 16 (§294.027(2))	No provision	Under 16: 7 p.m. (10 p.m. before nonschoolday and for minors not enrolled in school) to 7 a.m.	Director of the Division of Industrial Inspection of the Department of Labor and Industrial Relations (§294.090)

State	Minimum Age at Which a Child May Work (in specified occupations³ and/or at specified times)	Maximum Work Time Permitted at Indicated Ages	Issuance of Employment Permits	Requirements for Issuance⁴ of Employment Permits - Types of Permits Specified	Permitted Age for Issuance of Permits for Work During School Hours	Minimum Education Requirement for Employment Permit for Work During School Hours	Nightwork Prohibited for Minors of Ages Indicated and for Hours Specified	Enforcement Agency
Mont.	16 (mine, mill, smelter, workshop, factory, elevator, place where machinery operated as a messenger) (§10-2-1) 16 (during school hours) (by implication - §10.204)	No provision	Commissioner of Labor (§10.204) Age permits only.	No provision	No provision	No provision	No provision.	Commissioner of Labor or Bureau of Child and Animal Protection. (§.10-205)
Neb.	14 (in theatre, concert hall, place of amusement, mercantile establishment, store, office, hotel, laundry, manufacturing establishment, packing house, elevator, beet field, restaurant, drive-in, messenger; by implication permit generally not issued to minors under 14) (§§ 48.302, 49.304)	Under 16: 8 hours/day 48 hours/week (§48.310)	Local public school official (§48.303)	All minors under 16: school record (§48.302)	14 to 16 (§§ 48.302, 48.304)	6 grades can read and write simple English sentences (§48.304)	Under 14: 8 p.m. to 6 a.m. 14 to 16: 10 p.m. (beyond 10 p.m. before nonschoolday on special certificate) to 6 a.m.	Department of Labor (s.48.302)
Nev.	14 (during school hours; any labor whatsoever in store, shop, factory, mine or inside employment not connected with farmwork or housework) (§§609.220, 609.250)	Under 16: 8 hours/day 48 hours/week (§609.240)	Local public school official or district court judge (§§ 392.090, 392.111)	Employment must be for child's own or parent's support (§§ 392.090-392.110) see also: Column 5, "Permitted Age...")	14 to 17 (§§392.100, 392.110)	8 grades (§392.090)	No provision.	Commissioner of Labor (s.607.160)

State	Minimum Age at Which a Child May Work (in specified occupations[3] and/or at specified times)	Maximum Work Time Permitted at Indicated Ages	Issuance of Employment Permits	Requirements for Issuance of Employment Permits - Types of Permits Specified	Permitted Age for Issuance of Permits for Work During School Hours	Minimum Education Requirement for Employment Permit for Work During School Hours	Nightwork Prohibited for Minors of Ages Indicated and for Hours Specified	Enforcement Agency
New Hamp.	16 (in a dangerous area in manufacturing, construction, mining, quarrying, logging) 12 (general employment) (§§ 276-A:4III, 276-A:4V)	Under 16 enrolled in school: 3 hours/school-day; 8 hours/any other day; 23 hours/school week; 48 hours/week during vacation (276-A:4IV) Under 16 not enrolled in school, and 16 to 18 10 hours/day and 48 hours/week at manual or mechanical labor in manufacturing; 10½ hours/day and 54 hours/week at such labor in other employment (275:15)	Local public school official (§276-A:5) Age permits only	No permit provision. But see: §§ 275:25, 276-A:5 regarding age certificate requirements: 1) parental accompaniment; 2) physician's statement if under 16	No provision	No provision	Under 16: enrolled in school: 9 p.m. - 7 a.m.	Commissioner of Labor (§§ 276-A:6, 276-A:8)
New Jersey	16 (during school hours & at any time in factory) 14 (outside school hours in any gainful occupation, but not in factory or other prohibited occupation) 12 (agriculture) (§§ 34:2-21.2, 34:2-21.15)	Under 18: 8 hours/day 40 hours/week 6 days/week Under 16: 10 hours/day and 6 days/week in agriculture 8 combined hours of work and school/schoolday. (§34:2-21.5)	Local public school official (§34:2-21.7)	Types: 1) Regular-during school hours, 16 to 18 2) Vacation-outside school hours 14 to 16 Required for each of the above: 1) employer's statement; 2) physician's statement; 3) school record (§§ 34:2-21.7, 34:2-21.8)	No provision	No provision	Under 16: 6 p.m. to 7 a.m. 16 to 18: 10 p.m. (midnight in restaurants before non-schoolday and during vacation) to 6 a.m. except 11 p.m. for boys in nonfactory establishments during vacation.	Department of Labor and Industry (§§ 34:2-21.8, 34:1A-6)
New Mexico	14 (during school hours) (§59-6-1)	Under 14: 8 hours/day 44 hours/week (48 in special cases)	Local public school official (§59-6-8)	1) physician's statement; 2) necessity to the family of income if child 14 to 16 working during school hours; 3) work determined to be non-dangerous (§§ 59-6-1, 59-6-2 59-6-8)	14 to 16 (§59-6-2)	No provision	Under 14: 9 p.m. to 7 a.m. (§59-6-3)	Labor and Industrial Commission (§59-6-11)

State	Minimum Age at Which a Child May Work (in specified occupations[3] and/or at specified times)	Maximum Work Time Permitted at Indicated Ages	Issuance of Employment Permits	Requirements[4] for Issuance of Employment Permit - Types of Permits Specified	Permitted Age for Issuance of Permits for Work During School Hours	Minimum Education Requirement for Employment Permit for Work During School Hours	Nightwork Prohibited for Minors of Ages Indicated and for Hours Specified	Enforcement Agency
New York	17 (when school attendance required) 16 (in factory) 14 (any trade or business except those 12 to 13 working for parents in farm or in home) (Labor §§ 130, 131(1), 131(2), 132(1))	Under 16: 8 hours/day 40 hours/week 6 days/week 23 hours/schoolweek (Labor §§ 171(1)(a), 170(1)) 16 to 18: 8 hours/day 48 hours/week 6 days/week (Labor §172(1)) 16 attending day school 4 hours/schoolday 28 hours/schoolweek (Labor §170(2))	Local public school official (Education §3215(a))	Types: 1) Student non-factory: ages 14 to 15 attending school, work in trade or business or service which is not factory work; 2) Student general: ages 16 to 17 attending day school; 3) Full-time labor: ages 16 to 17; 4) Limited: physical limitation; 5) Special: incapable of profiting from further school attendance. Required for all of the above: 1) consent of parents; 2)physician's statement; 3)school record if full-time, or special permit. (Labor §§ 131, 132(2); Education §§ 3215, 3216, 3217. Permits also required for farmwork, ages 14 to 15, Education §3226; street trades, ages 14 to 18, Education §3227)	14 to 16 (Labor 131; Education §§ 3216(5), 3225)	No provision	Under 16: 7 p.m. to 7 a.m. (Labor §171(1)(b)) 16 to 18: Midnight to 6 a.m. (Labor §173(1))	Industrial Commissioner of Department of Labor (Labor §§21,140) Department of Education (Education §§ 3213, 3234)

State	Minimum Age at Which a Child May Work (in specified occupations and/or at specified times)[3]	Maximum Work Time Permitted at Indicated Ages	Issuance of Employment Permits	Requirements for Issuance[4] of Employment Permits - Types of Permits Specified	Permitted Age for Issuance of Permits for Work During School Hours	Minimum Education Requirement for Employment Permit for Work During School Hours	Nightwork Prohibited for Minors of Ages Indicated and for Hours Specified	Enforcement Agency
North Caro-lina	16 (during school hours and in factories and mines or with power-driven machinery) 14 (any gainful occupation except boys over 12 may sell newspapers) (§110-1)	Under 16: 8 hours/day 40 hours/week 6 days/week 8 combined hours work and school/school/day 16 to 18: 9 hours/day 48 hours/week 6 days/week (§110-2)	Local directors of social services (§110-10)	Types: 1) Regular - during school hours 2) Vacation - outside school hours Required for both of the above: 1) employer's statement; 2) school record (§§110-9, 110-12, 110-14)	No provision	No provision	Under 16: 7 p.m. (9 p.m. when school not in session) to 7 a.m. 16 to 18: Midnight to 6 a.m.	Department of Labor (§110-19)
North Dakota	14 (during school hours & at any time in factory, workshop, mercantile establishment, store, business, office, telegraph office, restaurant, hotel) (§34-07-01)	Under 16 and not exempted from school attendance: 3 hours/schoolday, 24 hours/schoolweek. (s.34-07-15)	Local public school official (§34-07-05)	Types: 1) Full-time: 1) employer's statement; 2) school record 2) Vacation: regularly attending school (§§34-07-02, 34-07-06 to 34-07-11)	14 to 16 (§§34-07-02, 34-07-08)	8th grade or attended 9 years (§34-07-09)	Under 16: 7 p.m. (9 p.m. June 1 through Labor Day) to 7 a.m.	Commissioner of Labor (§§34-07-19, 34-07-20)
Ohio	16 (during school hours except 14 if determined to be in best interests of child) 16 (factory, mill, workshop oil well, pumping station, cannery, bottling or preserving establishment, mercantile or mechanical establishment, store, office, laboratory, restaurant, hotel, laundry, et al.) (§§4109.23, 4109.10)	Under 18: 8 hours/day 48 hours/week 6 days/week (4109.22) Under 16: 9 combined hours of work and school/schoolday Under 14: 4 work hours/day (§4109.10)	Minors of compulsory school age must obtain age and schooling certificate including: 1) employer's statement; 2) school record; 3) physician's statement. (ss.4109.01, 3301.01, 3301.02)	Types of permits: Nonstandard: over 14, cannot profit from further instruction. (s.3301.03); 2) Certificate: over 16 who has completed 7 grades. (s.3301.04); 3) Part-time & vacation. (s.3301.05); 4)Limited: physical limitations. (s.3301.06).	14 to 16 (§3301.01, but see Column 1)	Completed vocational training (§3301.01; see also: Column 2 for additional educational requirements.)	Under 16: 6 p.m. to 7 a.m.(10 p.m. to 6 a.m. before nonschoolday) (§4109.22) 16 to 18: 10 p.m. (midnight before nonschoolday) to 6 a.m. (§4109.22)	Department of Industrial Relations, (§4101.02(B)); Inspectors of Workshops and Factories, attendance officers (§4109.08, 4109.43)
Okla.	14 (factory, factory workshop, theatre, bowling alley, laundry) (T.40, §71)	Under 16: 8 hours/day 48 hours/week (T.40, §75)	Local public school officials (T.40, §79)	Age and schooling certificate including: 1) parental accompaniment; 2) proof of physical fitness for job; 3) school attendance certificate (T.40, §§ 77-80)	14 to 16 (T.40, §79)	Under 16 - must be able to read and write simple English sentences (T.40, §74)	Boys under 16 and girls under 18: 6 p.m. to 7 a.m. (T.40, §76)	Commissioner of Labor (T.40, § 1)

State	Minimum Age at Which a Child May Work (in specified occupations[3] and/or at specified times)	Maximum Work Time Permitted at Indicated Ages	Issuance of Employment Permits	Requirements for Issuance[4] of Employment Permits - Types of Permits Specified	Permitted Age for Issuance of Permits for Work During School Hours	Minimum Education Requirement for Employment Permit for Work During School Hours	Nightwork Prohibited for Minors of Ages Indicated and for Hours Specified	Enforcement Agency
Oregon	14 (while school is in session and in factory, workshop, mercantile establishment, store, business, office, restaurant, bakery, hotel or apartment house.) (s.353.320)	Under 16: 8 hours/day 44 hours/week 6 days/week; emergency overtime allowed on special permit 16 to 18: 44 hours/week; emergency overtime allowed on special permit (§653.315)	Wage and Hour Commission (§635.307)	Types: 1) Full-time: (§353.307, §353.310) 2) Vacation: 12-14 year olds in suitable work during any vacation over a term of two weeks (§653.320(3)) Requirements by regulation	14 to 16 (§§ 353.320, 353.307)	No provision	Under 16: 6 p.m. (10 p.m. on special permit) to 7a.m.	Labor Commissioner (§651.050) Wage and Hour Commission (§653.520)
Penna.	16 (all employment that interferes with school attendance and in manufacturing and mechanical work, heavy work in building trades, railroads and on commercial boats) (T.43, ss. 42, 44)	Under 18: 8 hours/day 44 hours/week 6 days/week 16 to 18 enrolled in regular day school: 28 hours/schoolweek Under 16: 4 hours/schoolday 18 hours/schoolweek (T.43, § 46)	Local public school official (T.43, § 50)	Types: 1) General: during entire year 2) Vacation: outside of school hours Required for both of the above: 1) parental accompaniment; 2) physician's statement; 3) employer's statement (T.24, § 13-1391, T.43, § 49, §§ 51-56)	14 to 16 (T.24, § 13-1330(4))	Completion of highest elementary grade in district (T.24, § 13-1330(4))	Under 16: 7 p.m. (10 p.m. during vacation from June to Labor Day) to 7 a.m. 16 to 18 enrolled in regular day school: 11 p.m. (midnight before nonschoolday) to 6 a.m.	Secretary of Labor (T.21, § 567) State of Superintendent of Public Instruction attendance officers (T.43, §§ 62, 66, 70)
R.I.	16(factory, mechanical or manufacturing establishment) 16 (business establishments outside of school hours) (ss.28-3-1, 28-3-3)	Under 16: 8 hours/day 40 hours/week 16 to 18: 9 hours/day 48 hours/week (§28-3-11)	Local public school official (§28-3-3)	Special limited: age 14 outside of school hours. Form prescribed and provided by Department of Education. (§§28-3-3,28-2-5; see also: § 28-3-22, employment permit for street trades required for minors under 16)	No provision	No provision	Under 16: 6 p.m. to 6 a.m. 16 to 18: 11 p.m. to 6 a.m.	Division of Labor Standards (§28-3-18) Truant Officer (§21-32)

State	Minimum Age at Which a Child May Work (in specified occupations[3] and/or at specified times)	Maximum Work Time Permitted at Indicated Ages	Issuance of Employment Permits	Requirements for Issuance of Employment Permits[4] - Types of Permits Specified	Permitted Age for Issuance of Permits for Work During School Hours	Minimum Education Requirement for Employment Permit for Work During School Hours	Nightwork Prohibited for Minors of Ages Indicated and for Hours Specified	Enforcement Agency
South Carolina	16 (any gainful occupation during school hours) 16 (factory, mine, textile establishment) (s.40-161)	16 and over in cotton or woolen manufacturing establishments: 10 hours/day 55 hours/week overtime permitted with special authorization. (s.40-61)	No permits	No permit provision	No provision	No provision	Under 16: 8 p.m. (11 p.m. before nonschoolday in stores, domestic service, farmwork) to 5 a.m. (s.40-161)	Department of Labor (s.40-165)
South Dakota	14 (mercantile establishment during school hours) 14 (Factory, workshop, mine, but below 14 if necessary to support family) (ss.60-12-2, 60-12-5)	Under 16: 8 hours/day 40 hours/week (s.60-12-1)	Local public school officials (s.60-12-4)	Full-time; literacy. Part-time: child regular attendant at some school or during past 12 months has attended school as required. (s.60-12-4)	Under 16 (s.60-12-4)	Ability to read and write simple English sentences (s.60-12-4)	Under 14: After 7 p.m. in mercantile establishments. (s.60-12-2)	Department of Manpower Affairs (s.60-12-11)

State	Minimum Age at Which a Child May Work (in specified occupations[3] and/or at specified times)	Maximum Work Time Permitted at Indicated Ages	Issuance of Employment Permits	Requirements for Issuance[4] of Employment Permit - Types of Permits Specified	Permitted Age for Issuance of Permits for Work During School Hours	Minimum Education Requirement for Employment Permit for Work During School Hours	Nightwork Prohibited for Minors of Ages Indicated and for Hours Specified	Enforcement Agency
Tenn.	16 (during school hours unless legally excused) (§§ 49-1710, 50-727, 50-729 (c)) 14 (any gainful occupation) (§§ 49-1710, 50-727, 50-729 (c))	Under 18: 8 hours/day 40 hours/week 6 days/week Under 17; not exempted from school attendance: 4 hours/schoolday (5 on Friday) 28 hours/schoolweek	Local public school official (§50-733)	Types: 1) Regular – during school hours 2) Vacation -outside school hours Requirements: 1) employer's statement; 2) physician's statement; 3) school record; 4) parental accompaniment if under 16 (§§ 50-732 to 50-734) An exemption from the requirements of the child labor laws may be granted if employment is in the best interests of child, presents no danger to life, health or safety, and does not interfere with the child's education ... (§50-731)	14 to 16 (§§ 50-733, 49-1710, 50-727, 50-729(c))	No provision	Under 16: 10 p.m. to 7 a.m. 16 to 18: 10 p.m. to 6 a.m. (§50-729)	Department of Labor (§50-735)
Texas	15 (mine, factory, workshop, laundry, messenger service in towns over 15,000 population) (§5181(a))	Under 15: 8 hours/day 48 hours/week (§5181(d))	No permits	No permit provision. But see: §5181(e). Child may be exempted from school attendance by court order if: 1) child is over 14; 2) earnings are necessary for support of self or family; 3) child has completed 7th grade; 4) proof of suitable employment; 5) physician's statement (§5181(3))	14 (exemption) (§5181(e), but see Column 4)	7 grades (§5181(e))	Under 15: 10 p.m. to 5 a.m.	Commissioner of Labor Statistics (§5181(f))

State	Minimum Age at Which a Child May Work (in specified occupations[3] and/or at specified times)	Maximum Work Time Permitted at Indicated Ages	Issuance of Employment Permits	Requirements for Issuance[4] of Employment Permits - Types of Permits Specified	Permitted Age for Issuance of Permits for Work During School Hours	Minimum Education Requirement for Employment Permit for Work During School Hours	Nightwork Prohibited for Minors of Ages Indicated and for Hours Specified	Enforcement Agency
Utah	16 (during school hours) 14 (retail food service, automobile service station, public messenger service, janitorial custodial service, lawn care, use of hoists, non-dangerous areas of manufacturing (§§ 34-23-3, 34-23-5)	Under 16: 8 hours/day 40 hours/week 4 hours/schoolday (§34-23-3)	Local public school officials (§34-23-10) Age permits only	No provision	No provision	No provision	Under 16: 9:30 p.m. to 5 a.m. before schoolday	Industrial Commission (§34-23-11)
Vermont	14 (at any time in mill, cannery, workshop, factory, manufacturing establishment; outside of school hours in any other gainful occupation) T.21, §436	Under 16: 8 hours/day 48 hours/week 6 days/week (T.21, §434) 16 to 18: 9 hours/day 50 hours/week (T. 21, §440)	Commissioner of Industrial Relations (T.21, §431)	Employment during school hours: 1) school record; 2) physician's statement (T.21, §§ 431,432, 433)	Under 16 (T.21, §433)	Elementary school (T.21, §433)	Under 16: 7 p.m. to 6 a.m.	Commissioner of Industrial Relations (T.21, §446)
Va.	16 (during school hours and in manufacturing or mechanical establishment, commercial cannery, elevators, hospital, warehouse, laundry) 14 (outside of school hours in specified tasks) (§§40.1-78, 40-1-100(D))	Under 18: 8 hours/day 40 hours/week 6 days/week (§40.1-80)	Local public school official (§40.1-79)	Types: 1) General employment: ages 16 to 18, work entire year; 2) Vacation or part-time: ages 14 to 17, outside of school hours; 3) Work-training: ages 14 to 18; 4) Provisional employment ages 14 to 16, child found incapable of profiting from further instruction; 5) School and part-time employment. Required for all of the above: 1) parental accompaniment; if 16-17, consent sufficient; 2) employer's statement; 3) physician's statement (§§40.1-84,40.1-86 to 93;see also: §40.1-105 re: street trades)	14 to 16 (§40.1-90)	No provision	Under 16: 6 p.m. (10 p.m. before non-schoolday and June 1 to Sept. 1) to 7 a.m. except that minors 15 or older may begin work at 5 a.m. 16 to 18: Midnight to 5 a.m.	Commissioner of Labor (§40.1-114)

State	Minimum Age at Which a Child May Work (in specified occupations[3] and/or at specified times)	Maximum Work Time Permitted at Indicated Ages	Issuance of Employment Permits	Requirements for Issuance[4] of Employment Permits - Types of Permits Specified	Permitted Age for Issuance of Permits for Work During School Hours	Minimum Education Requirement for Employment Permit for Work During School Hours	Nightwork Prohibited for Minors of Ages Indicated and for Hours Specified	Enforcement Agency
Wash.	14 (factory, store, shop, or mine without written permission of District Court Judge) 15 (during school hours) (§26.28.060)	Under 16: 8 hours/day, 40 hours/week, when school is in session. In computing hours, total school attendance hours are included. 8 hours/day, 40 hours/week when school is not in session. 16 to 18: 8 hours/day, 40 hours/week, 5 days week. (Industrial Welfare Commission Order No. 49)	Local public school official (§28A.28.010)	During school hours: 1) needs of the family or welfare of child requires employment; 2) minor may legally engage in such employment (§§ 28A.27.090, 28 A.28.030; see also regulations)	15 to 18; 14 if child has completed 8th grade (§28A.27.090)	8 grades (§28A.28.030)	Under 16: 7 p.m. to 7 a.m. 16 and 17 attending school may be employed after 7 p.m. in authorized employment.	Industrial Welfare Commsssion (§49.12.030)
West Va.	16 (any gainful occupation) (§21-61-1)	Under 16: 8 hours/day 40 hours/week 6 days/week (§21-6-7)	Local public school officials (§21-6-3)	Types: 1) Work: anytime 2) Vacation work: school not in session; 3) Special non-factory employment: outside of school hours. Required for all of the above: 1) parental consent; 2) employer's statement; 3) school record (not required for special permit) (§21-6-3)	Under 16 (§21-6-3)	8 grades (§21-6-3)	Under 16: 8 p.m. to 5 a.m.	State Commissioner of Labor (§21-6-9)

State	Minimum Age at Which a Child May Work (in 3 specified occupations and/or at specified times)	Maximum Work Time Permitted at Indicated Ages	Issuance of Employment Permits	Requirements for Issuance of Employment Permits - Types of Permits Specified	Permitted Age for Issuance of Permits for Work During School Hours	Minimum Education Requirement for Employment Permit for Work During School Hours	Nightwork Prohibited for Minors of Ages Indicated and Hours Specified	Enforcement Agency
Wisc.	18 (during school hours in any gainful occupation) 14 (any gainful occupation at any time except street trades, agricultural pursuits, domestic service and as caddies) (§103.67)	Under 16: 8 hours/day, 24 hours/week, 6 days/week; except 8 hours/day, 40 hours/week, 6 days/week during school vacation. 16 to 18: 8 hours/day, 40 hours/week, 6 days/week; except 8 hours/day, 48 hours/week, 6 days/week during school vacation. (§103.68)	Department of Industry, Labor and Human Relations (§103.70)	Employer's statement (§§ 103.70, 103.71, 103.73; see also: regulations) Street trades (§103.25)	14 to 16 (§§ 103.71, 103.67)	High school (§103.71)	Under 16: 8 p.m. (9:30 p.m. before non-schoolday and during vacation) to 7 a.m. Girls 16 to 18: 11 p.m. (12:30 a.m. before non-schoolday and during vacation) to 6 a.m. Boys 16 to 18: 12:30 a.m. to 6 a.m. (except where under direct supervision of adult, and provided that minor receives 8 consecutive hours of rest between end of work and beginning of schoolday)	Department of Industry and Labor, and Human Relations (§§ 103.28, 103.66)
Wyo.	16 (during school hours) 14 (any gainful occupation outside school hours; minimum age set indirectly by permit provisions) (§§ 27-229, 27-226)	Under 16: 8 hours/day (§27-228)	Local public school or person authorized by Labor Commissioner (§27-226)	Employer's statement (§§ 27-225, 27-226)	No provision	No provision	Under 16: 10 p.m. (midnight before non-schoolday and for minors not enrolled in school) to 5 a.m. Girls 16 to 18: Midnight to 5 a.m.	Child Labor Commissioner (§27-227)
Dist. of Col.	Under 18: 14 (any gainful occupation except boys 10 and over employed in newspaper sale or delivery) (§36-201)	Under 18: 8 hours/day 48 hours/week 6 days/week (§36-202)	Director of the Department of School Attendance and Work Permits (§36-209)	Types: 1) Work: during school hours; 2) Vacation: outside of school hours. Required for all of the above: 1) employer's statement; 2) school record if under 16 (not required for vacation permit); 3) parental accompaniment if under 16; 4) proof of physical fitness (§§ 36-208, 36-210 to 212; see also: §36-219 re street trades	14 to 16 (§36-208)	8 grades and can read and write simple English sentences (§36.210(d))	Under 16: 7 p.m. to 7 a.m. 16 to 18: 10 p.m. to 6 a.m.	Department of School Attendance and Work Permits (§36-201)

State	Minimum Age at Which a Child May Work (in [3] specified occupations and/or at specified times)	Maximum Work Time Permitted at Indicated Ages	Issuance of Employment Permits	Requirements for Issuance[4] of Employment Permits - Types of Permits Specified	Permitted Age for Issuance of Permits for Work During School Hours	Minimum Education Requirement for Employment Permit for Work During School Hours	Nightwork Prohibited for Minors of Ages Indicated and for Hours Specified	Enforcement Agency
Puerto Rico	16 (any gainful occupation during school hours) 14 (gainful occupation outside school hours) (T.29, §432)	Under 18: 8 hours/day 40 hours/week 6 days/week 8 combined hours of work and school on school-day for minors attending school	Secretary of Labor (T.29, §436)	Types: 1) Regular: during school hours, ages 14 to 18 2) Vacation: outside of school hours Required for both of the above: 1) Parental accompaniment; 2) employer's statement; 3) physician's statement; 4) school record (T.29, §§ 432, 435, to 440) Peddlers (T.29, §443)	14 to 16 (T.29, §432)	No provision	Under 16: 6 p.m. to 8 p.m. 16 to 18: 10 p.m. to 6 a.m. (T.29, §433)	Department of Labor (T.29, §455)

APPENDIX F

Compilation of State Constitutional Provisions
Concerning Education

Alabama
Art. 14, §256

It is the policy of the state of Alabama to foster and promote the education of its citizens in a manner and extent consistent with its available resources, and the willingness and ability of the individual student, but nothing in this Constitution shall be construed as creating or recognizing any right to education at public expense, nor as limiting the authority and duty of the legislature, in furthering or providing for education, to require or impose conditions or procedures deemed necessary to the preservation of peace and order.

The legislature may by law provide for or authorize the establishment and operation of schools by such persons, agencies or municipalities, at such places, and upon such conditions as it may prescribe, and for the grant or loan of public funds and the lease, sale or donation of real or personal property to or for the benefit of citizens of the state for educational purposes under such circumstances and upon such conditions as it shall prescribe. Real property owned by the state or any municipality shall not be donated for educational purposes except to nonprofit charitable or eleemosynary corporations or associations organized under the laws of the state.

To avoid confusion and disorder and to promote effective and economical planning for education, the legislature may authorize the parents or guardians of minors, who desire that such minors shall attend schools provided for their own race, to make election to that end, such election to be effective for such period and to such extent as the legislature may provide.

Alaska
Art. VII, §1

The legislature shall by general law establish and maintain a system of public schools open to all children of the state and may provide for other public educational institutions.

Arizona
Art. XI, §§1, 6

The legislature shall enact such laws as shall provide for the establishment and maintenance of a general and uniform public school system, which system shall include kindergarten

schools, common schools, high schools, normal schools, industrial schools, and universities (which shall include an agricultural college, a school of mines, and such other technical
schools as may be essential, until such time as it may be
deemed advisable to establish separate state institutions of
such character). The legislature shall also enact such laws
as shall provide for the education and care of the deaf, dumb,
and blind. The University and all other State educational
institutions shall be open to students of both sexes, and the
instruction furnished shall be as nearly free as possible.

Provision shall be made by law for the establishment and
maintenance of a system of public schools which shall be open
to all the children of the state and be free from sectarian
control. The legislature shall provide for a system of common
schools by which a free school shall be established and maintained
in every school district for at least six months in each year,
which school shall be open to all pupils between the ages of six
and twenty-one years. (Art. XX, Ordinance, 7th Par.)

Arkansas
Art. 14, §1

Free school system. -- Intelligence and virtue being the
safeguards of liberty and the bulwark of a free and good government, the State shall ever maintain a general, suitable and
efficient system of free public schools and shall adopt all
suitable means to secure to the people the advantages and opportunities of education. The specific intention of this amendment
is to authorize that in addition to existing constitutional or
statutory provisions the General Assembly and/or public school
districts may spend public funds for the education of persons
over twenty-one (21) years of age and under six (6) years of
age, as may be provided by law, and no other interpretation shall
be given to it. [As amended by Amendment No. 53.]

California
Art. IX, §§1, 5

A general diffusion of knowledge and intelligence being
essential to the preservation of the rights and liberties of
the people, the legislature shall encourage, by suitable means,
the promotion of intellectual, scientific, moral and agricultural improvement.

(5) The legislature shall provide for a system of common
schools by which a free school shall be kept up and supported
in each district at least six months in every year, after the
first year in which a school has been established.

Colorado
Art. IX, §§2, 11

The General Assembly shall, as soon as practicable, provide for the establishment and maintenance of a thorough and uniform system of free public schools throughout the state, wherein all residents of the state, between the ages of six and 21 years, may be educated gratuitously. One or more public schools shall be maintained in each school district within the state, at least three months in each year; any school district failing to have such schools shall not be entitled to receive any portion of the school fund for that year.

The General Assembly may require, by law, that every child of sufficient mental and physical ability, shall attend the public schools during the period between the ages of six and 18 years, for a time equivalent to three years, unless educated by other means.

Connecticut
Art. VIII, §§1, 2

There shall always be free public elementary and secondary schools in the state. The General Assembly shall implement this principle by appropriate legislation.

The fund, called the school fund, shall be made a perpetual fund, the interest of which shall be inviolably appropriated to the Support and encouragement of the public schools, throughout the state, and for the equal benefit of the people thereof.

Delaware
Art. X, §1

The general assembly shall provide for the establishment and maintenance of a general and efficient system of free public schools, and may require by law that every child, not physically or mentally disabled, shall attend the public schools, unless educated by other means.

Florida
Art. IX, §1

Adequate provision shall be made by law for a uniform system of free public schools, and for the establishment, maintenance and operation of institutions of higher learning and other public education programs that the needs of the people may require.

Georgia
Art. VIII, §1

The provision of an adequate education for the citizens shall be a primary obligation of the state of Georgia, the expense of which shall be provided for by taxation.

Hawaii
Art. IX, §1

The state shall provide for the establishment, support, and control of a statewide system of public schools, free from sectarian control, a state university, public libraries, and such other educational institutions as may be deemed desirable, including physical facilities therefore. There shall be no segregation in public educational institutions because of race, religion, or ancestry; nor shall public funds be appropriated for the support or benefit of any sectarian or private instructional institution.

Idaho
Art. IX, §§1, 9

The stability of a Republican form of government depending mainly upon the intelligence of the people, it shall be the duty of the legislature of Idaho to establish and maintain a general, uniform and thorough system of public, free common schools.

Compulsory attendance at schools. -- The legislature may require by law that every child shall attend the public schools of the state, throughout the period between the ages of six and eighteen years, unless educated by other means, as provided by law.

Illinois
Art. X, §1

A fundamental goal of the People of the State is the educational development of all persons to the limits of their capacities.

The State shall provide for an efficient system of high quality public educational institutions and services. Education in public schools through the secondary level shall be free. There may be such other free education as the General Assembly provides by law.

Indiana
Art. VIII, §1

Knowledge and learning, generally diffused throughout a community, being essential to the preservation of a free government: It shall be the duty of the general assembly to encourage, by all suitable means, moral, intellectual, scientific, and agricultural improvement; and to provide by law for a general and uniform system of Common Schools wherein the tuition shall be without charge, and equally open to all.

Iowa
Art. IX, Pt. 1, §12

The Board of Education shall provide for the education of all the youths of the state, through a system of Common Schools and such schools shall be organized and kept in each school district at least three months in each year.

Kansas
Art. VI, §1

The legislature shall provide for intellectual, educational, vocational and scientific improvement by establishing and maintaining public schools, educational institutions and related activities which may be organized and changed in such manner as may be provided by law.

Kentucky
§183

The General Assembly shall, by appropriate legislation, provide for an efficient system of common schools throughout the state.

Louisiana
Art. XII, §1

The legislature shall provide for the education of the people of the state and shall establish and maintain a public educational program.

Maine
Art. VIII, §1

A general diffusion of the advantages of education being essential to the preservation of the rights and liberties of the

people; to promote this important object the Legislature are
authorized, and it shall be their duty to require the several
towns to make suitable provision, at their own expense, for the
support and maintenance of public schools; and it shall further
be their duty to encourage and suitably endow, from time to time,
as the circumstances of the people may authorize, all academies,
colleges and seminaries of learning within the state . . .

Maryland
Art. VIII, §1

The General Assembly, at its First Session after the
adoption of this Constitution, shall by law establish throughout the State a thorough and efficient System of Free Public
Schools; and shall provide by taxation, or otherwise, for their
maintenance.

Massachusetts
§91 (Pt. 2, ch. 5, §2)

Wisdom, and knowledge, as well as virtue, diffused generally among the body of the people, being necessary for the
preservation of their rights and liberties; and as these depend
on spreading the opportunities and advantages of education in
the various parts of the country, and among the different orders
of people it shall be the duty of the legislatures and magis--
trates, in all future periods of this commonwealth, to cherish
the interests of literature and the sciences and all seminaries
of them; especially the university at Cambridge, public schools
and grammar schools in the towns . . .

Michigan
Art. VIII, §§1, 2

Sec. 1. Religion, morality and knowledge being necessary
to good government and the happiness of mankind, schools and
the means of education shall forever be encouraged.

Sec. 2. The legislature shall maintain and support a
system of free public elementary and secondary schools as
defined by law. Every school district shall provide for the
education of its pupils without discrimination as to religion,
creed, race, color or national origin . . .

Minnesota
Art. VIII, §1

The stability of a republican form of government depending

mainly upon the intelligence of the people, it shall be the duty
of the legislature to establish a general and uniform system of
public schools.

The legislature shall make such provisions, by taxation
or otherwise, as, with the income arising from the school fund,
will secure a thorough and efficient system of public schools
in each township in the State.

Mississippi
Art. VIII, §201

The legislature may, in its discretion, provide for the
maintenance and establishment of free public schools for all
children between the ages of six (6) and twenty-one (21) years,
by taxation or otherwise, and with such grades as the Legislature may prescribe.

Missouri
Art. IX, §1(a)

A general diffusion of knowledge and intelligence being
essential to the preservation of the rights and liberties of
the people, the general assembly shall establish and maintain
free public schools for the gratuitous instruction of all persons in this state within ages not in excess of twenty-one years
as prescribed by law.

Montana
Art. X, §1

Section 1. Educational goals and duties. (1) It is the
goal of the people to establish a system of education which will
develop the full educational potential of each person. Equality
of educational opportunity is guaranteed to each person of the
state.

(2) The state recognizes the distinct and unique cultural
heritage of the American Indians and is committed in its educational goals to the preservation of their cultural integrity.

(3) The legislature shall provide a basic system of free
quality public elementary and secondary schools. The legislature may provide such other educational institutions, public
libraries, and educational programs as it deems desirable. It
shall fund and distribute in an equitable manner to the school
districts the state's share of the cost of the basic elementary
and secondary school system.

Nebraska
Art. VII, §§1, 4

The legislature shall provide for the free instruction
in the common schools of the state of all persons between the
ages of five and twenty-one years.

. . . [I]t shall be the duty of the Legislature to pass
suitable laws . . . to encourage schools and the means of
instruction.

Nevada
Art. II, §2

The legislature shall provide for a uniform system of
common schools, by which a school shall be established and maintained in each school district at least six months in every year
. . . and the legislature may pass such laws as will tend to
secure a general attendance of the children in each school district upon said public schools.

New Hampshire
Part II, Art. 83

Knowledge and learning, generally diffused through a
community, being essential to the preservation of a free government; and spreading the opportunities and advantages of education through the various parts of the country, being highly
conducive to promote this end; it shall be the duty of the
legislators and magistrates, in all future periods of this
government, to cherish the interest of literature and the sciences, and all seminaries and public schools, to encourage private and public institutions, rewards and immunities for the
promotion of agriculture, arts, sciences, commerce, trades,
manufactures, and natural history of the country, to countenance
and inculcate the principles of humanity and general benevolence,
public and private charity, industry and economy, honesty and
punctuality, sincerity, sobriety, and all social affections, and
generous sentiments, among the people . . .

New Jersey
Art. VIII, §4, ¶1

The Legislature shall provide for the maintenance and
support of a thorough and efficient system of free public schools
for the instruction of all the children in the State between the
ages of five and eighteen years.

New Mexico
Art. XII, §§1, 5; Art. XXI, §4

A uniform system of free public schools sufficient for the education of, and open to, all children of school age in the state shall be established and maintained.

Every child of school age and of sufficient physical and mental ability shall be required to attend a public or other school during such period and for such time as may be prescribed by law.

Provision shall be made for the establishment and maintenance of a system of public schools which shall be open to all the children of the State and free from sectarian control and said schools shall always be conducted in English.

New York
Art. XI, §1

The legislature shall provide for the maintenance and support of free common schools, wherein all the children of this state may be educated.

North Carolina
Art. I, §15; Art. IX, §§1, 2, 3

The people have a right to the privilege of education, and it is the duty of the State to guard and maintain that right.

Sec. 1. Religion, morality, and knowledge being necessary to good government and happiness of mankind, schools and libraries and the means of education shall forever be encouraged.

Sec. 2. The General Assembly shall provide by taxation and otherwise for a general and uniform system of free public schools which shall be maintained at least nine months in every year, and wherein equal opportunities shall be provided for all students.

Sec. 3. The General Assembly shall provide that every child of appropriate age and sufficient mental and physical ability shall attend the public schools, unless educated by other means.

North Dakota
Art. VII, §§147, 148

Sec. 147. A high degree of intelligence, patriotism,

integrity and morality on the part of every voter in a government
by the people being necessary in order to insure the continuance
of that government and the prosperity and happiness of the people,
the legislative assembly shall make provision for the establishment and maintenance of a system of public schools which shall
be open to all children of the state of North Dakota and free
from sectarian control. This legislative requirement shall be
irrevocable without the consent of the United States and the
people of North Dakota.

Sec. 148. The legislative assembly shall provide for
a uniform system of free public schools throughout the state.

Ohio
Art. VI, §§2, 3

The General Assembly shall make such provisions . . .
as . . . will secure a thorough and efficient system of common
schools throughout the state . . .

Provision shall be made by law for the organization,
administration and control of the public school system of the
state supported by public funds . . .

Oklahoma
Art. 1, §5; Art. XIII, §§1, 4

Provisions shall be made for the establishment and
maintenance of a system of public schools, which shall be open
to all the children of the State and free from sectarian control and said schools shall always be conducted in English.

The legislature shall establish and maintain a system of
free public schools wherein all the children of the state may
be educated.

The legislature shall provide for compulsory attendance
at some public or other school, unless other means of education
are provided, of all the children in the State who are sound in
mind and body between the ages of eight and sixteen years for at
least three months in each year.

Oregon
Art. VIII, §3

The legislative assembly shall provide by law for the
establishment of a uniform and general system of common schools.

Pennsylvania
Art. III, §14

The General Assembly shall provide for the maintenance and support of a thorough and efficient system of public education to serve the needs of the Commonwealth.

Rhode Island
Art. XII, §1

The diffusion of knowledge, as well as of virtue, among the people, being essential to the preservation of their rights and liberties, it shall be the duty of the general assembly to promote public schools, and to adopt all means which they may deem necessary and proper to secure to the people the advantages and opportunities of education.

South Carolina
Art. 11, §3

The General Assembly shall provide for the maintenance and support of a system of free public schools open to all children in the State and shall establish, organize and support such other public institutions of learning as may be desirable.

South Dakota
Art. VIII, §1; Art. XXII

The stability of a republican form of government depending on the morality and intelligence of the people, it shall be the duty of the Legislature to establish and maintain a general and uniform system of public schools wherein tuition shall be without charge, and equally open to all; and to adopt all suitable means to secure to the people the advantages and opportunities of education.

The following article shall be irrevocable without the consent of the United States and the people of South Dakota by their legislative assembly:

. . . Fourth, that provision shall be made for the establishment and maintenance of systems of public schools, which shall be open to all the children of this state and free from sectarian control.

Tennessee
Art. XI, §12

Knowledge, learning, and virtue, being essential to the preservation of republican institutions, and the diffusion of the opportunities and advantages of education throughout the different portions of the State, being highly conducive to the promotion to this end, it shall be the duty of the General Assembly in all future periods of this Government, to cherish literature and science. And the fund called common school fund, and all the lands and proceeds thereof, dividends, stocks and other property of every description whatever, heretofore by law appropriated by the General Assembly of this State for the use of common schools, and all such as shall hereafter be appropriated by the General Assembly of this State for the use of common schools, and all such as shall hereafter be appropriated, shall remain a perpetual fund, the principal of which shall never be diminished by Legislative appropriations; and the interest thereof shall be inviolably appropriated to the support and encouragement of common schools throughout the State, and for the equal benefit of all the people thereof; and no law shall be made authorizing said fund or any part thereof to be divested to any other use than the support and encouragement of common schools.

Texas
Art. VII, §1

A general diffusion of knowledge being essential to the preservation of the liberties and rights of the people, it shall be the duty of the Legislature of the State to establish and make suitable provision for the support and maintenance of an efficient system of public free schools.

Utah
Art. X, §1

The legislature shall provide for the establishment and maintenance of a uniform system of public schools, which shall be open to all children of the State, and be free from sectarian control.

Vermont
Ch. 2, §68

Laws for the encouragement of virtue and prevention of vice and immorality ought to be constantly kept in force, and duly executed; and a competent number of schools ought to be maintained in each town unless the general assembly permits other provisions for the convenient instruction of youths.

Virginia
Art. VIII, §§1, 3

The General Assembly shall provide for a system of free public elementary and secondary schools for all children of school age throughout the Commonwealth, and shall seek to ensure that an educational program of high quality is established and continually maintained.

The General Assembly shall provide for the compulsory elementary and secondary education of every eligible child of appropriate age, such eligibility and age to be determined by law . . .

Washington
Art. IX, §§1, 2; Art. XXVI, Par. 4

It is the paramount duty of the state to make ample provision for education within its borders without discrimination or preference on account of race, color or sex.

The legislature shall provide for a general and uniform system of public schools. The public school system shall include common schools, and such high schools, normal schools and technical schools as may hereafter be established.

Provision shall be made for the establishment and maintenance of systems of public schools free from sectarian control which shall be open to all the children of said state.

West Virginia
Art. XII, §1, 12

The legislature shall provide, by general law, for a thorough and efficient system of free schools.

The legislature shall foster and encourage moral, intellectual, scientific and agricultural improvement; it shall, whenever it may be practicable, make suitable provision for the blind, mute, and insane and for the organization of such institutions of learning as the best interests of general education in the State may demand.

Wisconsin
Art. X, §3

The legislature shall provide by law for the establishment of district schools, which shall be as nearly uniform as

practicable; and such schools shall be free and without charge
for tuition to all children between the ages of four and twenty
years . . .

Wyoming
Art. I, §23; Art. VII, §1; Art. XXI, §28

The right of the citizens to opportunities for education
should have practical recognition. The legislature shall suitably encourage means and agencies calculated to advance the
sciences and liberal arts.

The legislature shall provide for the establishment and
maintenance of a complete and uniform system of public instruction, embracing free elementary schools of every needed kind
and grade, a university with such technical and professional
departments as the public good may require and the means of the
state allow, and such other institutions as may be necessary.

The legislature shall make laws for the establishment and
maintenance of systems of public schools which shall be open to
all the children of the State and free from sectarian control.

Puerto Rico
Art. II, §5

Every person has the right to an education which shall be
directed to the full development of the human personality and to
the strengthening of respect for human rights and fundamental
freedoms. There shall be a system of free and wholly non-sectarian public education. Instruction in the elementary and
secondary schools shall be free and shall be compulsory in the
elementary schools to the extent permitted by the facilities
of the state. Compulsory attendance at elementary public schools
to the extent permitted by the facilities of the Commonwealth,
as herein provided, shall not be construed as applicable to those
who receive elementary education in schools established under non-
governmental auspices. No public property or public funds shall
be used for the support of schools or educational institutions
other than those of the state. Nothing contained in this provision shall prevent the state from furnishing to any child non-
educational services established by law for the protection or
welfare of children.

TABLE OF CASES

INDEX